THE YELLOW HOUSE

'Gayford brings together all the latest research . . . it is a story of such fascination that it can hardly fail, but this is clearly a labour of love and Gayford tells it vividly, intelligently and intelligibly' *Literary Review*

'Endlessly intriguing . . . Gayford gives us another sideways glance into the mystery of man's infinitely complex nature' *Sunday Express*

'Gayford brings this strange ménage wonderfully to life'
Evening Standard

'Remarkable . . . admirers of the protagonists will find a great deal to enjoy in this thoughtful and well-researched study' *Independent*

'Absorbing . . . it is the account of their art that grips' Sally Vickers, *The Times*

'Gripping account of art's most famous amputation'
Independent on Sunday

'The work of Van Gogh and Gauguin will never look quite the same'
Tablet

'Gayford has done a splendid job of harnessing a lot of fiddly information, including a back story full of obscure but critical detail'
Spectator

Martin Gayford has been Art Critic of the *Spectator* and the *Sunday Telegraph*. He is currently Chief European Art Critic for Bloomberg. Among his publications are *The Penguin Book of Art Writing*, of which he was co-editor, and contributions to many catalogues for exhibitions at the Tate, the Hayward Gallery, the Courtauld Gallery and the Musée d'Art Moderne, Paris. Martin Gayford lives in Cambridge with his wife and two children.

The Yellow House

Van Gogh, Gauguin and Nine Turbulent Weeks in Arles

MARTIN GAYFORD

PENGUIN BOOKS

PENGUIN BOOKS

Published by the Penguin Group

Penguin Books Ltd, 80 Strand, London WC2R ORL, England

Penguin Group (USA) Inc., 375 Hudson Street, New York, New York 10014, USA

Penguin Group (Canada), 90 Eglinton Avenue East, Suite 700, Toronto, Ontario, Canada M4P 2Y3
(a division of Pearson Penguin Canada Inc.)

Penguin Ireland, 25 St Stephen's Green, Dublin 2, Ireland
(a division of Penguin Books Ltd)

Penguin Group (Australia), 250 Camberwell Road, Camberwell, Victoria 3124, Australia
(a division of Pearson Australia Group Pty Ltd)

Penguin Books India Pvt Ltd, 11 Community Centre, Panchsheel Park, New Delhi – 110 017, India

Penguin Group (NZ), 67 Apollo Drive, Rosedale, North Shore 0632, New Zealand
(a division of Pearson New Zealand Ltd)

Penguin Books (South Africa) (Pty) Ltd, 24 Sturdee Avenue, Rosebank, Johannesburg 2196, South Africa

Penguin Books Ltd, Registered Offices: 80 Strand, London WC2R ORL, England

www.penguin.com

First published by Fig Tree 2006
Published in Penguin Books 2007

7

Copyright © Martin Gayford, 2006
All rights reserved

The moral right of the author has been asserted

Typeset by Rowland Phototypesetting Ltd, Bury St Edmunds, Suffolk
Printed in England by Clays Ltd, St Ives plc

ISBN: 978–0–141–01673–3

www.greenpenguin.co.uk

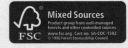

Penguin Books is committed to a sustainable future
for our business, our readers and our planet.
The book in your hands is made from paper
certified by the Forest Stewardship Council.

To Josephine

Contents

List of Illustrations

Unless otherwise stated, paintings are by Van Gogh.

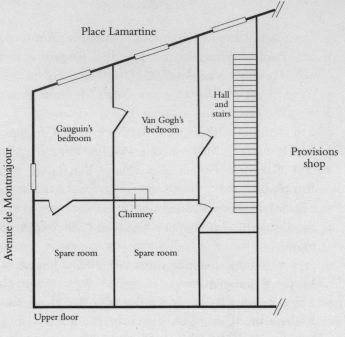

S

Place Lamartine

Avenue de Montmajour

Gauguin's
bedroom

Van Gogh's
bedroom

Hall
and
stairs

Provisions
shop

Chimney

Spare room

Spare room

Upper floor

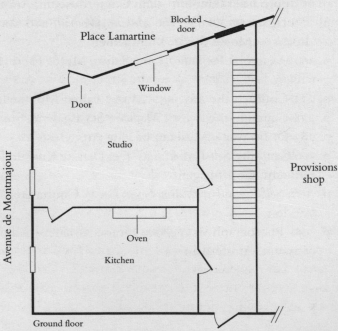

Blocked
door

Place Lamartine

Avenue de Montmajour

Window

Door

Studio

Provisions
shop

Oven

Kitchen

Ground floor

1. The Arrival

23 October 1888

While it was still dark, shortly after five o'clock in the morning, a train clanked into the station at Arles and a solitary, exhausted passenger got out. He had been travelling for nearly two days. His journey had begun the previous Sunday in Pont-Aven, near the Atlantic coast of Brittany, almost 700 miles away. Since then he had moved by stages from a damp, green region on the Atlantic coast to a flat plain near the point where the Rhône River met the Mediterranean.

The route had taken him right across France, via Nantes and Tours, Clermont Ferrand and Lyon. Although he was now in the sunny south, the night air was chilly – only 5°C. He stepped out of the station, turned left and walked under the railway bridge, then along the street until he came to a large open square. On his right was the embankment of a wide river – the Rhône. To the left was the house he was heading for, its shutters still closed. But just at the junction of the street and the square there were signs of animation in an all-night café. He opened the door.

It was bright inside because of the lamps hanging from the ceiling. The walls were red, the floorboards bare. Around the sides of the room were tables topped with marble; in the centre was a big billiard table; and at the back of the room a small bar covered with assorted bottles. On the wall above, over the entrance to an inner room, hung a handsome clock, still showing not much after five o'clock. The owner looked at the newcomer, then exclaimed, 'You're the pal. I recognize you!'

The speaker, Joseph Ginoux, was proprietor of the café – a new establishment that had opened only at the beginning of the year. He was talking to a forty-year-old artist with some reputation in the circles of the avant garde. Ginoux had identified him by means that – even in the 1880s – were old-fashioned. Earlier, he had been shown a painted portrait and been told to look out for its subject, who would soon be arriving.

Paul Gauguin settled down in the Café de la Gare to wait for dawn. When the sun finally rose, he went out, crossed over to number 2 Place Lamartine, whose yellow walls and green-painted woodwork could now be clearly seen, and knocked on the door. It was opened by Vincent van Gogh.

This was, it was safe to say, among the most exhilarating but also the most anxious moments of Vincent's life. No sooner had he signed the lease for the Yellow House, almost six months before, than Vincent had started to evolve a plan. He didn't want to live in the house alone; he desperately yearned for company. Right from the start, Gauguin had come to mind as the ideal companion. On that very day he had written to his younger brother, Theo, describing the house and floating a suggestion: 'Perhaps Gauguin would come south?'

The notion rapidly grew into an obsession. From the end of May for the following five months, by letter, Vincent plotted, cajoled, argued, pleaded and insisted that Gauguin journey to Arles and join him. He persuaded Theo – who was already supporting Vincent himself – to offer the penurious painter a deal: free board and lodging in exchange for pictures provided he agreed to live in 2 Place Lamartine, the Yellow House. Theo was working as an art dealer in Paris – one of the few who supported experimental painting – so he was in a position to help Gauguin a great deal.

In reply, Gauguin accepted, then – time and again – postponed his departure. A correspondence developed between the two painters, far more intense than their actual, physical acquaintance in Paris the previous winter. Ideas were exchanged and adopted, new paintings described. Vincent was euphoric with the hope that Gauguin would soon appear and cast down by the fear that he would not.

Recently – since Gauguin's departure had definitely been announced – Vincent had been consumed by the anxiety that, when the other actually arrived, he would not think much of Arles. Gauguin, Vincent feared, would find the area unsatisfactory in comparison to Brittany. He might find the scenery lacking in the rich possibilities he had discovered in the north. Instead of joining in Vincent's project and offering his companionship, there was the tormenting possibility that Gauguin would be angry and disdainful. Vincent's nervous tension had reached such a point that he feared he would become ill. Some explosion threatened. And now here Gauguin was, actually at the door. He entered.

The two men were a little disconcerted by each other. Both had built up their expectations, based on the evidence of paintings. In advance of Gauguin's arrival, Vincent had proposed an exchange of portraits. Gauguin had dispatched one south – the picture that had been shown to the café owner, Ginoux – and Vincent had in turn sent a painting of himself north to Brittany. But those self-portraits were not simply evidence of how the two men actually looked or who they actually were. One was a forty-year-old Frenchman with an estranged family and a background in financial trading, the other a thirty-five-year-old Dutch man who had tried his

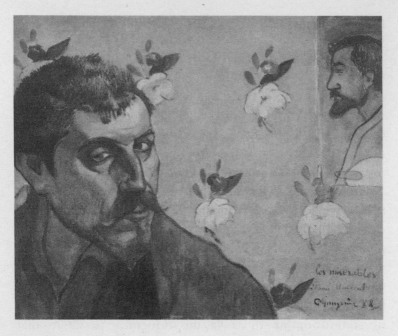

hand at various tasks. Both had come to painting relatively late in life. But the pictures were indices of how Gauguin and Van Gogh imagined themselves. Each had presented his image in character, as a figure from literature. One thing they had in common was an intense fantasy life in which their own real lives merged with their reading.

In the corner of his picture, Gauguin had painted above his signature the words, '*Les Misérables*' – a reference to the best-known of all French novels, Victor Hugo's masterpiece. This was an easy clue, as such things go. Gauguin meant to present himself as an artistic equivalent to the hero of that novel, Jean Valjean – convicted criminal, outcast, martyr and saint. Despite his having written the name of the novel on the picture, Gauguin still doubted whether all the nuances of his meaning would be understood.

So, ahead of the arrival of the portrait itself, Vincent had received a letter of explanation from Brittany in which Gauguin described the crucial aspects of the self-portrait: 'The face of a bandit like Jean Valjean, strong and badly dressed, who has a nobleness and gentleness hidden within. Passionate blood suffuses the face as it does a creature in rut, and the eyes are enveloped by tones as red as the fire of a forge, which indicate the inspiration like molten lava which fills the soul of painters such as us.'

The yellow wallpaper behind, with its bouquets of flowers, 'like that of a young girl's bedroom', symbolized – he went on – 'our artistic virginity'. As he saw it, Jean Valjean – oppressed by society but full of love and power – was just like an impressionist artist of the day.

And so, Gauguin concluded, in giving Valjean his own features, he was also painting a collective portrait of the tiny band of rebellious modern painters, who were poverty stricken for the most part, victims of society. They remained artistically as pure as virgins and were victims who responded to suffering – in a Christ-like manner – by doing good. They were creating the art of the future.

On reading Gauguin's description of his self-portrait, Vincent had concluded that the picture must be a masterpiece. But when it arrived he found it worryingly dark and sad. It was too close an echo of the anxious, harried feelings he had himself.

Vincent's self-portrait was even harder to decode. He had written no clue to its meaning on the canvas. He had simply presented his head and shoulders – his hair and beard unusually short – against a jade-green background. Of all the self-portraits he painted, this was the oddest.

Characteristically, when he described it to Gauguin, it was the colour that came first to mind. 'I have a portrait of myself, all ash-grey,' he had written three weeks before. This effect was the result of mixing green and orange on a pale jade

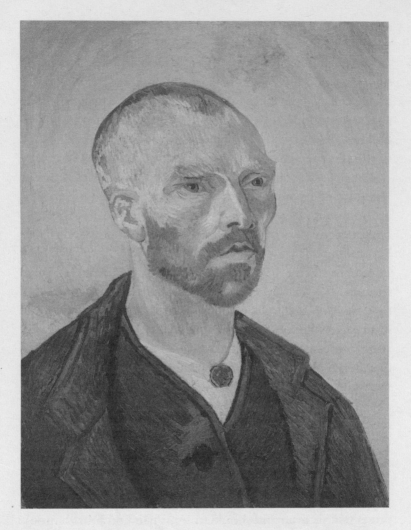

background, all harmonized with his reddish-brown clothes –
a difficult combination which had given him trouble.

   In the flesh of Vincent's neck and face, delicate strokes of
light green and pale rose mingled with the ginger of his hair
and its reflections. From a distance, these marks of the brush
fused into a unity that vibrated with life. The touches of

paint followed the contours of his face. And those features themselves were gaunt, the cheekbones strongly projecting.

An opalescent green seemed to radiate from the head, forming an icy halo. Vincent's eyes – yellow-brown, not blue-green as in his other portraits – were pulled up on either side in cat-like fashion, brush strokes radiating around them like lines of magnetic force. Their look was elusive. Was it nervous? Or timid? Or determined? It was an enigmatic self-depiction, with a touch of the convict or some other kind of institutional inmate about it.

He signed it, as he always did those pictures with which he was particularly pleased, and those he presented as gifts, 'Vincent'; the signature was later partially erased. Partly because no French tongue could negotiate his surname, and perhaps also partly because he felt disconnected from his pious, bourgeois Dutch family, he was always simply Vincent.

Few observers would have guessed the guise that the painter took on in this picture. Vincent had, he wrote to Gauguin, 'aimed at the character of a simple bonze worshipping the eternal Buddha'. That is, he had painted himself as a Japanese monk. No persona, on the face of it, might seem less probable for Vincent, an avant-garde Dutch painter living in the South of France. The idea had come from a book – then newly published and widely read – by the best-selling author Pierre Loti: *Madame Chrysanthème*.

This purported to be the memoirs of a French naval officer whose ship was temporarily stationed in Tokyo and who took a Japanese mistress in a purely financial arrangement. She became fond of him, and he almost developed a fondness for her; then he departed. The story was later to serve as the basis for Puccini's opera, *Madame Butterfly*.

Buddhist monks were not the heroes of *Madame Chrysanthème*; they merely had walk-on parts. They appear in a procession and in a later visit to a monastery. The life of such a Buddhist monk, the book revealed, did not exclude a little indulgence. The monks were fond of French liqueurs, and pictures of women. But the essential message of the portrait was that the sitter was leading a calm, orderly, contemplative life. He was a member of a spiritual order, under the discipline of a superior.

This was the reverse of the solitary existence that Van Gogh had been experiencing in Arles; it was more the expression of a hope: the Yellow House was to be a miniature monastic community dedicated to producing the art of the future. In this monastery there had to be an Abbot – to 'keep order', as Vincent put it – and that would naturally be Gauguin, with Vincent his humble adherent. But in reality, Vincent was not at all the tranquil being he depicted. On the contrary, he was often disquietingly worked up.

On actually seeing Gauguin, Vincent was surprised to find that his guest was much healthier-looking than he had anticipated. The portrait inscribed '*Les Misérables*' had created the image of desperation; so too had constant complaints in Gauguin's letters about a debilitating disease – probably dysentery – that he had picked up the year before while painting in Martinique. But Gauguin seemed finally to have shaken that off.

The impression Gauguin generally made on people was of contained power, both bodily and psychological. Physically, both Gauguin and Van Gogh were small, even by the standards of nineteenth-century France. The French navy, in which he had once served, recorded Gauguin's height as 1.63 metres (a little over 5 foot 4 inches), but he thought of himself as long-legged and tall. Archibald Standish Hartrick, a Scot who encountered him in Brittany, thought Gauguin 'a fine figure of a man'.

Vincent made the opposite impression. At home in Holland he had been called, mockingly, '*het schildermanneke*' or 'the little painter'. True, a Dutch neighbour remembered him, though short, as 'squarely built', but that was not how most others recalled him over subsequent years. Hartrick considered him 'a rather weedy little man, with pinched features'. One of the staff at the hospital at Arles – Dr Félix Rey – found him a yet more unimpressive specimen – 'miserable, wretched . . . short and thin'.

Although Gauguin was inclined to impress on an initial meeting, not everybody liked him on closer acquaintance. Many in the small coterie of advanced Parisian painters were suspicious, even hostile. Camille Pissarro, for instance, who had at one stage taken Gauguin under his wing, came to think of him as a thief of other artists' ideas, and the young painter Paul Sérusier felt there was something dubious about him, a touch of play-acting and also of ruthlessness. 'He made you think of a buffoon, a troubadour, and a pirate all at once.'

Gauguin was measured in manner. His voice was sombre and husky. He had, a writer named Charles Morice noted, 'a large, bony, solid face with a narrow forehead'. His mouth was straight and thin-lipped, and he had 'heavy eye-lids that opened lazily over slightly bulging, bluish eyes that rotated in their sockets to look to the left and right almost without the body or the head having to take the trouble to move.'

Vincent, in contrast, was prone to disquietingly fast and jerky behaviour. Hartrick remembered:

He had an extraordinary way of pouring out sentences, if he got started, in Dutch, English and French, then glancing back at you over his shoulder, and hissing through his teeth. In fact, when thus excited, he looked more than a little mad; at other times, he was inclined to be morose, as if suspicious.

Hartrick and his cronies thought him 'cracked' but harm-less, perhaps not interesting enough to bother much about.

But some found redeeming inner qualities when they got to know Vincent better. He had found a few friends in Arles that year – a soldier, a postal worker and three other painters. But sometimes he went for days without speaking to anyone, and there were painful persecutions by the local youths which he did not confess, even to his brother Theo.

Years later, Monsieur Jullian – by then the respectable librarian of Arles – felt guilt for the way he and his teenage friends had treated Vincent. They would shout abuse at him as he went past, 'alone and silent, in his long smock and wearing one of those cheap straw hats you could buy every-where.' Vincent had decorated his hat with ribbons, 'some-times blue, sometimes yellow'. This touching mark of his faith in colour was bound to provoke the local youths. Vincent's habit of 'continually stopping and peering at things' – natural in a painter – excited the ridicule of his tormenters:

I remember and I am bitterly ashamed of it now – how I threw cabbage stalks at him! What do you expect? We were young, and he was odd, going out to paint in the country, his pipe between his teeth, his big body a bit hunched, a mad look in his eye. He always looked as if he were running away, without daring to look at anyone.

Vincent caused no disturbance, M. Jullian recalled, 'except when he had been drinking, which happened often'. Looking back, the librarian saw that he was 'really a gentle person, a creature who would probably have liked us to like him, and we left him in his terrifying isolation, the terrible loneliness of genius.'

Adding to Vincent's general air of eccentric vagrancy was

his lack of teeth, ten of them having been extracted in Paris eighteen months before and replaced by false ones. Years of rough living had left him looking older than his thirty-five years (his birthday, on 30 March, had fallen that year a month after he arrived in Arles).

Gauguin, too, had had his share of sufferings – including near-destitution at times in the previous few years – and his draining tropical disease. But these had not yet destroyed his air of dynamism and strength. Few considered Gauguin other than formidable. No one seems to have thought the same of Vincent. His brother Theo was perhaps the only person in the entire world who believed he might become a significant painter.

Vincent had been accepted as a colleague and a friend in Paris before he left for Arles by such promising younger artists as Paul Signac, Henri de Toulouse-Lautrec and Emile Bernard. But there was no hint that any of them thought he had the potential for greatness.

Indeed, on 23 October 1888 neither Gauguin nor Vincent had large reputations in the world of art. They were both members of a loose coterie of experimental, mainly youthful painters based in and around Paris. This was the forerunner of what came to be called the avant garde (though that term was not yet used). These new artists no longer formed a single school, as a critic noted a few years later. They reminded him of the geometric patterns of a kaleidoscope, now fusing, now flying apart, but all revolving within 'the circle of the new art'. All of them were searching for a something beyond Impressionism, the dominant radical movement of the older generation. The Impressionists themselves – Monet, Renoir, Pissarro – were now in their late forties and fifties.

The embryonic and emerging younger artists exhibited not in the annual *Salon*, where established, academic painters showed, but in less formal shows, some in cafés and on the premises of friendly magazines. Even in this little world, Gauguin and Vincent were not the most prominent figures. The leading innovative painter in Paris was the twenty-nine-year-old Georges Seurat, who had devised a new method of painting based on dots of pure colour.

In comparison, Gauguin was just beginning to establish himself as a force. In the past couple of years he had attracted a small following of much more youthful painters, all searching for a new art that did not yet have a name. These disciples were on the point of calling him 'master'.

Vincent himself, at thirty-five, had almost no reputation at all. He was known to a circle of fellow painters, Gauguin among them, as an odd fellow with intriguing ideas. He had been working as an artist for less than a decade, mostly in isolation, and his work had been seen in public only twice, on both occasions in exhibitions he had organized himself in Montmartre drinking-spots.

Nobody, including the painter himself, realized that, in October 1888, Vincent van Gogh was engaged in one of the most astonishing creative sprints in Western art. During his year and a bit in Arles, he produced some 200 paintings – around a third of the number Gauguin executed in his entire life – and many of those pictures were masterpieces. Although some had been dispatched to Theo in Paris, the bulk of them were there in the Yellow House. The pictures were everywhere – tacked to the walls, hung in frames, stacked in storage. There was much to talk about and do as the sun rose on 23 October 1888, but the most startling novelty for Gauguin was those extraordinary paintings. Very few people alive were in such a good position as Gauguin to comprehend Vincent's achievement; and no one had better reasons to admire it, assimilate it – or resist it.

★

Sun poured in through the south-facing windows of the Yellow House that Tuesday morning, a fine, clear autumn day. The light in the front room downstairs, which one stepped into straight from the street, was among the attractions of the place. Vincent had chosen it as his studio. So there were his easel, palette and all he needed to paint. The room smelt of his pipe smoke as well as of turpentine, pigment and Vincent himself. This was an era before the invention of deodorants, the climate was hot and washing arrangements limited.

The windows of this work room faced straight out on to the street, so passers-by could peer in. But Vincent – at least in his more ebullient phases – did not mind being watched while he painted. He felt people might then understand that he was doing a real job of work.

The space was permeated by noises as well as odours and the life of the street. While working there one could hear chatter outside, mostly in Provençal. Occasionally, a farm wagon or horse-drawn carriage would rattle past. Whenever a train went over the bridge just down the Avenue de Montmajour, its chugging was clearly audible. The steam whistles were loud at night.

Gauguin recalled a chaotic untidiness in the studio. 'I was shocked,' he wrote. 'His box of colours barely sufficed to contain all those squeezed tubes, which were never closed up.' In this reaction Gauguin wasn't alone. Theo had complained that after his brother moved into his flat in Paris, the place deteriorated because Vincent was so 'dirty and untidy'.

Vincent had been working in the studio at the Yellow House since the previous May – although he had only begun living in the building on 16 September. There had been plenty of time for him to deposit debris all around him, like the active volcano Gauguin compared him to and which, in a way, he was.

This domestic confusion was part of the zone of disturbance

Vincent created around him – by his manner, the rhythm of his speech, his movements, the insistence with which he expressed his views. Despite the disarray, however, there was a pleasant simplicity about the house with its white walls, blue doors and floors of local red tile.

The studio – like the other rooms at the front of the Yellow House – was an irregular shape. The walls of the building followed the arrangement of the streets outside, which were not at right angles, so though the jaunty little classical structure looked foursquare, it was actually askew.

The two long, narrow bedrooms upstairs faced the square. Vincent's was furnished with a puritanical sobriety – a plain deal bed, a couple of chairs, a simple washing stand with hair-brushes and shaving gear, a towel on a hook, a mirror. Six days before, Vincent had completed a picture of this interior.

Gauguin's room was next door – in fact, one had to pass through Vincent's to reach it. It was smaller and had no fireplace but was more opulently appointed, with a walnut bed, dressing-table and matching picture frames. Both rooms looked straight out on to one of the little parks outside, which had an oval pond in the middle. When the green shutters were open on a fine day such as that one, sun poured in. But that was not the overwhelming thing.

It was the paintings that were astonishing. Those, Gauguin wrote later, 'shone out' from the surroundings, indeed, there was hardly any gap between them; the whole room was only 2.25 by 3.4 metres – not much bigger than a boxroom – and it contained six big canvases. There were four landscapes of the gardens in the Place Lamartine – not as they were that fine autumn morning, with the leaves beginning to fall, but as they had been a month before when the greens were already starting to turn to gold.

These were on the side walls of the room, but the paintings

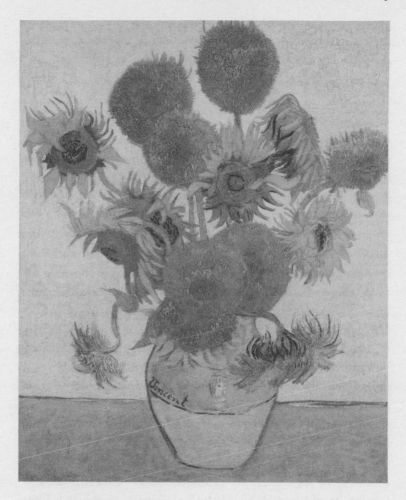

that really caught Gauguin's attention and stayed in his mind were at either end, beside the window and above the bed-head.

'In my yellow room,' he wrote six years later, using a little poetic licence:

sunflowers with purple eyes stand out on a yellow background; they bathe their stems in a yellow pot on a yellow table. In a corner

of the painting, the signature of the painter: Vincent. And the
yellow sun that passes through the yellow curtains of my room
floods all this fluorescence with gold; and in the morning upon
awakening from my bed, I imagine that all this smells very good.

Gauguin's description was not exact. There were actually
two sunflower paintings in the bedroom, and only one of the
pictures was yellow on yellow; the other had a turquoise
backdrop. But both were crackling with electricity in a way
that no floral paintings had ever done before.

Vincent had arranged the decoration and furnishing of the
Yellow House after long and careful thought. On first arriving
in Arles at the end of February he had taken a room at the
Hôtel-Restaurant Carrel in the Rue de la Cavalerie, just
inside the medieval gate of the city before Place Lamartine.
He paid five francs a week for the room. Later, that was
reduced to four – but he still felt he was being overcharged.
He didn't like the food, which he also thought expensive
(Vincent tended to be strange about eating and suffered from
pains in his stomach).

Often, walking out of town towards Montmajour, Vincent
had passed the Yellow House, standing in the sun on the
corner of the square. Eventually, on 1 May, he signed a five-
month lease for the empty right-hand part of the building.

If he couldn't yet live in the unfurnished rooms of the
Yellow House, at least he could soon use it as a studio. Six
days later – the dispute about overcharging at the Hôtel-
Restaurant Carrel having grown acrimonious – he moved to
the Café de la Gare along the street, where he slept and ate
from then on. He became a member of the little community
of Place Lamartine.

Hardly had Vincent rented the Yellow House – for fifteen

francs a month – than he began to think about furnishing and
equipping it. The building had been shut up and uninhabited
for a long time and was in poor condition. Vincent, despite
his dishevelled appearance, had pronounced nest-building
tendencies. In Paris, where he had shared a flat with his
brother, Theo, he had filled it with carefully selected objects.
When later his sister-in-law was shown the apartment, every
vase or ornament she praised turned out to be something that
Vincent had found and thought pretty.

But what Vincent thought pretty – just like his own paintings – was much rougher and simpler than what most people
liked. 'What a mistake,' he exclaimed, 'Parisians make in
not having a palate for crude things.' He loved 'common
earthenware', for example, and often posed his flower subjects
in vases made of it. Early in May, out of his limited allowance
– all provided by Theo – he bought two chairs, a table and
'things for making a little coffee and soup at home'.

These starred in a new painting:

a still life of a blue enamelled iron coffee-pot, a royal blue cup and
saucer, a milk jug with pale cobalt and white checks, a cup with
orange and blue patterns on a white ground, a blue majolica jug
decorated with green, brown and pink flowers and leaves.

Although he still had no furnishings or beds and the place
badly needed decorating, Vincent bought table linen for the
house, selecting a hard-wearing variety.

On 27 May Vincent agreed to contribute towards the costs
of having his half of the building repainted, inside and out.
He paid his half of the bill – ten francs – on 10 June. From
that point, the Yellow House, previously dilapidated, became
visibly much fresher and brighter than the twin, left-hand
side of the structure, occupied by a grocer's shop.

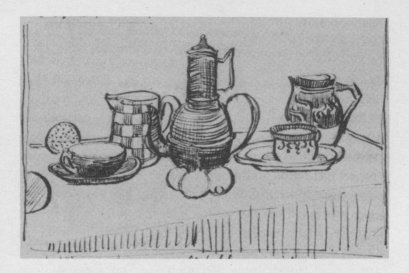

The outside walls were the fresh, almost edible colour of butter. The shutters were vivid green, the doors inside a soothing blue. There, in and on the house, were the major notes in the colour scale – yellow, green, blue, and the rich red of the studio floor. From that moment, the ground-floor front room became Vincent's studio. The studio and its furniture took on roles in his pictures. The strength of the colours suited his mood that summer.

Just before Gauguin arrived Vincent had gaslight installed in the studio and kitchen at a cost of twenty-five francs. He planned to paint portraits indoors at night, just as he had recently painted after dark in the central square and beside the Rhône, the glow of the streetlight eked out by candles on his hat.

It was not until September that Vincent could afford to furnish the two bedrooms upstairs. On Saturday 8 September, advised by his friend, the postal supervisor at the station, Joseph Roulin, and his wife, he bought two beds. Vincent selected a simple one made of white deal for his room and a more luxurious walnut one for the guest room – with luck

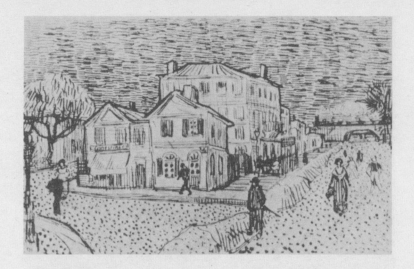

to be occupied by Gauguin. They were big double beds in the local style, not iron bedsteads. This gave them, Vincent felt, 'an air of solidity, permanence and calm'.

He also bought two mattresses and – because the beds came to 150 francs and his money was running short – sheets and blankets for only one. That same day he bought a mirror – because he had the self-portrait in mind – a few bits and pieces and twelve chairs. The latter figure, however, might have been just in Vincent's mind; he thought he painted twelve sunflowers, though that was not the real amount. He was apt to be absent-minded about factual details. He wrote Rue de Laval on an envelope instead of Rue de Lepic, which was Theo's correct address, presumably because he had been thinking about Charles Laval, a painter friend of Gauguin's. Describing the yellow of the sun that burnt in the sky above his house, Vincent accidentally wrote 'souffre' not 'soufre' – not 'sulphur' but 'suffering' – perhaps an insignificant slip. Twelve was a suitably apostolic number for gatherings connected with the Yellow House.

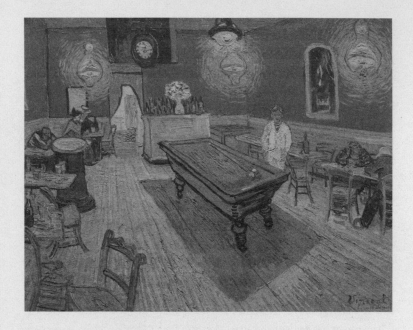

On that Saturday Vincent had received a generous 300 francs enclosed in a letter from Theo. By Sunday only fifty remained, but the house was almost ready. A few days before, he had been feeling despondent and ill; now, suddenly, he felt a rush of confidence and energy.

For three nights, he sat painting in the Café de la Gare – to the entertainment of Ginoux and the other habitués, who included local streetwalkers and their clients. This was a room in which Vincent had spent many evenings – reading, writing letters, thinking, talking, drinking – amid the prostitutes and the drunks who snoozed on the little tables. His picture, he wrote, was intended to 'express the terrible passions of humanity'.

'I have tried to express the idea that the café is a place where one can ruin oneself, go mad or commit a crime.' Someone who saw the *Night Café*, Vincent reflected, would

conclude that its painter had full-blown delirium tremens –
and it was true that Vincent's consumption of drink was
sometimes out of control.

Vincent was always reading newspapers, magazines and
novels. Another painting from that year was a portrait of his
books, piled up on the table-top, some open, some closed.
Most of them were yellow-covered paperback editions of his
favourite modern authors, men such as Gustave Flaubert, the
brothers Goncourts, Alphonse Daudet, Guy de Maupassant
and, above all, Emile Zola. When he looked around in Arles,
the works of these men came back to him. The Café de la
Gare no doubt reminded him of Zola's novel *L'Assommoir*,
about the degradation, derangement and death brought on
by drink.

As soon as Vincent had bought the bedroom furniture, his
mind was racing with ideas for the poky, rented, skewed four
rooms on Place Lamartine. 'I have it all planned,' he wrote
on the evening of 9 September, excited by his purchases, and
sitting in the Café de la Gare. 'I really do want to make it –
an artist's house, but not affected, on the contrary, *nothing
affected*, but everything from the chairs to the pictures full of
character.'

The notion of a house for an artist was in the air. Edmond
de Goncourt, the survivor of the two brothers, had published
a deluxe, two-volume account of his own house in Paris. But
in the Yellow House – quite different from de Goncourt's
luxurious house – everything was to be simple. That was an
ideal as well as a matter of necessity. The rush-bottomed
chairs, for example, were just the same as the ones Vincent
sat on when he took his dinner in the Restaurant Venissat,
next door to the Café de la Gare. They were ordinary, unpretentious Arles chairs. But that kind of simplicity – apart from
its being unavoidable for reasons of cost – pleased Vincent. It

spoke to him of monastic life and of the spare interiors in Japanese dwellings (the bonzes in *Madame Chrysanthème* lived among plain yellow walls and unframed pictures).

His new home, Vincent decided, would be an artist's house in the most direct way – by being filled with his art. His pictures would form a *décoration* for the walls. By that, he meant not just that they would be decorative, but that they would evoke multiple meanings and emotions – amounting to his whole world – through their contrasting colours and subjects. Some paintings depicted the immediate neighbourhood – the parks outside, the banks of the Rhône, the Café de la Gare – all of which reminded him of Zola and the artist Honoré Daumier, whose lithographs also hung on the walls of the Yellow House, in company with Japanese prints and Vincent's pictures. Other paintings portrayed Vincent's friends. The *décoration* was a fitting backdrop to Vincent's most ambitious plan: the Yellow House would be home to a miniature community. Most often, Gauguin was Vincent's imagined housemate, but there were other possibilities. Perhaps Emile Bernard would come. Then there was Charles Laval, the friend of Gauguin's who had shared in his intrepid painting adventure to Martinique.

In Vincent's mind, the Yellow House expanded. There were two other tiny compartments, cupboards really, on the upper floor. Surely it would be possible to fit everybody in? Another visitor might be his brother, Theo, coming down from Paris to recuperate from ill health and the exhaustion of his art-dealing life.

The Yellow House would house a new artists' colony. That, of course, was not a new idea. Northern Europe, especially the cheaper coastal fringes, was strewn with the rookeries of bohemian painters. But to found such a group in the remote Midi, land of blazing sun and brilliant colour – that was absolutely new, and Vincent's own idea. His would be a studio of the *South*, a band of brother artists whose work was so new and unknown it did not even have a proper name. Vincent called them the 'painters of the Petit Boulevard' after their Parisian haunt, the Boulevard de Clichy, rather than the smart Boulevard Montmartre. Some were painters who used simplified shapes and colours in the manner of the Japanese prints that were then so fashionable and widely collected among the up-to-date – among them, Vincent.

It seemed obvious to him that the artists of the Petit Boulevard should work in the bright, clear light of the south, which was, he imagined, exactly like that of Japan. He and the others would live and paint together – different in individual style but sharing a common aim, exchanging ideas, commenting on each other's work just as Vincent, Bernard and Gauguin now did by letter. However, to coax his friends to Arles seemed an impossible task. There were moments at which Vincent wondered whether it might be easier for him to migrate to Pont-Aven.

The Paris–Lyon–Méditerranée Railway, or PLM, was Vincent's means of contact with the outside world. Its trains carried his mail to the north, where his brother and artist friends lived, and their mail back to him in the south. (In cases of dire emergency, there was also the telegram.) Letters were picked at regular intervals, from five in the morning until ten at night. And there were four postal deliveries a day, so Vincent and his circle could transmit ideas and information to each other with some rapidity. The only aspect difficult to convey by post – and a vital matter to Vincent and his fellow painters – was colour, which was why their letters were full of detailed descriptions of pictures, shade by shade, hue by hue, and their drawings were carefully labelled '*bleu*', '*orange*', '*violet*' or '*vert*'.

★

In the month after he moved into the Yellow House, Vincent worked furiously. During the warm days of mid September, he painted day after day in the public gardens of Place Lamartine and, as he did so, a chain of extravagant associations formed in his mind. He had read an article about the medieval Italian writer Boccaccio in a magazine. Soon, it struck him that he was like Boccaccio, and Gauguin resembled Boccaccio's wise and noble friend, the poet Petrarch. These little parks were Provençal gardens of love, especially the one in the corner nearest the brothel district, which filled him with erotic thoughts. Gauguin would be the new poet of the South! Together, they would make a new Renaissance.

During the second week of October alone, Vincent painted five large paintings, then felt completely exhausted; his eyes were so tired he could scarcely see properly. On the night of Saturday 13 October, he slept for sixteen hours at one stretch in his new bed. A violent mistral wind was blowing, whipping up clouds of dust and keeping him indoors. He had had, as he put it, a 'queer turn': some sort of attack or collapse.

It gave him the idea for a new picture. 'This time,' he wrote, the subject was simply his bedroom – the colour alone made it seem simple and grand and suggestive 'of *rest* or of sleep in general'. But, actually, the picture did not give an entirely tranquil impression.

Partly, that was due not to Vincent, who painted what was before his eyes, but to the architecture of the Yellow House. The end wall of the room was not at right angles to the sides but slanting. The rushing perspective of the room, however, was Vincent's. And, more than rest and repose, the painting suggested furniture and fittings hurtling along under the impact of some tremendous force.

Vincent feared, not for the first time, that he was going mad. He needed to eat more regularly, he felt, and paint less for a few days; otherwise, he might become 'ill'. He confided to Theo that if he did go mad it would not take the form of persecution mania, which rather suggested that he had wondered whether it might. It was at this point, on the day that he finished the *Bedroom* – Wednesday the seventeenth – that Gauguin, after delaying so many months, announced his imminent departure from Brittany.

The obstacles to his leaving had suddenly cleared. Theo had sold some of his ceramics, so Gauguin could pay off a proportion of his debts for food, lodgings and medicine (he was surprisingly punctilious about that sort of thing). His illness – which had been causing painful stomach cramps and discharges of blood into his chamber pot – had cleared up. He had already sent his trunk containing his fencing gear and heavier possessions. He himself would soon follow.

Writing to his friend Emil Schuffenecker, Gauguin expressed his satisfaction at the way things were going. 'However fond of me Van Gogh may be he isn't falling over himself to send me to the Midi board and lodging paid just for my fine blue eyes.' To Gauguin, Theo was always 'Van Gogh', and Vincent was just Vincent. He saw the former as a 'cool Dutchman' who had studied the art market and concluded that he, Gauguin, was the coming man. Finally, everything was going his way.

'You know well that in art I am always fundamentally right. Mark this well, at the moment among *artists* a wind is blowing which is most decidedly favourable to me.' Gauguin was even enthusiastic about the South. He had written a little poem in one of his recent letters to Vincent, an ode to the sun of the Midi. It began, 'Oh chrome God!' and continued through multiple crossings-out. Poetry was not Gauguin's *métier*.

So they were in very different states of mind, the two men who met that morning in the Yellow House, one full of renewed health and confidence, the other teetering on the edge of derangement. They had a lot of talking to do. After a while they went out, so that Gauguin – who had only walked the few yards from the station to Place Lamartine, and in the dark at that – could take a look at the town of Arles.

2. Beginning and Carrying On
24–28 October

Wednesday 24 October turned out to be another fine autumnal day. Winter was coming but was not here yet. It was good painting weather. The two men set to work. Normally, they got up early – Gauguin regarded a seven o'clock start as later than usual.

In Brittany, he was accustomed to come down to breakfast around seven and then start work, breaking for lunch at eleven-thirty and resuming painting at one-thirty or two, then carrying on until five. Vincent sometimes stayed out in the fields at his easel all day, snacking off a little bread and milk since he thought it too much bother to go back into town.

But if he was frugal about food, Vincent was very fond of coffee – in fact, he was addicted to it. When short of cash he had lived on little else, except bread. One of the first items he bought when he rented the Yellow House was coffee-making equipment. In Arles he sometimes ate a couple of eggs for breakfast, which he thought good for his stomach. Gauguin's habitual morning meal was *café au lait* with bread and butter.

On that first day, Vincent – though perhaps not Gauguin – went out into the fields to paint. But first he needed to assemble his outdoor painting equipment. This included a portable easel – not the more bulky type used indoors – a box filled with tubes of paint, brushes, turpentine, sticks and other paraphernalia. As a result, when fully loaded, he looked – he thought – like a bristling porcupine. He wore workmen's clothes – either a blue workman's jacket and trousers or white, both liberally marked with dabs of pigment as a result of carrying wet canvases. Vincent topped off his outfit with a straw hat such as the local shepherds wore. If he took a left turn out of the front door of the Yellow House, another left into the Avenue de Montmajour, after a few minutes Vincent would be in the plain of the Crau.

He had come to have many powerful feelings for this place; oddly, because it was difficult to say exactly why he had settled in Arles. His reasons for coming to the South of France were clearer, though – characteristically, mixing the personal and the aesthetic in a fashion that, to a superficial observer, would have seemed downright peculiar.

'My dear brother,' he reminded Theo. 'You know that I came to the south and threw myself into work for a thousand reasons.' He was 'looking for a different light', partly because he 'believed that observing nature under a brighter sky might give one a more accurate idea of the way the Japanese feel and draw'. Japanese prints, with their bright, flat, clear colours, were a source of inspiration to many European artists of the time and a passionate interest of Vincent's. When his train had approached the Midi the previous February, Vincent had stuck his head out of the window in his excitement, hoping to see the landscapes of Japanese prints.

He had wanted to see a 'stronger sun', then, for artistic reasons, because he felt the 'colours of the prism' were 'veiled in the mists of the north'. It would help him to understand not only Japanese art but also the intense colours of Delacroix, another artistic hero. But he needed the light for personal reasons, too. Like many Northerners, he craved the southern warmth and radiance. The previous winter in Paris, he had had some sort of breakdown, he had felt 'mental weariness', emptiness, he was 'dimmed with sadness'. Vincent felt the

country was a better and a healthier place than the town and
that the southern countryside in particular would be more
carefree than the gloomy North (he had gathered as much
from a favourite book, *Tartarin de Tarascon* by Alphonse
Daudet).

But none of these factors really explained why he settled
in Arles, which was far from being the most obvious choice.
It wasn't on the coast; it wasn't especially picturesque. Many
people found it tawdry despite its ancient monuments, a
run-down town which had once been great – for an instant
it was capital of the Western Roman empire – but struggled
to find a role in the modern world. Gauguin decided it was
'the dirtiest town in the whole south' and with, in Vincent's
view, 'uncommonly good reason'. The sharp stones of its
twisting streets hurt the feet. The hotels were grubby.

Quite why Vincent had got off the train here, nobody ever
knew. Perhaps Toulouse-Lautrec, who came from the South,
had mentioned it. Degas, who had never been here, had told
him he was looking forward to painting the famous women
of the place. But perhaps it was just on a whim that Vincent
came here, liked what he saw, and stayed. He told an acquaintance that he only wanted to interrupt his journey in Arles
for a short time, but he became fascinated by the possibilities
of the area.

The landscape was calculated to appeal to the eye of a
Dutchman. The plain around Arles was, like much of the
Netherlands, reclaimed land. Until the drainage canals had
been dug in the sixteenth century the town had risen almost
like an island from the surrounding wetlands. The Roman
name of the place, Arlate, simply meant 'town in the marshes'.

The very flatness of this landscape appealed to Vincent. It
reminded him – as it would remind anyone brought up on
Dutch painting – of the landscapes of the great painters of the

seventeenth century – Ruysdael, Hobbema, Philips Koninck. He was fascinated especially by the view across the plain from the heights at Montmajour. In the summer, he went there again and again, to that 'flat landscape, where there was nothing but . . . infinity – eternity'. Gauguin, however, had no fond memories of low country.

Naturally, the contrast in terrain between Brittany and Provence was a topic of conversation between the two painters. For the time being, Vincent meekly accepted what Gauguin had to say about the Breton scenery – namely that it was larger, more pure and 'definite' than the 'shrivelled, scorched and trivial' surroundings he found in the South.

This was discouraging. But Vincent took comfort from the fact that Gauguin sensed artistic possibilities in his new surroundings and especially the female inhabitants. 'Above all things,' he reported to Theo, 'he is intrigued by the Arlésiennes.' At least Gauguin seemed to be settling in, and that was the main thing.

The size of the picture Vincent now began – a thirty – was a sign of ambition. Parisian dealers in art materials classified the sizes of the pre-prepared canvases they sold by number. It was a system derived from the widths produced by looms, arranged to suit the suppliers, not the painters. But artists had grown used to it. A size thirty was a large one, suitable for inclusion in an important exhibition. That was the size Vincent had selected for the *décorations* of the Yellow House.

He finished two new paintings over the next few days, 'a new study of a sower, the landscape quite flat, the figure small and vague', and a 'study of a ploughed field with the stump of an old yew tree'. He never said which came first, but for both meteorological and psychological reasons, it was probably the *Sower* that he began on that first morning of Gauguin's stay.

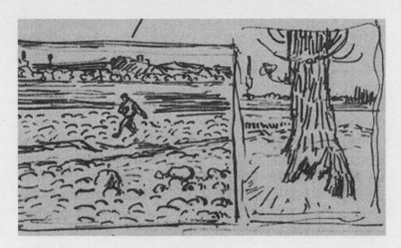

The sky was almost clear on the twenty-fourth – just a little light cloud – and the temperature balmy, which were the conditions to be seen in that picture. Psychologically, too, the subject was an apt beginning to a new phase of work.

This was a stretch of countryside bordering the road to Tarascon, and a continuation of the road that went past the Yellow House, which Vincent had painted again and again through the year. It was familiar territory in every way: almost exactly the place – with the violet Alpilles and the medieval ruins of Montmajour behind – where he had painted the best of his harvest pictures and also his *Ploughed Field*. Those were among the works from the whole year with which he was most pleased.

In addition, the sower broadcasting his seed was an image that had been with him almost since he had become an artist. It stood for a painter – or an evangelist – sowing the seed of new beauty and truth. With great excitement, Vincent had painted a picture on this theme in the summer, but eventually he had decided it was a failure. He still had the ambition of painting a truly successful *Sower*.

As a choice of subject, it was significant, suggesting Vincent's determination to show his own art at its best before he was influenced – as he expected to be – by Gauguin. The *Sower* represented his highest ambitions for his work in Arles, and was all the more timely because it was actually painted during the sowing season.

This *Sower*, however, was not the masterpiece he planned. The figure hurries along in a way quite unlike the measured confidence of the earlier violet man standing in the sun, bringing regeneration. His right leg is badly drawn. The brushwork has a flurried quality, perhaps reflecting Vincent's anxious condition.

In the post that Wednesday was a letter from Theo, replying to Vincent's last appeal for cash and the worrying remarks he had made about his state of mind. Theo, who was on the point of dashing off to Brussels on business, diagnosed one reason for Vincent's attack of nerves: 'It is to be supposed that you have worked too hard, and consequently have forgotten to take proper care of your body.' As often, Theo enclosed money – fifty francs, which would temporarily calm Vincent's most urgent source of anxiety.

Unfortunately, his letter also contained three pieces of information likely to disturb Vincent further. One was that a Dutch painter, Meyer de Haan, was going to stay in Theo's flat. That is, he was going to take up Vincent's former position as his brother's flatmate and would soon, Theo predicted, 'become the central figure of a group of young people'. That was just what Vincent himself had done – form a circle of young artists. He was being supplanted.

Vincent had been hostile to this alter ego, de Haan, and his friend Isaacson, also an artist, the moment Theo had mentioned them. He had leapt to the conclusion that they

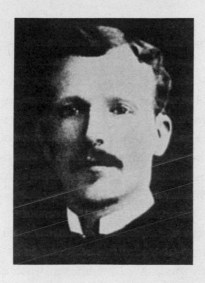

were brash know-alls from Holland with none of his own knowledge of contemporary French painting. Now, he accepted Theo's mild defence of the two of them: it was all Theo's fault, he must have given the wrong impression. It would be just as well, Vincent noted, for Theo to have a companion, 'especially since the winter will soon be here'.

Vincent and his brother suffered from a syndrome he called 'melancholy'. In becoming a painter, instead of giving in to despair, Vincent felt he had chosen an 'active melancholy', but he particularly dreaded the cold, dark months of winter, which were always a bad time for him. Fortunately, he now had someone to share this sombre season. It was good that Theo did too.

Theo mentioned more agitating news: another dealer – *père* Thomas – had shown no interest in buying Vincent's work (the second time Theo had tried recently). On the other hand, Theo himself had sold a big picture by Gauguin, *Breton Girls in a Ring*, to a collector named Dupuis. The artist's share was 500 francs. He had sent a letter about it to Gauguin in Brittany, but that message was still following the painter south to Arles.

The question of sales was an extremely sensitive one for Vincent. In reality, he had sold virtually nothing in his entire career as a painter to date, just a handful of works sold or exchanged for a few francs with his friend, the dealer Tanguy. His notion of the prospective value of his paintings was subject to drastic fluctuations, depending on his mood. A few weeks before, his estimates had been buoyant; now he computed them with the arithmetic of depression.

Then, in a state of elation, he had calculated the worth of fifteen of the *décorations* in the Yellow House at 10,000 francs, but now he estimated only 100 francs for each of his pictures. The consequences of this low price were dismal. If, over fifty years, Vincent spent 100,000 francs – low outgoings of 2,000 francs per year, less than he was already spending – that meant he must paint and sell 1,000 pictures at 100 francs each. It was a heavy burden, especially as he wasn't selling any at all. And now the longed-for sale had come – but to Gauguin, not to him.

Agonized by anxieties – and not only financial ones – Vincent was not as elated by Gauguin's arrival as one might have expected. He mentioned it to Theo, only with a wry twist. 'Gauguin has arrived in good health. He gives me the impression he is even better than me.' Altogether, given the intensity with which he had anticipated Gauguin's arrival, Vincent's enthusiasm was perfunctory.

'Gauguin is very, very interesting as a man,' Vincent declared. He would probably produce a great deal of paintings in Arles and, he added tentatively, 'I hope perhaps I shall too.' Then Vincent launched into a long and bitter lament about his financial predicament, his weariness, both physical and mental, his wasted efforts, his whole futile existence:

I myself realize the necessity to produce even to the extent of being morally crushed and physically drained by it, just because after all I have no other means of ever getting back what we have spent. I cannot help it that my pictures do not sell.

His debts were poisoning his life, even if he did succeed in paying them off – which seemed unlikely. 'The pains of producing pictures will have taken my whole life from me, and it will seem to me then that I have not lived.'

The one thing that cheered him up was a painting that had arrived in Gauguin's baggage trunk: Emile Bernard's most important work of the summer, *Breton Women in a Meadow*. This caused a lift in Vincent's morale. It was, he thought, 'magnificent'. He added, with a momentary flicker of better spirits, 'after all, we must all be of good cheer.' He very much admired what he saw, 'those Breton women walking in a meadow so beautifully composed, the colour with such naive distinction.'

This was one of the most radical paintings yet produced by a European artist; it had emerged from a creative conjunction of artists that summer in Pont-Aven. While Vincent was producing his astonishing *Sunflowers* in Arles, hundreds of miles north, Gauguin and Bernard were at work on equally audacious projects. They had indeed been a virtual trio, with Vincent taking part at a remove, by post.

It had been on his suggestion that Emile Bernard had joined Gauguin and Laval in August. Bernard, an extremely precocious twenty-year-old, was already acquainted with Gauguin but knew Vincent much better. They had been good friends at art school in Paris and afterwards. The proposal that Bernard should link up with Gauguin was typical of Vincent's urge to interfere benignly in his friends' affairs, but it had proved directly contrary to his other plan: to get Gauguin to come to Arles.

For several years Gauguin had had an idea of the kind of art he wanted to make: not an evocation, like Impressionism, of naturalistic appearances and shimmering visual sensations but of feelings and dreams. It would be an art that resembled music: an 'abstraction', a word that he used in a letter to Vincent a few weeks before Bernard arrived.

Gauguin could imagine it, but he couldn't actually paint it. And young Bernard brought just the clue Gauguin was looking for. A devout Catholic, Bernard was fascinated by medieval art as well as Japanese prints. The simple, strong outlines and flat, bright colours of stained glass and other medieval art offered an example of a mystical, non-naturalistic way of working.

Under the stimulus of Gauguin's company and that of the innovative artists who had already gathered around him, Bernard produced *Breton Women in the Meadow*. It depicted local women in their traditional costumes, but they were set in the solid green of the grass like figures in a thirteenth-century window. There was little perspective, not much light and shade: just figures thickly outlined in black, floating in a parallel universe of green.

Within a week or two, it seemed, Gauguin went one better and painted the *Vision of the Sermon*. Gauguin's painting resembled Bernard's in its simplification but had much greater intensity. Instead of a flat green background, Gauguin substituted a brilliant red. He activated that scarlet space with a tree that curves diagonally across the canvas. And he added two other elements: mystery and ambiguity.

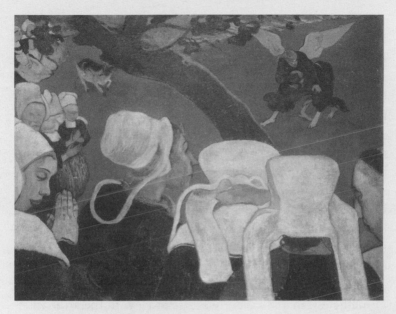

For all its formal boldness, Bernard's painting was essentially what the title says it is – a lot of women in a field. In Gauguin's picture, there were at least two levels of reality. In the foreground and on the left are the Breton women (plus a priest who may or may not be a self-portrait). In the middle of the deep-red field Jacob wrestles with the angel, an open metaphor for spiritual struggle or the striving of the artist.

It was a painting that was impossible to pin down. Was it religious in spirit or a snide attack on superstition? Gauguin seemed to believe the former, as he attempted to present it to two local churches, one after the other. But, to no one's surprise, it wasn't accepted by the priest responsible for either. Meanwhile, hearing by letter of these feats of painting, Vincent was half inclined to set off for Brittany himself. But, instead, thinking about stained glass, he plunged into the *Sunflowers*, a foray into pure yellow as bold as Gauguin's voyage into absolute red.

The painting Gauguin had sold wasn't the *Vision*, of which he was very proud. That had yet to arrive at Theo's gallery. It was an earlier, less radical work. But he still had every reason to be overjoyed. This sale was exactly the result that he had been scheming for since the summer. In 1888 the market in new, experimental art was itself a novel thing. The art market itself, for which Theo worked and Vincent himself had worked, was large, powerful and international. Works by old masters and respected stars of the annual *Salon* could reach astonishing sums. In 1876 a painting by Jean-Louis-Ernest Meissonier – an artist Vincent admired and Gauguin despised – had fetched 380,000 francs – making him the most expensive living artist.

In comparison, the only Impressionist who made a really good income was Claude Monet, the shrewdest businessman. Nonetheless, in 1888 there was a firm view in the art market that Impressionist prices were going to rise. The idea, the basic strategy of the trade – as of many other markets – was to buy low and to wait until prices went up. And the fundamental idea of artists, if they could afford it, was to set a high price and sit tight. Vincent and Gauguin both understood this principle.

Vincent felt that to find – or paint – a good painting was as difficult as finding a diamond. 'It requires pain and one must risk his life as a dealer or as an artist.' Once one had done so, however, the thing to do was to keep one's nerve and hold out for the right price. 'Art,' wrote Gauguin to his sceptical wife, Mette. 'It is my capital.' The problem was how the artist was to survive until that distant day when the world accepted his work at his own valuation.

Vincent, in practice, depended entirely on his allowance, and extra hand-outs, from Theo. But earlier in the year, after long discussions in the bars of Montmartre, he had elaborated a scheme. It was a self-help society for avant-garde painters. More established artists such as Monet and Degas would contribute canvases, as would their struggling colleagues. Profits would be pooled, from which the less established could live. Vincent still thought, however impractically, like a merchant in art.

Hearing of this proposal, Gauguin came up with his own variation: new art would be floated, like a company on the stock market. Speculators would invest in new artists and, when their reputations rose, draw a handsome dividend. This drew on Gauguin's own experience of a decade working in the Parisian financial markets. He was so proud of this idea that he swore Schuffenecker to secrecy about it. From these exercises in hopeless impracticality, two points can be deduced. First, Vincent's and Gauguin's minds ran on similar but slightly divergent lines. Second, that Gauguin had a capacity to take up the other's ideas, almost unconsciously, as his own.

The Van Gogh brothers came from a family of art dealers. Two of their uncles, Hein and Cent, were in the business. Uncle Cent, after whom Vincent had been named, was a big wheel in the international picture trade.

This other Vincent van Gogh had gone into partnership with the Parisian art-dealing firm run by Adolphe Goupil. He had retired in 1872, but his old firm was the obvious one for his brother's eldest son to enter. Thus, extraordinary though it would seem in 1888, to anyone looking at the outlandishly bohemian tenant of the Yellow House, Vincent had begun his adult life as a respectable businessman with, apparently, excellent prospects. He had started in the art trade at the age of sixteen in 1869 and carried on until 1876, when he was sacked.

Vincent's temperamental unsuitability for and lack of interest in selling art had become obvious, but his dismissal was a source of shame and anxiety to his parents. Theo, on the other hand – more diligent, practical and balanced – had followed the same path with success. He had also begun at sixteen, but he had progressed steadily, moving to Paris in 1875. Now, still only thirty-three, Theo was one of the more prominent of the dealers in Paris who took an interest in experimental painting.

Vincent had not forgotten the lessons of his first profession. His ideas might seem wild, but he kept an eye on the market. Two years before, in the early spring of 1886, Vincent had unexpectedly arrived in Paris from Antwerp, where he had been living. To Theo's alarm, he moved in with him.

Then, Vincent had known nothing of Impressionism and its successors, but he rapidly accumulated a group of radical young artists around him. Most of them were contemporaries at the Atelier Cormon, where Vincent attended life classes for a while – among them Henri de Toulouse-Lautrec and Emile Bernard. None had much of a reputation.

The brothers Van Gogh began collecting pictures – Vincent always talked about 'we' in this context – partly through exchanges of work between Vincent and his friends, partly through purchases using Theo's money. They tried to corner the market in Adolphe Monticelli, a neglected painter from Marseilles whom Vincent hugely admired, and they speculated in Gauguin. It looked as if they had been shrewd about the second.

As far as Gauguin was concerned, the sale of a picture proved that his affairs were finally improving. Gauguin's first letter to his friend Schuffenecker was mainly about prices. He was a little anxious that Schuff, who had plenty of his pictures, might sell them low and spoil the newly founded impression that a Gauguin was worth 500 francs. 'Vincent also recommends you not to let anything of mine go at a vile rock-bottom price.'

Gauguin decided to use the 500 francs to pay off his debt to the inn at Pont-Aven run by the widow Gloanec. The letter was short because Gauguin was still shattered from his long train journey. 'I am too tired and my head is too done in,' he concluded, 'to write any longer.' Only then, in a postscript, did he mention the Yellow House. Could Schuff fetch a couple of his ceramics from Theo's gallery – one with the figure of Cleopatra and some pigs on it, the other with horns – put them in a parcel and send them to Arles? 'We are in a nice enough little home here and I'd like to have a bit of pottery in front of my eyes.' Schuff was used to running these errands, and to putting Gauguin up at short notice.

It was not much, but it was positive. Gauguin was reasonably content with his new lodgings. Looking around the Yellow House, so densely packed with Vincent's work, Vincent's ideas, Vincent's dreams, Vincent's taste and Vincent's clutter, he saw a 'pleasant enough' little dwelling. But evidently he felt a need to put his own mark on it.

Gauguin, like Vincent, was an enthusiastic homemaker. When still living with his wife, Mette, and the children, he had designed and carved idiosyncratic furniture for their apartment. With Schuffenecker in Brittany, he had just decorated a sideboard with scenes of Adam and Eve in Paradise. Vincent's paintings were everywhere in the Yellow House, but there was only one painting of his – the *Self-Portrait 'Les Misérables'*. If this was going to be his home, it required at least a couple of pieces of his pottery.

These ceramics were the most original creations Gauguin had produced – at least until the *Vision*. Like many of his works, they were hard to pin down. They were rough and raw like the handiwork of primitive man, or the simple earthenware vessels that Vincent admired. Simultaneously, they were full of the imaginative fantasy – bulbous, meandering shapes, naked figures – that was subsequently to be dubbed '*l'art nouveau*'.

In a couple of these ceramics, Madame Schuffenecker, wife of his friend Emil, was encircled by a snake. Quite a few people, looking at that sensual and unnerving portrayal – the bourgeois housewife as pagan goddess – wondered whether there had been an affair between Gauguin and the beautiful, domineering wife of his good and long-suffering friend Schuff.

The two pieces he had selected for the Yellow House were among the more bizarre he had produced. More than simply ornaments, they were subversive, aggressive, dark in hue, awkwardly made. The Cleopatra pot was a roughly moulded square, half vase, half sculpture, on one side of which a naked woman reclined. The 'horned' vase was even odder. From its side protruded the faces of two rats and from its top waved not horns but the tails of the rodents.

In addition to homemaking, Gauguin was also keen to put some order into the administration of finances at the Yellow House (for all his haughty bohemianism, he had a practical side). He had not been there long, as he later remembered, before he noticed that the household accounts were a muddle. They were just as disorderly as the Yellow House, and for the same reason – Vincent.

What, Gauguin asked himself, was he to do? Obviously, the situation was delicate. There was a risk of wounding 'that very great susceptibility of Vincent's'. It was thus with many precautions and much gentle coaxing, of a sort Gauguin considered very 'foreign' to his nature, that he approached the matter. But, in the event, Vincent readily agreed to his proposal. He was greatly impressed; he thought Gauguin had a 'marvellous way' of apportioning expenses from day to day. Gauguin described this system:

We kept a box – so much for hygienic excursions at night, so much for tobacco, so much for incidental expenses, including rent. On top of it lay a scrap of paper and a pencil for us to write down virtuously what each took from this chest. In another box was the rest of the money, divided into four parts to pay for our food each week.

This was an orderly arrangement, reminding one that Gauguin, as well as having been a stockbroker, had also been a sailor.

Just as seamanlike were the first necessary expenses that came to Gauguin's mind: 'hygienic' nocturnal excursions. That meant, to the brothel. The theory that sexual activity, at least occasionally, was healthy was a popular one then, and afterwards. Sigmund Freud was a contemporary – three years and two months younger than Vincent. But in reality, sex in a provincial brothel was far from hygienic. Syphilis was common, and incurable.

These establishments were known as *maisons de tolérance*, because they were tolerated rather than approved of by the authorities. A little old-fashioned in Parisian eyes, they were still very popular with soldiers and, since Arles had a large barracks, it also had no fewer than six brothels. These were gathered conveniently close to the Yellow House in the warren of streets just inside the old town walls from Place Lamartine.

Some were large establishments with servants, cooks and up to six *filles soumises* or resident prostitutes. The latter, according to the census of 1886, were women in their twenties and thirties, mainly French but a few Spanish and one German in nationality, but French in name, so presumably from the occupied territories of Alsace-Lorraine. Such was the female companionship offered to the two painters in Arles after dark.

Both Gauguin and Van Gogh smoked a pipe – the

bohemian and proletarian alternative to a cigar – so tobacco was a regular purchase. There was a tobacconist, a forty-year-old woman named Maria Ourtoul, trading conveniently in Place Lamartine. For Vincent, smoking was a great solace. He often recommended it as a source of comfort and a remedy against melancholy. So, too, was painting directly from life. As he had written to Theo, when he did that and all went well, he could lose himself in an ecstasy. 'The emotions are sometimes so strong that one works without knowing one works.'

Gauguin was dependent on tobacco. In Brittany, he had a special ceramic jar to contain a pound of it at a time. When it was empty, Gauguin became silent and melancholy, hoping his young disciples would fill it up again. In Arles, the matter was dealt with efficiently, as part of the monthly budget.

In the future, the painters planned to cook at home. But for the time being, Gauguin and Vincent continued to eat at the Restaurant Venissat, which was almost next door. Vincent had formed the habit of eating there in the summer. It was a pink building, with green shutters, set back a little from Place Lamartine on a side road. It reminded Vincent, as so many things did, of painting.

'This restaurant,' he wrote to Theo one day while he was sitting there:

is very queer; it is grey all over; the floor is of grey bitumen like a street pavement, grey paper on the walls, green blinds always drawn, a big green curtain in front of the door which is always open, to stop the dust coming in. So it already has a Velásquez grey – like in the *Spinners* – and even the very narrow, very fierce ray of sunlight through a blind, like the one that slants across Velásquez's picture, is not wanting. Little tables of course, with white cloths.

And behind this room in Velásquez grey you see the old kitchen, as clean as a Dutch kitchen, with floor of bright red bricks, green vegetables, oak chest, the kitchen range with shining brass things and blue and white tiles, and the big fire a clear orange. And then there are two women waitresses, both in grey. In the kitchen, an old woman and a short, fat servant also in grey, black, white. I don't know if I describe it clearly enough for you, but it's here, and it's pure Velásquez.

In front of the restaurant was a pretty little garden, which Vincent described, paved with red brick, and on the walls 'wild vine, convolvulus and creepers'. Vincent not only liked the southern look of it, he liked the food and believed it had built him up (something he felt Gauguin needed). One ate there for one franc or one franc fifty, which Vincent considered quite a lot. But he felt that at Restaurant Venissat you got value for your money.

Rent was obviously a monthly requirement, to be paid to Bernard Soulé, the manager of the hotel on Avenue Montmajour, a big, square four-storey structure just behind Vincent's house. After rent, there were two other major items of expenditure in the household of the Yellow House – food and painting materials.

There was also the expense of going out for a drink at the Café de la Gare or one of the other Arlésienne bars. Gauguin was not much of a drinker. At this time, according to an acquaintance in Brittany, a drink for him 'never went beyond a few small and rare glasses of cognac, which he did not abuse and which were served to him more for appearance's sake than for its taste'. But for Vincent, alcohol was both a solace and a problem. While living in Paris in the two years before he came to Arles, he felt he had become 'almost an alcoholic'. Here, initially, Vincent cut down on his drinking. The aim of coming south was in part to settle his nerves in the peace of the country. In any case, at first he found that in the climate of Provence one glass of brandy was enough to make him tipsy.

As the year wore on and his work rate went up, his consumption increased again. This was partly a reaction to the stresses and anxiety of work itself but also a way of quieting his mental turmoil. When worried about 'disastrous possibilities', he threw himself into painting. He worked in any case so as not 'to suffer too much mentally'. And, he added, 'if the storm within gets too loud, I take a glass too much to stun myself.'

It was his wildly fluctuating moods that seemed to lie at the root of the trouble. In Paris he had suffered so severely they made him fear for the future. At times he put them down to 'bad wine'; possibly it was actually too much wine. Vincent complained repeatedly that his blood had not circulated, which he cannot have meant literally. Metaphorically, he seemed to be talking about the terrible lethargy of depression. When he was in this state, alcohol was enlivening; conversely, when he was agitated, it soothed him. But in neither case was it doing him any good.

In those first days, Vincent was keen to introduce Gauguin to one of his few local friends – Paul-Eugène Milliet, a junior military officer in the 3rd Regiment of Zouaves stationed in the barracks on the other side of Arles – particularly as Second Lieutenant Milliet was leaving on 1 November. Vincent always wanted his friends, however heterogeneous, to meet each other.

In the days before Milliet left, he and Gauguin struck up at least an acquaintance. Probably they met either in one of the cafés – the Café de la Gare being the most convenient –

or the brothels, which were social centres as well as a source of other pleasures.

Gauguin and Milliet had one important thing in common: they had both been to the tropics. Gauguin, born in Peru, had recently visited Martinique; Milliet had been in Tonkin – it was the first thing that Vincent ever mentioned about him. Later known as Indochina, then Vietnam, Tonkin was the most recent object of French imperial expansion. Previously, it had belonged to China.

Milliet had been stationed there for a year with his regiment and had returned in the spring. Two of his comrades had been murdered in a brawl outside the brothel in Rue de Bout d'Arles that March, shortly after Vincent arrived. Milliet himself had impressed Vincent by spending the night before an important examination relaxing in a bordello. He had recently been bidding fond farewell to every strumpet and trollop in town as he was due to be posted to North Africa the following month.

Milliet was the sort of confident, virile type Vincent admired. (The young officer reminded him of General Boulanger, a military strongman and notorious philanderer who seemed about to seize control of France.) For his part, Milliet accepted Vincent and had accompanied him on sketching excursions to the Alpilles.

Theirs was an odd friendship, but it worked – perhaps because Milliet was much younger and therefore not a challenge to Vincent's views. Vincent had more trouble with equals and superiors. As it was, the painter became testy on the occasions that Milliet questioned his opinions on painting.

Vincent wanted to meet up with friends not only in cafés and brothels but also at the Yellow House, which was cosier since he had had the new gas lighting put in. To Theo, he mused, 'I like the look of the studio, especially in the evening, with the gas burning.' The thought of this domestic refuge immediately suggested the *décorations* that he would like to put in it – so he asked Theo to look out for more prints of earthy ordinary people by Daumier to hang on the wall.

Vincent planned that he and Gauguin would paint just such pictures in the Yellow House. He looked forward to creating these 'portraits of people in the light of a gas lamp'. The subjects would be his little circle of friends – the Ginouxs from the bar, Roulin the postal supervisor and his family, a few fellow drinkers and frequenters of the brothel.

There was no question that the social possibilities in Arles were limited, especially in comparison with Pont-Aven, with its cosmopolitan colony of painters (with many of whom Gauguin, admittedly, was not on good terms). Vincent's circle of acquaintances was tiny and about to get even smaller with Milliet's departure.

Language was an element that cut Vincent and Gauguin off from the people around him. The mother tongue of most inhabitants of Arles was Provençal – another name for Occitan. It was much closer to Catalan than to standard French. Arles was, in fact, the centre of a revival of this language and culture, initiated by a poet, Frédéric Mistral, and his followers, who were called the *Félibriges*. Poems and writings appeared in the local press; there was one in one of the town's two weekly newspapers, the *Forum républicain*, that Sunday, lauding Arles as a city that had seen Caesar and Constantine. Vincent dreamed that these *Félibriges* might come one day to the Yellow House, realizing that he and they had a common goal: a renaissance in the South.

From day to day, the language barrier had a more immediate effect: when their neighbours spoke amongst themselves, Gauguin and Vincent could not understand what they said.

Vincent, however, liked the sound of what he didn't comprehend: 'the dialect of these parts,' he observed, 'is extraordinarily musical in the mouth of an Arlésienne.'

But Gauguin tended to become irritated with those who did not speak pure, Northern French. He told an anecdote about an earlier visit to the Midi. He had been drawing on the beach near the Spanish frontier. 'A gendarme from the Midi, who suspects me of being a spy, says to me, who comes from Orléans: "Are you French?" "Why, certainly." "That's odd. *Vous n'avez pas l'accent* (lakescent) *français.*"' When it came to linguistic snobbery, Gauguin emphatically did not count himself a 'savage from Peru'. He thought Vincent's French accurate, however, to the point of grammatical pedantry; indeed, Vincent wrote French more beautifully than Gauguin did. It was the language Vincent spoke, and even used to his Dutch brother and younger sister.

In Arles entertainments were few. Sometimes a play was put on; a troupe of actors from nearby Nîmes was to perform the following week, for example, though if Vincent and Gauguin went to the theatre, they never mentioned it. Gauguin was a keen fencer – in Brittany he helped out in a little fencing school – and had brought his masks, gloves and foils with him. They were kept in the small cupboard in the Yellow House.

Gauguin could hold forth about this sport at length, and probably did. Essentially, his views on swordplay and painting were the same. It was a matter of strategy – the winner was the one with the best head, not the fastest hand or arm. The fencing gear, with its sharp blades, made Vincent nervous. He hoped that Gauguin would never use these 'infantile weapons of war' in earnest. Gauguin's other favoured athletic contest was boxing.

In the evenings in Brittany, he and his companions liked

to play board games such as draughts, for which he drew his own board on a piece of newspaper, or play music. He had taught himself piano and mandolin, the former very slowly. He could pick out such pieces as Schumann's *Berceuse*.

Vincent, in contrast, was not a musician, though he had begun to learn the piano, nor a player of sports or games. His leisure activities were walking, reading, writing and talking. He liked the kind of verbal wrangle for which he used the Dutch word, '*wrijving*' (friction). But he longed to find a soulmate with whom he could reach complete agreement, or as he put it, say together, 'That's it.'

Gauguin had also started work on that first day, but it always took some time for his ideas to coalesce. Whenever he changed location he needed a 'certain period of incubation' in which to discern the inner essence of his new surroundings. Gauguin didn't expect to do serious work for a month – until then, everything he painted would be an experiment. And, indeed, it was several weeks, he remembered, before he was able 'to catch distinctly the sharp flavour of Arles and its surroundings'. But that did not hinder him from working hard (though not as hard as Vincent).

He began two pictures, one of which, according to Vincent, was a 'Negress' – so she was clearly not an Arlésienne. This was a significant choice of subject, since it was as a painter of tropical subjects from Martinique that Gauguin had made his initial impact on Vincent and Theo. They had bought one of these, and he had given them another. It was indeed these pictures that had brought Vincent and Gauguin together.

Vincent and Theo had met Gauguin soon after he returned to France, penniless and still ill, in mid November of the previous year (if they had not bumped into each other before in the hurly-burly of Parisian bohemia). The work that Gauguin had brought back from the Caribbean made a huge impression on Vincent, most of all a picture of four black women gathering mangoes, with a band of deep-blue sea in the background. This – which they dubbed 'the Negresses' – was the one the brothers Van Gogh bought. Gauguin also swapped another Martinique landscape for one of Vincent's earlier pictures of sunflowers painted in Paris (obviously, he had always loved Vincent's depictions of that bloom).

From the moment they had seen those paintings from Martinique, Vincent was convinced Gauguin was the great painter of the future – a master of richer colours, and hotter, paradisiacal lands. 'Everything his hands make,' Vincent declared to Bernard, 'has a gentle, pitiful, astonishing character. People don't understand him yet, and it pains him so much that he does not sell anything, just like other true poets.' So – to please Vincent, or to assert himself or both – Gauguin began work on a picture of a black woman. But it was not a success. Later, Gauguin probably painted another picture over it – a portrait of Roulin's wife – so as to save the canvas.

His other picture, a landscape, was also a five-finger exercise, very far from the 'abstraction' and audacity of his *Vision*. It was a picture of a typical local farmhouse, known as a *mas*, with a large haystack in front and a tall, twisting cypress behind. The partially cloudy sky depicted the weather conditions of Thursday and Friday.

This was a subject that Vincent had painted and drawn during the summer. He had sent one of these drawings – each swirl and whorl of the pen filled with intense vitality – to Bernard, who had passed it around in Pont-Aven. But Gauguin's picture was nothing like that drawing. It was calm and orderly, the haystack a carefully constructed cone. His handling – in serried rows of brush strokes – was also very far from Vincent's, but close to another painter of the South: Paul Cézanne.

The style of Cézanne was Gauguin's default position. As a collector – in wealthier days, he had bought Cézanne's pictures and was still, despite financial problems, loath to part from one. The older man had been one of Gauguin's most important earlier influences; indeed, at one point, he had – half laughingly – suggested that Pissarro administer a sleeping draught to Cézanne so that they could interrogate him about his secrets while he slumbered. Gauguin was markedly curious about other artists' innovations. In this case, Cézanne had become so suspicious of Gauguin's inquisitiveness that he had departed suddenly for Aix-en-Provence.

To Gauguin, it went without saying that Cézanne – and not the eccentric Dutch newcomer with whom he had just moved in – was the great painter of southern French landscapes. He admired Cézanne's disciplined, rational approach: it was a way of working ruled by the head (as he felt art, and fencing, should be).

Vincent, for his part, had a low opinion of Cézanne. He found his parallel brush strokes 'almost timid' and 'conscientious'. Cézanne and Van Gogh, according to Émile Bernard, did not hit it off. One day they had met over lunch at the shop of the art dealer and colour merchant, *père* Tanguy. Vincent boldly showed the older man his work. 'After inspecting everything, Cézanne, who was a timid but violent person, told him, "Honestly, your painting is that of a madman."'

Vincent also painted a landscape, another view in the fields outside Arles, during the first few days of Gauguin's stay. It had a sky of lemon yellow – dawn or sunset – streaked with bands of cloud. In the foreground there was an ancient yew tree: a massive, venerable trunk, grey and gnarled, that rose up like a human being, dominating the picture and the furrowed field behind. (See his sketch on p. 31.)

Yew trees had two common associations – they were grown in cemeteries and, even when old, they had the power to throw out new shoots. Thus, they suggested both death and regeneration. Which, if either, was it here?

Vincent was immensely aware of the emotional and spiritual connotations of flowers and trees. He could see rampant sexuality in shrubs and tragic suffering in willows. This yew tree resembled a man: a stricken arboreal hero. Branches stuck out like arms, the root advanced at the front like a leg – indeed, much like Vincent's own leg when he had painted himself in the summer on the road to Tarascon.

It was doubtful whether this old tree was capable of much new growth. It had a few brownish leaves, it was true. But there were funereal cypresses on the horizon, and the wintry light in the picture was very far from the ecstatic blaze of the summer *Sower*, in which the sun flooded the world with gold. True, Vincent's violets were originally richer; he used poor-quality red, which later faded. Even so, this – like the new *Sower* – was an autumnal painting, hope and energy flagging. By the end of the week, however, Vincent's own spirits were rallying.

On Saturday the twenty-seventh, Theo got back to Paris after a business trip to Belgium. There, waiting for him, was the long lament of despair and anxiety that Vincent had composed just after Gauguin had arrived. But Theo was 'overjoyed' to discover that Gauguin had finally come to Arles.

Theo tried to staunch the stream of financial anguishes that had flowed from Vincent's pen. First, he sent yet another postal order. He was worried that if money ran out, his brother might act as he had earlier in the autumn – virtually ceasing to eat, living on endless cups of coffee and crusts of bread while sending frantic letters to Paris. Now there was a danger that he might have two penniless painters in Arles to rescue from semi-starvation. Theo could not always be there, ready to send money at a moment's notice, since he was obliged to travel on business. Vincent, moreover, had shown an ability to run through cash at a rapid and unpredictable rate.

Theo implored him to get food on credit if his cash ran low. There was no need to starve. Money would always arrive. It was odd that Vincent hadn't thought of this obvious notion; there was something almost masochistic about the way he behaved.

Theo tried as hard as he could to reassure Vincent by post:

Now I see from your letter that you are unwell, and that you are worrying a good deal. I want to tell you something once and for all. I look upon it all as though the question of money and the sale of pictures and the whole financial side did not exist . . .

Thinking about money only led to 'misery'; the best thing would be for Vincent to rid his mind of it, and also to avoid other 'excesses' and the 'diseases' that resulted. This sounded like a warning against the heavy drinking to which Vincent was prone. Theo's message to Vincent was simple. He was not to concern himself with money, or with sales, just to get on with painting.

'You speak of money which you owe me, and which you want to give back to me. I won't hear of it. The condition I want you to arrive at is that you should never have any worries. I must work for the money.' Theo then threw in a word of caution. He felt Vincent spent too much time, energy, and cash on other people and their problems:

You don't know how much pain you give me when you say that you have worked so hard that you feel as though you had not lived. In the first place I don't believe this is true, for in point of fact you are living *and* living like the great ones of the earth and the aristocrats. But I beseech you, warn me in time, in order that you may not feel that you have been living in misery, and that you have fallen ill because you lacked a piece of bread to keep alive. I hope Gauguin's company will be pleasant for you, and that you will recover within a very short time.

It was a noble letter. And that last part was true: Vincent was living the free and fulfilling life of the artist. It could have been an idyll – except for the turmoil within him.

On Saturday Gauguin wrote to Theo – Monsieur Van Gogh to him – acknowledging his earlier letter about the sale, which had just arrived, and letting him know as tactfully as possible that his brother's mental state was odd.

'Your brother is, as it happens, a little agitated, and I hope to calm him down bit by bit.' He noted that Vincent had received the money order and, since he had many things to tell his brother in Paris, he would also be writing. Otherwise, Gauguin's letter was all about his own affairs – naturally enough, since he was reporting to his dealer. He was anxious to hear what Theo thought of the pictures, including the *Vision*, he had just dispatched from Brittany. Their roughness of execution, he wanted to point out, was intentional, part of a conscious strategy.

Vincent also wrote to Theo, with a hint that his morale was rising. 'My brain is still feeling tired and dried up but this week I am feeling better than during the previous fortnight.' He then plunged straight into what was now on his mind: wide-eyed admiration of his new housemate:

I knew well that Gauguin had made sea voyages, but I did not know that he was a regular mariner. He has passed through all the difficulties, and has been a real able seaman and a true sailor. This gives me an awful respect for him and a still more absolute confidence in his personality.

What could Gauguin have been telling Vincent? Viewed coldly, his youth wasn't all that much to boast about. A difficult, fatherless boy, Gauguin had wanted to go to sea. But he did too badly at school to enter the French Naval Academy, the standard path to a career as an officer. So instead, in December 1865, he joined a merchant ship as a trainee pilot. He then made several voyages across the Atlantic to South America before joining the navy, in which he served through the Franco-Prussian war.

Gauguin later recorded a little of his life at sea, and what he did relate – like his pictures – took the form of evocative yarns:

On my first trip as a pilot's apprentice on the *Luzitano* [one began] bound for Rio de Janeiro, it was part of my apprenticeship to do the night watch with the lieutenant. He told me the following.

He had been a cabin boy on a ship that made long voyages in the Pacific with cargoes of all sorts of cheap goods. One fine morning, while he was washing the deck, he fell into the sea without anyone's noticing it. He did not let go of his broom, and thanks to this broom the boy kept afloat for forty-eight hours in the ocean. By an extraordinary chance a ship happened to pass and save him.

Then, some time later as this ship had put in at a hospitable little island, our cabin boy went for a walk and stayed a little too long. So he remained for good and all.

Our little cabin boy pleased everybody, so there he was settled, with nothing to do, forced to lose his virginity straight away, fed,

lodged, petted and flattered in every way. He was very happy. This
lasted two years; then one fine morning another ship happened to
be passing and our young man wanted to go back to France.

'My God, what a fool I was,' he said to me. 'Here I am, obliged
to fight my way against wind and wave . . . And I was so happy!'

In his letter to Theo, Vincent suggested a precise literary
analogy for Gauguin – rugged sailor and man of action.
Gauguin had, he thought 'an affinity' with a book called
Pêcheur d'Islande, or *Icelandic Fisherman*, by Pierre Loti. This
was a bestseller from the year before last, 1886. It was Loti's
most recent publication, *Madame Chrysanthème*, that had
greatly influenced Vincent's ideas about the furnishing of the
Yellow House and his self-portrait as a Japanese monk. Now,
Icelandic Fisherman also took a place among the cult books of
the Yellow House.

The connection between Gauguin and this book was not
– as one might have imagined – one of Vincent's astonishing
associative leaps. It was one that Gauguin had made himself,
at least by implication. His own life and that of the author
ran on almost embarrassingly parallel tracks.

Loti was a *nom de plume*. The writer's real name was Julien
Viaud. He was two years younger than Gauguin, and he too
was a sailor, an officer in the French navy. At one point he
had served in the same flotilla as Gauguin. Loti/Viaud had
published a series of books. The second, which really made
his name, described the 'marriage', according to local custom,
of a British naval officer to a fourteen-year-old girl on Tahiti.

Loti was one of those authors who are destined to be forgotten after their deaths but who purvey some vital dream to their
contemporaries. Vincent and Gauguin were of precisely the
generation to whom Loti spoke most seductively. The fantasy
he presented was one of escape: a route out of the financial

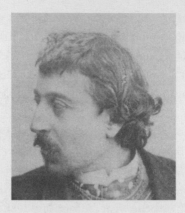

and sexual constraints of middle-class European life into a distant Eden. This was something both Vincent and Gauguin yearned for; indeed, Gauguin had already tried to live out the dream in Martinique, with decidedly mixed results.

Loti did not only write of remote locations. *Mon Frère Yves* from 1883 described the life of a semi-literate, hard-drinking Breton sailor. The ringing of wooden Breton clogs recurs throughout the book, 'hammering the hard granite paving-stones'. Brittany, time and again, is described as 'primitive' and 'savage'.

These are just the words and sounds that Gauguin had singled out when writing to Schuffenecker from Pont-Aven:

You're a true Parisian. Give me the country. I love Brittany. I find here the savage and primitive. When my clogs clang on this granite earth, I hear the dull, muffled tone, flat and powerful, that I try to achieve in painting.

It was all very 'sad', and sadness was his character as an artist.

Gauguin had taken over Loti's entire package: a new, ready-made identity for an ex-businessman. He even dressed as a Breton fisherman, in fisherman's jersey, beret and clogs.

Gauguin frequently emphasized that he was a savage, a primitive man. He wasn't quite sure, or too concerned, exactly what type of savage he was – French or Peruvian – but it was a Breton sailor's costume that he wore. As it happened, Vincent also thought of his own life as a voyage in a frail boat on perilous seas.

For the time being, everything that Gauguin had to say was fascinating to Vincent. Gauguin's tales of the tropics struck him as 'marvellous'. 'Surely,' he reflected, 'the future of a great renaissance in painting lies there.' He decided that the tropics were the place for Meyer de Haan and Isaacson – those two Dutch painter friends of Theo's whom he had never met, whose work he had never seen and of whom a few days before he had been highly suspicious. Now they had turned into a couple of surrogates for himself.

Vincent's notion of the future of painting took a nationalistic form: if French artists such as Gauguin worked in French colonies such as Martinique, it followed that Dutch painters ought to go to the Dutch territories in the East Indies and found a school of colourist painting in Java. 'What things could be done there!' Vincent exclaimed. He would go there himself if he were ten or twenty years younger.

As usual, his maths was off; twenty years before, he had been fifteen. Evidently, however, Vincent didn't feel up to further travelling. Instead, he would remain in Arles, and others would visit him before sailing from Marseilles: 'Now it is most unlikely that I shall leave the shore and put to sea, and the little yellow house here in Arles will remain a way station between Africa, the Tropics, and the people of the North.'

3. Lessons among the Tombs

28 October–4 November

Vincent and Gauguin had now been living together in the Yellow House for six days. Gauguin had begun to settle in and they were establishing a routine. It was time to tackle a new and important subject together. Now, they would begin to do what Vincent had always hoped for: work side by side, a few yards apart, on parallel subjects. This was the real initiation of the Studio of the South.

The two painters could learn from one another and, especially, Vincent would gain from Gauguin's example. Still, there was an undercurrent of rivalry. Both men possessed huge talents but neither their ideas nor their temperaments were identical. Apparently, Gauguin was the master; in reality, and most of the time – though he did not entirely know it – Vincent was the greater painter, though his confidence was low and Gauguin's high.

As Vincent had long planned, they were going to paint the autumn foliage of Arles, which was looking magnificent. His project for the *décorations* of the Yellow House included pictures showing the changing seasons. But so far, apart from a couple of canvases done in the days of exhaustion before Gauguin's arrival, he had painted only spring and summer in the area. Also, the two of them were going to work in a new place, one that Vincent had never depicted.

They issued from the Yellow House, Vincent wearing his paint-daubed working clothes and straw hat, and festooned with his working equipment, Gauguin dressed as a Breton sailor. They carried their portable easels, boxes of paints, brushes and primed canvases across town to the other side of Arles, where a Roman cemetery called Les Alyscamps was located. This – with the ancient arena and theatre – was counted among the most notable sights of the city.

'*Les Alyscamps*' was a mutation into Provençal of '*Elisii Campi*', or the Elysian Fields – the blessed land where the virtuous dead of the classical world were believed to spend eternity. It had been built, as was normal Roman practice, outside the city walls, along the Via Augusta that led to Rome. Consequently, when the first Christians appeared in Arles, it was an ideal place for secret meetings.

On one occasion, it was believed, Jesus Christ himself had attended and left the miraculous imprint of his knee on the lid of a sarcophagus. As a result of this holy relic, Les Alyscamps became the most highly regarded cemetery in early medieval Europe. Bodies were shipped there from distant places, among them, according to legend, that of the hero Roland and other paladins of Charlemagne. But the place that Gauguin and Vincent entered on that warm October day was much diminished since those days of glory.

For many years, the authorities of Arles had made a habit of presenting the most beautifully carved sarcophagi to visiting notables; others had been removed to museums. When the Craponne Canal – named after its engineer, Adam de Craponne – was dug in the sixteenth century, it had cut across the cemetery, destroying much of it. In 1848 the railways had been built in a great arc around Arles, and they too had scythed into Les Alyscamps.

Finally, the Paris–Lyon–Mediterranée railway had decided to site its main southern workshop for manufacturing locomotives and rolling stock just in this location. The result was

a big industrial complex, far larger in extent now than the
dwindling cemetery. This now comprised the Allée des Tombeaux – the avenue of tombs – a walk shaded by poplar trees
with a medieval arch at the entry and a Romanesque chapel
at the end. Between the poplars and the canal ran an embankment a couple of metres high. Gauguin clambered to the top
of this and set up his easel. By doing so he obtained a view
past the autumnal trees to the Romanesque chapel of Saint-
Honorat. The painting that he began on the top of the bank,
however, represented only a small part of what he could see,
and that not accurately. But then, Gauguin was not especially
interested in reality.

He ignored the great workshop just to his left, from which
a din of clattering and hammering could be heard, since this
was a weekday and a thousand men were at work, and edited
out the avenue of old tombs at the bottom of the bank which
was the main point of Les Alyscamps for most visitors.

Instead, Gauguin painted open woodland, with the tower
of Saint-Honorat rising mysteriously above the foliage. At
first glance, it was not even clear that this was a church. The
domed structure seemed vaguely classical,. and also vaguely
exotic. To the side of the painting rose a great wall of yellow
leaves: the poplars of the avenue. Low down on the right side
was a bush of a red so vivid it exceeded anything that even
that October in Arles could boast.

This intensification of colour was one of the lessons that
Gauguin taught to younger painters. This, Vincent felt, was
part of the *abstraction* he and Bernard had been pioneering in
Brittany:

They will not ask the correct tone of the mountains, but they will
say: 'In the Name of God, the mountains were blue, were they?
Then chuck on some blue and don't go telling me that it was a

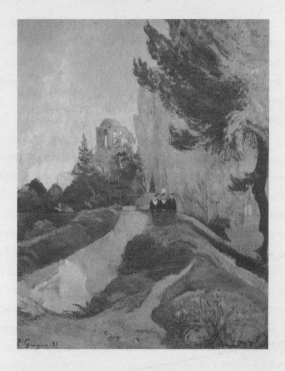

blue rather like this or that, it was blue, wasn't it? Good – make them blue and it's enough!'

That was evidently exactly what Vincent now heard being expounded by his new companion:

Gauguin is sometimes like a genius when he explains this, but as for the genius Gauguin has, he is very timid about showing it, and it is touching the way he likes to say something really useful to the young.

Timid or not, shortly before he left for Arles, Gauguin had given precisely this kind of advice to a young man called Paul Sérusier, who had returned to Paris and showed his amazed friends a cigar-box lid, painted under Gauguin's instructions with a little landscape. It was entirely covered in pure, bright colours such as purple, vermilion and Veronese green, and became known to Sérusier and his circle as the Talisman — a touchstone of a new way of painting.

Vincent already believed that the painter did not have to copy the colour he saw before him. He could alter it, or omit it, or anything else, in order to make the picture more expressive. But Gauguin had pushed this indifference to reality very far in his *Vision*, with its field of unbroken vermilion.

Vincent was doubtless looking with great interest at Gauguin's new painting as it progressed. Gauguin's art, Vincent came to feel, was something to live up to, 'that a good picture should be equivalent to a good deed, not that he says so, but it is in fact difficult to be much in his company without being mindful of a certain moral responsibility'. And, despite his vagueness and piratical shiftiness, there was indeed a heroic aspect to Gauguin's determination, his willingness to sacrifice everything for a new kind of painting; the same was of course true of Vincent.

In the middle distance of his picture of the Alyscamps Gauguin placed three figures wearing black and white. They were women of Arles, Arlésiennes, who were just as notable among the attractions of the town as the ancient ruins. So, not surprisingly, the women of the town were among the first sights that Gauguin wanted to inspect after he had arrived. He was already angling to persuade one of them to pose.

Their traditional costume could just be made out in Gauguin's rather abbreviated version. Everyday clothes · — there were others for brides, young women and special occasions — comprised a black dress and shawl with full white muslin stomacher and a very small lace cap at the back of the hair, bound round with broad black velvet or ribbon, fastened with gold or jewelled pins. This mode of dress was believed to be very ancient. In reality, like many 'traditional' customs, it was relatively new – a provincial version of Parisian women's eighteenth-century wear.

Like their clothes, the women of Arles themselves were thought to be survivals from the remote past. Arles was itself an ancient place, a Greek town, Theline, before it was the Roman Arlate. In addition to its architectural relics, it had produced one famous sculpture – the *Venus of Arles* – dug up in the seventeenth century on the site of the Roman theatre. This sculpture, second in fame only to the *Venus de Milo*, created a lasting association between Arles and the goddess of love. Consequently, the living women of Arles came to be seen as younger sisters of Venus, possessing a stately Grecian beauty and a powerful, potentially dangerous, attraction.

A literature had grown up around the subject of the Arlésiennes. Alphonse Daudet, one of Vincent's favourite authors, had written a short story in his book *Letters from My Windmill* about a young farmer from the Crau who kills himself out of hopeless passion for a girl from Arles. Daudet had then transformed this into a play – *L'Arlésienne* – with music by Bizet, which had recently been successfully revived on the Parisian stage. The Arlésienne was a Provençale cousin to Carmen – as alluring, as fatal.

Gauguin saw them as figures from the classical past, as he reported to Bernard in a letter that very week:

The women here, with their elegant coiffure, evoke Greek beauty. Their shawls fall in folds like the primitives, and evoke the parades of ancient Greece. The girls walking in the streets are as much ladies as any born, and as virginal in appearance as Juno.

He thought he saw a way to transform them into art 'in the modern style'.

Some of these erotic and classical associations were hinted at in the title he gave the painting: the *Three Graces at the Temple of Venus*. Was this a joke? Perhaps, partly, but the subject of Venus and the Three Graces was one to appeal to Gauguin. It had been painted by Botticelli, one of his favourite painters of the past.

Gauguin, as was his habit, worked methodically. He began by systematically drawing out the composition in Prussian blue. Then he covered sections in colour, which sank into the absorbent ground of the canvas he was using. Over that he put on another layer of colour, with regular vertical or diagonal strokes. He brushed, an acquaintance remembered, 'with a velvety, supple and feline gesture.' It looked like a cat playing with a mouse. The whole process usually took several days.

Meanwhile, a few yards away, Vincent was working to a very different rhythm. His mood was much better. He wrote that day or the next to reassure Theo. 'About falling ill,' he began, it wasn't that he thought he would, just that he might have if his financial worries had carried on.

Vincent was fired by excitement at the things and people he saw. He knew some people thought he painted too quickly, but he defended the habit. It was emotions that fired him, so that sometimes the strokes flowed as his words did when he was full of ideas. When that happened, one had to take advantage, because the mood would reverse. There would be 'hard days, empty of inspiration'.

It looked as though he had been working like that on his first picture in the Alyscamps – at top speed. He had placed his easel down a little to the right of the path up the centre of the Allée des Tombeaux and looking – like Gauguin – at

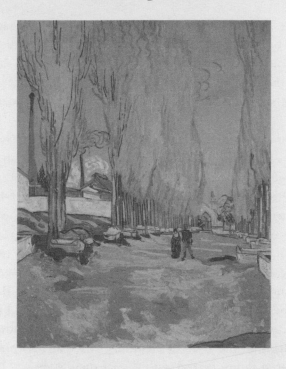

the chapel of Saint-Honorat. Vincent, however, emphasized just those aspects of the place that his friend had omitted.

Gauguin had ignored the railway workshop and the Roman tombs. Vincent painted a perspective view between the two lines of ancient coffins. And the factory, seen through the poplars, is such a prominent part of his picture that it is almost the subject of it. The chimneys, with dynamic swirls of smoke, and the red roofs of the workshops attracted the eye more than the chapel's triangular eave and low tower.

Vincent's picture looked like a direct depiction of what he saw in front of him. But, in fact, it was as much an edit of reality as Gauguin's. The tower of the church was shifted from one side to the other to help his composition, and also to complete his comparison of the ecclesiastical and functional structures. From where he stood, the tower was actually masked by the poplar trees. Where Gauguin depicted thick vegetation, Vincent revealed the workshop buildings through gaps in the ragged line of poplars. Thus he emphasized precisely what Gauguin left out – the ugly evidence of the railway age.

Down the promenade of tombs advances a pair of lovers – a Zouave from the barracks close by and a local woman. They were a perfectly naturalistic pair to place in this spot, which was one of the lovers' lanes of Arles. But, when one looked at the picture, a symbolic narrative came to mind. The lovers walk away from the religious past, and – in the logic of the picture if not in the topography of the Alyscamps – towards the busy, secular present.

Around this time, Gauguin mused in his letter to Bernard about the differing approaches to art of himself and his new housemate: 'It's strange, but Vincent sees opportunities here for painting in the style of Daumier, whereas I see in terms of coloured Puvis, mixed with the Japanese style.'

This was painter's shorthand. Puvis de Chavannes was an artist of an older generation, and an example to many painters who wished to move away from the Impressionist style. He painted carefully composed pictures with a clear classical line – in that, he resembled many academic painters. But Puvis's paintings were so pale, and so simplified, that they seemed radical.

Gauguin imagined Puvis's clarity with the brighter colours and flatter forms of Japanese prints. In Arles Vincent felt the urge to work in the manner of Honoré Daumier (1798–1879), a draughtsman and painter whose work was filled with passions – rage, resignation, misery, melancholy – and drawn with vehement intensity. His brush strokes, like Vincent's, were emotional calligraphy: an index of energy and impulse.

Daumier was one of the presiding spirits of the Yellow House. His prints hung in the studio and were a constant inspiration; Vincent had recently asked Theo to look out for more. Like Daumier, Vincent was intensely interested in the lives of his fellow beings. Gauguin was less so.

The difference in approach Gauguin was talking about was a matter of nuance. Gauguin also admired Daumier, and Vincent idolized Puvis de Chavannes little less than he did the other artist. Gauguin was happy to abstract away from what was in front of him; Vincent was more attached to what he saw: 'In the open air, exposed to the wind, to the sun, to people's curiosity, one works as best one can, one fills one's canvas regardless. Yet that is how one captures the true and the essential – the most difficult part.' But Vincent was also willing to adapt what he had done later, more reflectively, in the studio. This retouching made the painting 'more harmonious and pleasant to look at', and he could add 'whatever serenity and happiness' he felt.

Gauguin believed, as he went on to explain to Bernard, that it was quite unnecessary for a painter to transcribe precisely what he saw in front of his eyes. Bernard had asked whether Gauguin thought one should paint shadows. By no means, was Gauguin's answer – unless you want to. It's all a matter of what the artist thinks best for his picture. But in general he thought that the new art ought 'vigorously' to avoid 'anything mechanical such as photography'. 'For that reason I would avoid as far as possible anything that gives the *illusion* of something, and since shadow creates the *illusion* of sunshine I am inclined to suppress it.' Painting was, after all, in Gauguin's view, an intellectual matter: 'Do not paint too much from nature,' he advised. 'Art is an abstraction; extract it from nature, while dreaming in front of it.'

★

It was clear that Gauguin was calming Vincent down. One of his biggest fears must have been that Gauguin would leave straight away, either because he loathed Arles on sight or because, having sold a Breton picture, he no longer needed to share expenses in the Yellow House. But Vincent's mind had been put to rest on both scores. 'So have no fear for me,' he instructed Theo, 'nor for yourself either.'

Now, Gauguin had declared his intention to stay, and he had decided to make use of the cost-cutting regime in Arles to save money so that he could return to Martinique. 'He will wait here very quietly, working hard, for the right moment to take a great step forward. He needs rest as much as I do.' He found Gauguin's quiet command of himself 'astonishing'.

The house was 'getting on' very well indeed – no doubt ordered a little by Gauguin. It was 'becoming not only comfortable but an artist's house too'. Vincent's only uncertainty was what Gauguin thought of his pictures, the *décorations*. He had been trying to get him to give an opinion but could only get him to say he admired certain ones: the *Sower* (he didn't say which one), the *Sunflowers*, and the *Bedroom*.

After a few days of life with Gauguin, Vincent was beginning to look towards the future: 'I venture to hope that in six months Gauguin and you and I will all see that we have founded a little studio which will last.' Meanwhile, two could live as cheaply as one: '*Together* we shall not spend more than 250 fr. a month.' In the next paragraph Vincent suggested 150 francs each as a monthly allowance. This seemed to add up to 300 francs a month, but finance definitely wasn't Vincent's subject.

Gauguin, who was more business-minded, dispatched a sizable sum to Bernard to distribute to his creditors there: to the Pension Gloanec, his lodging, 280 francs, to another creditor, 35 francs; 5 francs for sending pictures; five for

Bernard and Laval to drink his health. But this still left him with money in hand apart from the monthly allowance he would get from Theo. He spent part of this surplus on a crucial purchase: 20 metres of coarse jute sackcloth. His idea was that he and Vincent would paint on it.

Over the coming weeks, the two painters cut off square after square from this roll – most of their new paintings were to be done on it. Jute had various possible advantages, among them that it was amazingly cheap – 50 centimes a metre as against at least 2 francs 50 for commercial canvas.

One thing Vincent and Gauguin had in common was that neither had had much formal instruction as a painter. They had picked it up from other artists and, in Vincent's case, from life classes at which he tended to clash angrily with the teachers. Essentially, they were self-taught, and that made them more open to innovations of every kind: stylistic, spiritual, technical.

The consistency of the paint, the weight and texture of the canvas, the nature of the surface put on top of that canvas, the light in which it took place, the speed at which it was done – all these variables affected the result. To Gauguin and Van Gogh, these technical matters were crucial, both financially and artistically. Painting, after all, was a physical affair.

Jute was a material which had virtually never been used as a support for painting before. But, by chance, Gauguin was extremely familiar with this fabric thanks to one of the more incongruous episodes in his earlier life. After embarking on a career as an independent artist, in December 1884 he had found himself in Copenhagen with a disillusioned spouse, dwindling resources and disappointed in-laws. He also had a new and supremely unsuitable job as sales representative for a French firm, Dillies et Frères of Roubaix, near Lille, who were manufacturers of tarpaulin and heavy textiles.

As a result of his own lack of Danish, the Danes' habit of taking an inordinate time in deciding to place orders and his employer's incompetence, Gauguin made almost no money at all from this humiliating post, but it left him with an intimate knowledge of jute – from which tarpaulin and sackcloth were made.

Over the centuries before Gauguin arrived at Vincent's door, the procedures for making a picture in oils had slowly been refined. The paints were generally applied to a piece of taut cloth – a canvas (although, on occasion, wood, metal or some other substance was used). Canvas (stout cloth of cotton or linen) came in many different grades, qualities and sizes, the choice of which had an effect on the appearance of the final picture.

Big Parisian colour merchants and painters' suppliers produced catalogues itemizing a profusion of canvases, pigments, brushes and other requirements, such as the wooden framework – the stretcher – on which the canvas was pulled tight. But in moving to remote Arles, Vincent had removed himself from easy access to these supplies. No sooner had Vincent arrived than he began to worry about obtaining materials. Although the town was not a well-known artists' colony as was Pont-Aven, there were a few other painters around. A local bookshop and grocer's sold paints. Vincent also considered buying canvas locally.

One place where he could do this was the Grand Magasin de Nouveautés Veuve Jacques Calment et Fils, the best fabric and furniture shop in the region. There, a thirteen-year-old girl named Jeanne Calment was introduced to an uncharming Dutch painter by her cousin and husband to be, the son of the owners of the shop. One hundred years later, she still recalled the painter, who must have been a regular customer. She thought him very ugly, ungracious, impolite, crazy and bad-smelling – which was characteristic of the impression poor Vincent made on people, especially the opposite sex.

For his second picture of the Alyscamps Vincent boldly took one of the new sackcloth canvases and tried it out. His subject was almost a repetition of the first picture, except that, instead of looking up the avenue of poplars towards the chapel of Saint-Honorat, he now looked in the other direction. And instead of two lovers, he painted a scattering of passers-by.

This picture was less successful than the first. Vincent was still painting rapidly, but the rough texture of the weave seemed to slow his brush strokes – much as sand or wet ground would hamper a walker's feet. The result – unusually for Vincent – was a little dull. Vincent would learn to work on jute successfully, but for him it was a question of overcoming its roughness; that same texture actually helped Gauguin attain the effect he wanted: a matt surface a little like that of a fresco or tapestry.

Though the *Three Graces* was probably unfinished, Gauguin decided to try out the new jute (a form of canvas he was to use at intervals for the rest of his life). He set up his easel in front of the Romanesque entrance arch beside the chapel of Saint-Honorat (with Vincent working behind him). He then painted what he very seldom attempted: a fleeting effect of light and colour of the kind in which Impressionists such as Monet specialized.

By then, the leaves were falling, as Vincent reported, 'like snow'. The sun was still brilliant, the sky remained clear. Right in front of Gauguin was a tree whose foliage had turned a vivid orange-red; the path below was covered with fallen leaves which swirled in the air. His painting caught the movement of the little flecks of scarlet and gold fluttering to the ground. This was more like Impressionism than 'abstraction'.

It flickered and dazzled, as immediate an image as Gauguin ever painted, quivering with life and full of the exhilaration of those early autumn days. But behind and below, providing structure, was an armature of blue-grey trunks and walls. On the left, carefully observed, was the twelfth-century arch. Gauguin, unlike Vincent, was fascinated by the Middle Ages, their art and their architecture.

On Thursday, Second Lieutenant Milliet was to depart for a remote garrison in Algeria. Before he left, the young officer was charged with a task. Emile Bernard was soon due to do his military service; and Vincent, always keen for all his stray friends and acquaintances to link up somehow, had decided that Milliet should arrange for Bernard to join his regiment, the 3rd Zouaves, and subsequently smooth his path.

Vincent and Gauguin both instructed Bernard to write to Milliet, Gauguin adding a characteristically vague address, 'M. Milliet sous-lieutenant de Zouaves, Guelma, Afrique.' Gaugin wrote separately to Bernard that he had chatted to the Zouave and believed 'in Africa you will have a fairly easy existence and very beneficial to your art.' In thanks for his help in taking some finished canvases to Paris in August, Vincent gave Milliet a painting, and Gauguin presented him with a drawing in exchange for an illustrated copy of Loti's *Madame Chrysanthème*. But when he came to read this book – which had so impressed Vincent and affected his ideas about the Yellow House – Gauguin thought Loti had misunderstood the Japanese, as indeed he had.

One of the advantages of the Yellow House was that it had running water (not always the case in Arles in 1888). But one of the disadvantages was that there was no bathroom, and, naturally, no hot water except what was boiled in a kettle.

Gauguin and Vincent's morning ablutions were performed at the wash stands in their bedrooms.

Vincent regarded having baths as a healthy measure. When living in Brussels, years before, he had taken one as often as two or three times a week and felt it did him good. He recommended bathing to Theo, while confessing that he himself did not always follow his own advice:

Now for us who work with our brains, our one and only hope of not breaking down too soon is this artificial eking-out by an up-to-date hygienic regimen rigorously applied, as much as we can stand. Because I for one do not do everything I ought. And a bit of cheerfulness is better than all the other remedies.

For those who wanted them, at Arles, there were public baths (one of which had a pretty garden Vincent had drawn).

Gauguin enjoyed sea-bathing, when he could. He was spotted on the beach in Brittany wearing trunks and beret, 'with his 40-year-old man's belly'. To Hartrick, Gauguin looked like a porpoise in the water. But there was no scope for swimming at Arles.

To visit the lavatory, Gauguin and Vincent had to go out and walk round the side of the Yellow House, where a large weed grew out of the pavement, and into the hotel behind, to which the Yellow House was little more than an annex.

Vincent did not think much of this facility but felt it was typical of the region he was living in. 'In a southern town I feel I have no right to complain of it, since these offices are few and dirty, and one cannot help thinking of them as nests of microbes.'

The fine autumn weather left at the same time as Second Lieutenant Milliet. On Thursday, at 3.25 in the morning, a

violent storm broke, followed by torrential rain. This down-
pour brought a halt, as one of the two local newspapers,
L'Homme de bronze, noted, to the work of the sowers in the
fields (which Vincent had painted the previous week). It also
made work in the Alyscamps impossible. Rain reduced the
promenade to a quagmire into which the wheels of carriages
sank up to their axles. The wet spell continued through the
rest of the day and also Friday 2 November. Thursday was
one of the darkest days ever recorded in Arles; certainly one
for working indoors with Vincent's new gaslight on.

In the studio during the next few days, Vincent completed
two more pictures of the Alyscamps. Both were seen from
the top of the bank, looking down through the poplars and
along the path. In colour, they were variations on an autumnal
theme – yellow-orange leaves and path in contrast to blue-
violet tree trunks. These were the best that Vincent had
produced since Gauguin had arrived and markedly unlike
anything he had done before (or, for that matter, afterwards).
They were in a way the first true products of the Studio of
the South in the Yellow House: the result of the teamwork
for which Vincent had hoped and planned.

'By *collaboration*,' he informed Emile Bernard, he did not
necessarily mean several painters working on the same picture.
He meant a pooling of thoughts and techniques, so that the
community of artists would create 'paintings that differ from
one another yet go together and complement one another'.
More and more paintings would 'probably be created by groups
of men combining to execute an idea held in common'.
Accordingly, Vincent's two paintings of *Falling Leaves* in the
Alyscamps mingled ideas of three artists – himself, Gauguin
and the absent Bernard. These pictures were 'a collaboration'.

They were a pair, designed to be hung together; Vincent
had an important position in mind for them. The pictures

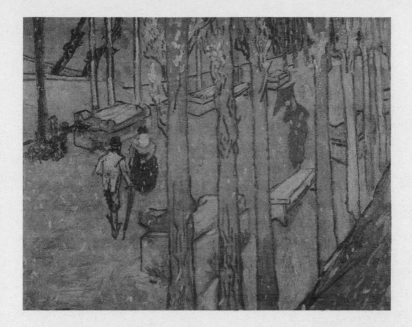

rhymed in form: a regular palisade of trees divided each one up like beats in a bar of music. In colour, the *Falling Leaves* were an exercise in compare and contrast, built up of complementary, or opposite, colours: green and red, violet and apricot. The bluish poplar trunks in one balanced the expanse of yellowish path in the other. There were certain colours, such as these, he had explained to his sister, 'which cause each other to shine brilliantly, which form a *couple*, which complete each other like man and woman'.

The insistent weave of the jute came through Vincent's brush strokes and gave the finished works a texture like tapestry or embroidery. Another link with Gauguin was the steep angle of vision, just like that in his *Vision*. In the *Falling Leaves*, Vincent looked down sharply on the yellow and orange of the Alyscamps avenue, just as Gauguin had on the deep-vermilion field where Jacob wrestled with the angel.

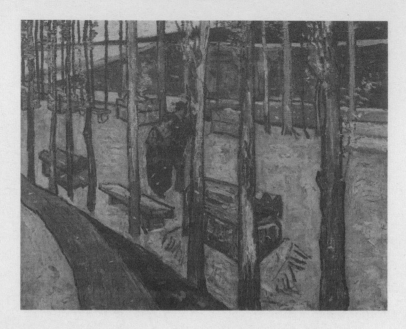

The motif of a landscape seen through tree trunks had been tried out by Emile Bernard. Gauguin told Vincent about one of his latest paintings; it showed the painter's seventeen-year-old sister reclining in the Bois d'Amour with, behind her, a grove like the one in Botticelli's *Primavera*. Gauguin's description made such an impact that Vincent was able to draw the picture from memory months later.

Vincent recalled how Gauguin had analysed the painting in terms of colour and construction:

On a grassy foreground, the figure of a young girl in a blue or whitish dress, lying stretched out full-length; on the second plane the edge of a beech wood, the ground covered with fallen red leaves, vertical grey-green tree trunks across it. Her hair, I think, is in a tint that serves as a complementary colour to the white dress: black if that garment is white, orange if it is blue.

'Well,' Vincent said to himself. 'What a simple subject and how well he knows how to create grace from nothing!' Gauguin also described another of Bernard's works of the weeks before: 'Just three trees, the effect of orange foliage against a blue sky, but with very clear outlines, very strictly divided into planes of contrasting, clear colours – splendid!' Vincent's *Falling Leaves* aimed to do just the same.

The third ingredient in the *Falling Leaves*, however, was Vincent's contribution: the novel-reader's touch. In both compositions he included vignettes from everyday life. In one painting, a thin man with an umbrella – elderly and bony, as Vincent ruefully thought of himself – accosted a woman of the 'fat hen' type with which he occasionally thought of settling down. Further up the Alyscamps a woman in harlot red approached. In the other, a couple walked between the tombs while a lemon-yellow sunset filled the sky.

Each of these incidents is of the kind that Vincent admired in Daumier's lithographs and found in his beloved novels. For example, in *La Fille Eliza*, by Edmond de Goncourt – a favourite of Vincent's – the tragic climax occurred in an old cemetery where the heroine, a prostitute, stabs her lover to death.

The *Falling Leaves* were considered a success. Technically and conceptually, they were the most assured pieces Vincent had produced since his *Bedroom*. Creatively and emotionally, he was once more swinging upwards. Vincent described them with pride to Theo and thought that Gauguin liked them. Gauguin believed that Bernard would admire them. They were hung in a position of pride: on the wall of Gauguin's bedroom. Unless the *Sunflowers* and the *Poet's Garden* had been moved, the walls of that little space were getting very crowded.

★

In the evenings, by gaslight in the studio, or with a candle by his bed, Vincent was reading *The Dream* – the latest work by the celebrated novelist Émile Zola. Zola's works were among Vincent's favourite books, and for once he was not alone in his tastes. The recent publication of *The Dream* had been a national event.

Over the previous few weeks there had been plenty of articles about it in the newspapers. But *The Dream* was one of the strangest, as well as the shortest, of Zola's fictions, and Vincent did not much like it. The setting, an old town with a medieval church covered in carvings of martyred saints, depressed him. Vincent enjoyed the account of the golden-haired heroine stitching embroidery, but her lover didn't much impress him. Characteristically, he saw the whole book in terms of colour contrast, between gloomy blues and the radiant hue of the sun.

Plagued by financial insecurity and guilt though he was, one thing on which Vincent never economized was reading matter. The Yellow House was full of it.

No doubt, Gauguin was also dipping into Vincent's hoard of books and magazines. Their tastes were different. For example, Gauguin later expressed distaste for Zola, whose style he found false. But it was difficult to have much contact with Vincent without being bombarded with literary recommendations.

Vincent told his sister Wil that he had got into the habit of reading for a few hours every night (though he felt it was his duty as an artist to be looking at the world around him and thinking about it): 'Driven by a certain mental voracity, I even read the newspapers with fury.' Indeed, old newspapers lay around in his house, eventually to be used to wrap up pictures whose paint was coming off.

There were the local papers, *L'Homme de bronze* and *Forum républicain*, which both appeared on Sundays at 5 centimes each, and also the national press from Paris, easily available at the station. Vincent read newspapers of varied editorial leanings – *Le Figaro*, which was right of centre, the radically republican organ *L'Intransigeant*, and *La justice*, which supported another radical politician, Georges Clemenceau. Gauguin favoured yet another paper, *L'événement*.

Politically, both men were unhappy with the current dispensation. Vincent was an admirer of the leaders of the movement for reform of the Republic, General Boulanger and Henri Rochefort – founder of *L'Intransigeant*. But, characteristically, he thought of them not as practical politicians but as suffering, would-be 'martyrs'.

Vincent dreamt, it seemed to Bernard, of 'a future filled with goodness and love, when all human beings would embrace one another, and personal struggles, always so bitter and bloody, would come to an end'. But he wasn't really a socialist – indeed he stated that he wasn't in a letter to his sister Wil. In his mind, art became a substitute for Christian salvation. Or, as Bernard put it, 'his artistic nature sought to make a religion and aesthetic credo out of the notion of social harmony.'

Gauguin had divided feelings about the French Republic, too. His father had been a supporter of the failed Revolution of 1848 (that was why the family had fled to Peru). But the new Third Republic – which had been founded only after the defeat in the Franco-Prussian war and was only seventeen years old – seemed to him a shabby trick, like a cheaply illusionistic picture. 'Philosophically speaking, I think the Republic is a *trompe l'oeil* (to borrow a term in painting), and I hate *trompe l'oeil*.'

In some notes he wrote for his daughter four years later, Gauguin expressed disdain for the vulgar rulers of modern

France, a country in which there was no place for an artist such as him. 'The democrats, bankers, ministers and art critics masquerade as protectors and don't protect anything; they haggle like fish buyers at the market.' So, he explained, 'instinctively and without knowing why', he was a snob – as an artist. 'Art is only for the minority, therefore it has to be noble itself.' As usual, Gauguin had ended up in a party of one.

In the newspapers, Vincent noted items of all kinds, particularly those with a bearing on the art world. Reading the literary supplement published by *Le Figaro* on Saturday 15 September (around the time he moved properly into the Yellow House), he was amazed to learn of an Impressionist building of violet glass:

With the sunshine reflected in it, and the yellow refractions, the effect was incredible. To support these walls of glass bricks, shaped like violet-coloured eggs, they had invented a support of black and gilt iron representing the weird branches of Virginia creeper and other climbing plants. This violet house was right in the middle of a garden where all the paths were of bright yellow sand.

This gave him food for thought about his own, simpler artists' house. But he also noted the weather and political events connected with the man of the hour, General Boulanger. Gauguin, with his experience of 'banking in Paris', noted, as the autumn wore on, that the financial state of the country was ominous. The French company founded to dig a canal through Panama, the Compagnie Universelle du Canal Interocéanique, was slowly foundering. It finally collapsed in December. Gauguin feared this would have a bad effect on the art market.

The other topic in the newspapers that autumn was murder. In France, an infamous murderer, Prado, was about to come to trial for the vicious slaying of a prostitute. Meanwhile, across the Channel, an even more sensational series of murders was taking place: the violent dismemberment of prostitutes by a man who signed himself 'Jack the Ripper'. This made international news and was extensively covered in France.

Probably Vincent read some of these reports. It was just the kind of low-life subject that his literary tastes encouraged (Guy de Maupassant, one of his heroes, was moved to write a story about the Ripper). Also, Vincent had actually been to Whitechapel, where the crimes took place, during a brief period as a spare-time evangelist near London.

His eye may have fallen on a macabre detail concerning one of the victims, Catherine Eddowes, killed on 30 September. The corpse was extensively hacked about and one ear cut right off. On 3 October, in one of several lengthy reports about these sensationally horrible crimes, *Le Figaro* had published a full translation of one of the letters to the police purporting to come from the Ripper himself. It contained a macabre and badly punctuated threat: 'The next job I do I shall clip the ladys ears off and send to the police officers just for jolly wouldn't you.'

Reading was one constant occupation in the Yellow House; writing was another. Bernard was receiving such a frequent correspondence from Arles that he almost counted as a third inhabitant of 2 Place Lamartine. And, as a sign of how well things were going, on Friday the second or Saturday the third, the two painters collaborated on his next letter. Vincent wrote a great deal and Gauguin added a little at the end.

Vincent was still meditating on the personality of his guest. He confided some startling conclusions to Bernard:

Gauguin interests me very much as a man – very much. For a long
time now it has seemed to me that in our nasty profession of
painting we are most sorely in need of men with the hands and the
stomachs of workmen; men who have more natural tastes – more
loving and more charitable temperaments – than the decadent
dandies of the Parisian boulevards. Well, here we are without the
slightest doubt in the presence of a virgin creature with savage
instincts. With Gauguin blood and sex prevail over ambition.

From a factual point of view, this characterization of
Gauguin was bizarre. It revealed Vincent's capacity – especially when in an excited mood – to run together all manner
of disparate associations in his mind, connecting real people
with books and images. Thus, in this case, the middle-class
Gauguin had the hands and stomach of a workman (unlike
Vincent himself, whose weak stomach was a sign of poor
health).

In Vincent's eyes, Gauguin – failed businessman/tarpaulin-
salesman – was as robust as the proletarian heroes of Zola and
Loti's fishermen. Simultaneously – though the real Gauguin
had spent much of his life in Paris – he was a rustic sage, not
a decadent metropolitan. He was a 'savage' from Peru (where
his great-great-uncle had been governor-general).

The scheming Gauguin was a noble primitive in whom
'sex and blood' prevailed over ambition. He also had 'a more
loving and more charitable temperament' than corrupt
dandies of the big city. And Gauguin, the married father of
five children, was a 'virgin creature'. No doubt, Vincent
meant 'undefiled by European civilization', but it was an odd
choice of word.

Of course, Gauguin himself had come up with much of
this farrago – emphasizing his 'primitive' persona like that of
a Breton fisherman, and his 'artistic virginity' symbolized by

the wallpaper 'like that of a young girl's bedroom', in his portrait *Les Misérables*. But he commented modestly in his postscript on Vincent's effusion, 'Don't listen to Vincent; he is as you know easily roused to admiration and indulgence.' But he didn't entirely disagree.

One of the main topics of conversation between the two painters was the scheme, which they both imagined they had originally invented, for a cooperative community of painters. 'The terrible subject of an association of certain painters,' as Vincent described it. Vincent favoured a pooling of resources in which more established artists subsidized poorer ones; Gauguin wanted to bring in investors: 'This association must or may have, yes or no, a commercial character.' Vincent summarized these discussions: 'We haven't arrived at any conclusion yet.'

Vincent's vision of a peaceful monastery of artists, co-operating at the birth of a new art, merged easily with another hobby-horse: that the new art would come into being in hot, new-found lands. This, too, was a fantasy the painters in the Yellow House had in common. Of course, Gauguin had actually worked in tropical Martinique whereas Vincent's ideas were entirely speculative – Provence was as close as he ever got to the Equator. But there was a sweeping, evangelical ring to Vincent's theories. The Studio in the Tropics blended into a biblical land where the lion would lie down with the lamb:

As for me, with my presentiment of a new world, I firmly believe in the possibility of an immense renaissance of art. Whoever believes in this new art will have the tropics for a home. I have the impression that we ourselves serve as no more than intermediaries. And that only the next generation will succeed in living in peace.

Even though he had first-hand experience of the problems of working on tropical islands – the fevers, the isolation, the danger of running out of cash – Gauguin found Vincent's preaching infectious. He told Bernard as much. 'His idea of a new generation of painters in the tropics seems absolutely right to me and I still have the intention of returning there when I have the means. Who knows – with a little luck?' Gauguin's great project for the future was taking firmer shape in his imagination as he listened to Vincent.

Vincent's description of Gauguin as 'virgin' was strictly meta-phorical: another evening occupation of the two painters, apart from reading, writing and talking, was brothel-visiting. They had already, as Vincent reported to Bernard, made 'several excursions'.

The brothel at No. 1 Rue du Bout d'Arles, one of the six establishments in Arles, was run by the not very aptly named Madame, Virginie Chabaud. It had, as was common with such places, a more spartan reception room for poorer customers, which reminded Vincent of a village school, with its plain bluish-white walls, and a smarter salon for the bourgeoisie. There was a cash desk at the door. Inside, drinks were avail-able. Its normal clientele was colour-coded, as Vincent noted with his painter's acumen: there were military men in red and citizens of Arles in black.

Gauguin described a different brothel in the same street run by a fifty-two-year-old man, Louis Farce, with his wife, cook, servants and six prostitutes.

Gauguin found the decor and entertainment there suitably tawdry – 'panelling with false gilt, rowdy songs, incoherence, art for the mob'. The bedrooms upstairs were functional, with their 'washbasins, bidets, *vinaigre de Bully*' (a fragrant substitute for eau de Cologne).

'Old Louis' himself proudly showed Gauguin, a favoured customer, the 'special' red drawing-room with its highbrow decorations. These were prints reproducing famous paintings (marketed by Theo's firm, Goupil's) by the sugary academic painter, Bouguereau. One depicted the Madonna, the other, Venus – suitably contrasted female ideals for a Provençal knocking-shop.

Gauguin especially despised the work of Bouguereau. He waxed ironic on the subject of the Bouguereaus in the brothel: 'In this instance old Louis had shown himself a man of genius. Like the magnificent brothel keeper he was, he had understood the far from revolutionary art of Bouguereau and just where it belonged.' It was more intriguing, however, in view of the disaster that was soon to overtake Vincent, that there was a picture of the Madonna on the wall at Farce's brothel.

Despite the low opinion he had of the decor, Gauguin was enjoying himself at the brothels. He had been apart from his wife for two and a half years and had apparently had little sexual life in the interim. Now he had money in his pocket and regular access to the women of Rue du Bout d'Arles.

In a semi-fictionalized account of a brothel in Arles which he wrote years later when he was dying on the other side of the world, he described his visits in animal terms: 'I was strong as a bull and lazy as a snake.' It was a sentence that evoked real sensual pleasure.

When he first arrived in Arles, Vincent had been inclined to consider abstention from women as well as from alcohol to be healthy. It was a couple of weeks before he even peeped inside a brothel. Thereafter, his references to these places became more frequent. He noted that fate was as inexorable as the doorman at these places: 'The brothel keeper, when he kicks anyone out, has similar logic, argues as well, and is always right, I know.' Had Vincent been thrown out?

He wondered whether prostitutes, apparently so degraded, might still be capable of love: 'She is seeking, seeking, seeking – does she herself know what? Might she be transformed one day like a grub into a butterfly?' (This was one of Vincent's favourite metaphors.) For that matter, he would have liked to know what he was the larva of himself.

The idea of regular brothel-visits had always been part of Vincent's plan for his studio. It was part and parcel of the 'monastic' nature of his fantasy. The artists would be bachelors, dedicated to their art, sharing spartan lives, but still, he believed – as he had found in his own life – there was a need for a sexual outlet. Hence the emphasis he laid on a visit to the brothel at least once a fortnight. An inhabitant of Arles remembered, perhaps unfairly, that he was 'always hanging round the brothels'.

These excursions were not, however, only 'hygienic'. They also had an artistic purpose. Gauguin and Vincent felt that they would probably often go to the brothels to work. That project, however, was not entirely their own. They were both taking their cue from the absent Bernard.

Up to now, Vincent had had little luck in finding sitters to pose for him. In eight months in Arles he had recruited only six: an old lady; Milliet; another Zouave (probably courtesy of Milliet); Roulin the postal supervisor; an adolescent girl he imagined as a little Japanese whore, a *Mousmé*; and a handsome woman who had taken his money and then not turned up.

Vincent's unsettling personality was not the only reason for this difficulty. There was a superstition among the people of Arles, Vincent was told, that having one's likeness taken was unlucky. It would attract the evil eye. In 1888 many people around the world felt the same: the inhabitants of rural Somerset firmly believed that being 'a-lookt' by an artist might result in illness and death. In Arles, they thought the same.

But that weekend, Vincent got his wish. On Saturday the third or Sunday 4 November a model – a female model at that, and one dressed in full traditional costume – gave a sitting in the studio of the Yellow House. Vincent had hinted before that Gauguin had 'almost got his Arlésienne'. But the model so triumphantly lured into the Yellow House was far from being the youthful southern *femme fatale* of Daudet's play and Bizet's music. She turned out to be none other than Marie, wife of Joseph Ginoux, proprietor of the Café de la Gare.

At forty, Marie Ginoux was a little younger than her husband, who was forty-five. She was a mature Arlésienne, but then, the distinctive costume was already falling out of fashion amongst younger women. The teenage Jeanne Calment preferred modern, colourful clothes. And Vincent also – with his distaste for the past and affinity for the modern – liked the look of the girls in town who wore violet, lemon or pink dresses rather than the traditional black and white.

There was a simple reason why Madame Ginoux was suddenly posing in the Yellow House after all these months. Gauguin, not Vincent, had asked her. He wanted to draw her in preparation for a painting of the Ginoux' bar, with, as Vincent put it, 'figures seen in the brothels'. This café was a place where streetwalkers – women not regularly attached to a *maison de tolérance* such as No. 1 or Louis Farce's establishment – would go for a drink and a chat with a client. If not actually a brothel, this was a similarly lowlife subject. In the two *Falling Leaves*, Vincent had used ideas of Gauguin's and Bernard's. In this project, Gauguin was going to borrow from Vincent and Bernard. Collaboration was proceeding according to plan.

This was Gauguin's sitting, as was clear from the way that

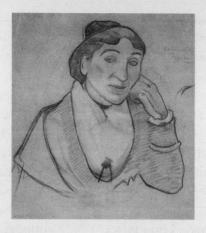

Madame Ginoux sat facing him. Vincent's less dominant role was obvious from his position. His easel was to her left, so he viewed Madame Ginoux from an angle. In his painting, she appeared to be staring into space in a thoughtful fashion. Actually, she was looking Gauguin straight in the eye. But Vincent's junior position – as an intruder, almost, in his own studio – was belied by the results.

During the sitting, Gauguin systematically and methodically produced a drawing. First, he sketched the outline of Madame Ginoux's head and torso in grey chalk. Then he went over this in stronger black conté chalk and charcoal, creating a firm, decisive outline. Then he put in highlights here and there in white chalk to bring out the forms. Finally, he considered the study and noted a few modifications to be made when he incorporated it in the finished painting he was planning: 'The eye less to the side of the nose. Stop sharply at the nostril.' This was the first stage in the evolution of a *tableau*, a proper picture.

In the same amount of time, Vincent turned out a whole completed canvas, a big one on the scale generally reserved for important exhibited works. It was a remarkable feat, of which he was proud. He claimed at first that the picture had been completed in an hour. A couple of months later he reduced the estimated painting time to forty-five minutes.

However long it actually took, the picture was painted at a tremendous pace; there are many areas – particularly on the white blouse over her bosom – where the coarse jute of the canvas shows clearly through the rapid thrusts of Vincent's brush, or palette knife. So the phrase he used to describe the process – 'slashed on', '*sabré*', or applied with a sword – might have been close to the literal truth.

That word was also a challenging reference to Gauguin and his fencing. The other painter, sitting a few feet away from Vincent, believed that both his favourite sport and his chosen art were best advanced by a cool mind, '*de tête*'. Well, then, here was a different sort of painterly swordsmanship – a dazzling feat of intuitive and intellectual brilliance, carried out at a speed that was almost unbelievable. Vincent's *L'Arlési-enne* was achieved by methods the absolute opposite of those that Gauguin advocated.

This was a work that by all conventional criteria should have been just a study, an *étude*, a stepping stone to something more considered. But, instead, Vincent executed, at an almost magical rate, a painting on the scale and with the authority of a fully pondered portrait. It was built with tremendous logic. The orange chair and green table were built with the solidity of a house, brush stroke by brush stroke against the light yellow background, which perhaps resulted from the newly installed gaslight shining on the studio wall.

Marie Ginoux herself appeared a figure of nobility and also of melancholy, with a hint of a smile and shadow of pain, wearing the traditional costume. The Arlésienne cap – *capello* in Provençal – crowned the wearer's head, with ribbons fluttering behind, and a white shawl or *gazo* covers her front.

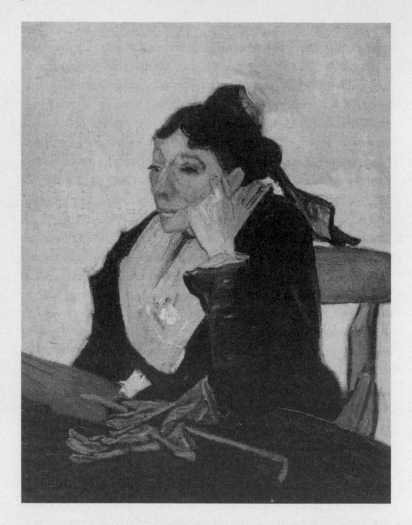

One ribbon, fluttering backwards, was a crucial part of Vincent's pictorial architecture. Without it, the painting would have lost energy. It was dashed in with a few decisive passes of a heavily laden brush.

On the table in front of Madame Ginoux, Vincent placed the rest of her Arlésienne accessories – a jolly red parasol and green gloves. On her front he placed a single oleander – the flower that spoke to Vincent of southern love. Though no longer young, Madame Ginoux was of an age and type to which Vincent was susceptible. The mistress of his Paris period, Agostina Segatori, owner of the Café du Tambourin in Montmartre, had been in her late forties.

Vincent made Marie Ginoux much more than a figure of local folklore. She was a relatively humble person – the wife of the owner of a rough sort of café with a dubious clientele. But even these people – dregs, bar-flies, riff-raff – are treated with full seriousness in the books of Zola and the Goncourts.

This was what Vincent wanted to achieve in his portraits: to portray ordinary modern people in all their suffering and individuality, as souls. The picture of Marie Ginoux was weighted with her thoughts and feelings. When he repeated this portrait the following month, perhaps as a gift for Marie Ginoux herself, he replaced the parasol and gloves with books, thus connecting her with his private literary world.

Vincent had always been a great – even an astonishing – walker. In his youth he had walked from Ramsgate to London, and from Isleworth to Welwyn, where one of his sisters was living. In Arles, he walked incessantly – perhaps its situation on the outskirts of town, almost in the fields, was one of the attractions of the Yellow House.

Vincent hated big cities and had ambivalent feelings about Paris. 'When I saw it for the first time,' he told his sister, Wil, 'I felt above all the dreary misery, which one cannot wave away, as little as one can wave away the tainted air in a hospital, however clean it may be kept.' Later, he realized that it was also a hugely stimulating place, a seedbed of new ideas. 'Other cities become small in comparison with it, and it seems as big as the sea.' But, still, he found the crowding and the tension of Parisian life unbearable. That had been one reason, he felt, for his breakdown the previous year: 'one thing is certain, *nothing is fresh there.*' He craved the space and ease of the countryside. Gauguin also liked to emphasize his dislike of Paris, where he had lived for many years, and his love of Brittany – 'Give me the country.'

By midsummer Vincent had already walked out the mile or two to Montmajour at least fifty times, to explore the ruins and – even more – to look back across the plain of the Crau, which reminded him, like the sea and the starry sky, of infinity. He did this walk several times with his friend Second Lieutenant Milliet, and also with Gauguin.

On that Sunday, in the late afternoon, Gauguin and Vincent took that very road towards Montmajour and the Alpilles. As the sun was setting they looked back over the vineyards that were sited on the lower slopes, the very place that Vincent had painted at the height of the grape harvest a month before.

The prospect was spectacular. The gold and green of the sky contrasted richly with the purple hue of the autumnal vine leaves. The slanting rays of light caught the puddles of water still lying around from the heavy rain of Thursday and Friday. In Vincent's eyes, 'It was all red like red wine.' In the distance the wet earth turned yellow with violet shadows, 'sparking here and there where it caught the reflection of the setting sun'. Vincent believed that the colours of the sunsets in the South were more varied and clearer than in the North.

The sight gave both painters ideas – quite different ones – for new pictures. At the moment the sun dipped beneath the horizon it was just before five-thirty. They walked back to Arles through the gathering night. Vincent and Gauguin had been living together for thirteen days. So far, everything was going well.

4. Collaboration

5–10 November

For the time being, the urgent financial problems of the Yellow House were over. Gauguin had nearly 200 francs left over from the 500 he had got from his sale, so there was even some extra money to hand. Over the previous week, he had been buying various things for the house.

This was part of Gauguin's plan to improve the domestic arrangements – as was his simple system for regulating the finances with the box of money, list of expenses and pencil. In addition to the 20 metres of jute, Gauguin had bought a chest of drawers, 'and various household utensils'.

In other words, as Vincent reflected slightly dubiously to Theo, 'a lot of things that we needed' or 'that at any rate it was more convenient to have'. Vincent felt that in due course – at New Year or perhaps Easter – Gauguin should be repaid for this expenditure on the house. That would help him save up for his second voyage to Martinique, and the Van Gogh brothers would own the chest of drawers and cooking implements.

Gauguin was assembling his kitchen equipment because the day was approaching when he was going to cook his first meal in the house. Vincent announced this development to Theo with jubilation in a letter which was probably written on Monday 5 November: 'Gauguin and I are going to have our dinner at home today, and we feel as sure and certain that it will turn out well as that it will seem to us better or cheaper.'

Gaugin had given the same news a day before to Bernard. If the latter didn't have to go to Africa to do military service, he could come to Arles and enjoy 'a fairly easy existence'. He had looked into the 'question of money', he added, and concluded that 'we can get by cheaply by doing what I shall be doing from tomorrow, by doing the cooking at home.' Clearly, he was content in Arles – and taking on Vincent's projects as his own.

The notion of eating at home had been part of Vincent's plan since the idea of forming a community of artists in the Yellow House first came into his head. Eating in restaurants was extravagant, he felt. But, he poignantly noted, it was hard to cook at home for just one.

In Vincent's mind, the job of chief cook in the Yellow House had always been allocated to Gauguin, who had done naval service and knocked around the world a bit. So from that day on they gave up going to the Restaurant Venissat. Instead, Gauguin made their supper on the gas stove which Vincent had had installed at the same time as the lighting.

The kitchen and dining room was behind the studio, a smaller space, which Vincent had briefly used to work in. He had drawn one of Milliet's Zouave soldiers in it, hunkered down on a little chair in front of the old oven and chimney. It contained a table – useful for writing letters – and chairs. But the bits and pieces which Vincent had bought for making coffee and soup were not sufficient, Gauguin clearly felt, for serious cooking. The chest of drawers, since there already was one in both bedrooms, was perhaps to store the cutlery, crockery and the rest of Gauguin's *batterie de cuisine*. A big frying pan was one of the requirements Vincent had noted before his guest arrived.

Gauguin had not only served in the navy for years, he had also kept house for himself and his six-year-old son Clovis when the two of them had returned from Copenhagen in 1885 (subsequently, Clovis had been farmed out with relatives, and then gone back to Denmark). Skill in the kitchen was not unknown in male artists of the period. Vincent's friend Toulouse-Lautrec was a renowned amateur chef. Moreover, Gauguin had a genuine feeling for food.

In Denmark, he noted, the best thing was — assuredly — not his mother-in-law, but 'the game she cooked so admirably'. The Nordic fish he also found 'excellent'. In his mind, good food implied liberality, jollity, feasting — 'No mean woman,' he declared, 'can cook well. It calls for a generous spirit, a light hand, and a large heart.' — whereas Vincent thought of what he ate medicinally, as a health tonic, or the reverse. At best, it was the fuel that kept him in condition to paint.

Vincent's job was to buy the food. And to do that, as Gauguin commented, 'he did not have to go far.' Indeed, he only had to step next door, to the other half of the building that contained the Yellow House. There, a man named François Crevoulin and his wife Marguerite kept a grocer's shop in premises that were almost, but not quite, a mirror image of the Yellow House.

His neighbours, Vincent had mentioned to Theo, 'strongly resembled' the Buteaux. This was a coded reference that packed in a great deal of information. Buteau was a character in Zola's novel about peasant life, *La Terre* (or *The Earth*), which had been published the year before. In French the name suggests '*buté*' or 'pig-headedness', and in the book Buteau was bullying, lustful, lying, hard-working and possessed jaws like a gorilla. He and his wife Lise, who was also his cousin, were murderers. Now, for the first time, Vincent went to this shop to buy the ingredients for a meal for two. Afterwards, in theory at least, he should have noted down the amount he had spent on the piece of paper beside the money box.

From now on, every evening Gauguin would stand at the stove boiling and frying, then eat with Vincent at the kitchen table. Neither painter recorded any of the recipes that Gauguin cooked, but they may well have eaten some fish when they could get it, since Vincent thought the fish at Stes-Maries de la Mer, at the mouth of the Rhône, was outstanding, and some of it came upriver to Arles. Vincent bought such things as crabs to pose for his pictures. He had also acquired a taste for that Mediterranean staple, the olive.

Throughout Vincent's life, eating had been a difficult issue, for reasons which it was hard to untangle – part ascetic zeal, part genuine penury, part illness, part incompetence, part neurosis. During his phase of religious exaltation, he had eschewed all but the simplest meals. Later, having gone back to live with his elderly parents and sister, he would insist on eating separately from the rest of the family, consuming nothing but dry bread and cheese. Either because he had wrecked his stomach through semi-starvation or because there was something else wrong with him, Vincent complained frequently about the state of his digestion.

Soon Vincent was sending Theo enthusiastic reports about Gauguin's food: 'He knows how to cook *perfectly*, I think I shall learn from him, it is very convenient.' But that last plan did not work out well. According to Gauguin, Vincent made only one attempt to produce a meal himself. He decided to make soup. 'How he mixed it I don't know; as he mixed his colours in his pictures I dare say. At any rate, we couldn't eat it. And Vincent burst out laughing and exclaimed: "Tarascon! The cap of Father Daudet!"'

This was a reference to the comic novel *Tartarin de Tarascon*, by Alphonse Daudet, the book that had been one of the reasons Vincent had wanted to come to Provence in the first place. The book related how the men of Tarascon had wiped out all game in the vicinity, so, instead of hunting, they went out into the country and took pot shots at their headgear. 'Every man plucks off his cap, "shies" it up with all his might, and pops it on the fly with a No. 5, 6 or 2 shot, according to what he is loaded for.' Vincent was saying that his culinary disaster was a similar piece of happy-go-lucky southern craziness. Looked at objectively, however, the connections he made – between soup and hunting, Tartarin and himself – were extremely far-fetched.

There was one profound and obvious difference between Vincent and Gauguin, which was reflected in their two paintings of the sunset over the vineyard. One of them had been brought up a devout Protestant, the other a pious Catholic.

Gauguin said little later of the 'theological studies' of his youth, but they were doubtless intense. He had studied from the ages of eleven to sixteen at the Petit Séminaire de La Chapelle-Saint-Mesmin outside Orléans. There, he applied himself, among other subjects, to Catholic liturgy, the latter subject being taught by the Bishop of Orléans himself, Félix-Antoine-Philibert Dupanloup.

This man was a big wheel in French religious education. A charismatic teacher, he devised new methods of inculcating faith in the young. He wanted his pupils to develop 'supernaturally-infused' powers of imagination, to focus within, on otherworldly truths. A favourite analogy of his was the spiritual harvest: an inner light that came from the planting of God in the soul.

At the heart of the bishop's system was his new catechism, a series of questions the boys were to ponder inwardly again and again: What is grace? What is death? There were three questions more fundamental than the rest: 'Where does humanity come from?' 'Where is it going?' 'How does humanity proceed?' Once embedded in the youthful mind, Dupanloup believed, this catechism would never be erased.

In the case of at least one pupil, Dupanloup was correct. Near the end of his life, on the other side of the world, Gauguin painted a huge painting, like a fresco, on jute: his testament. Its title was, *'Where Do We Come From? What Are We? Where Are We Going?'*

These were conundrums that tormented not only Gauguin, but his age, and the one that came afterwards. It was a period when to many thinking people, the certainties of Christian religion seemed to be disintegrating with alarming speed. Matthew Arnold, an English poet who had died that very year, 1888, put the matter well. The Sea of Faith, he wrote, was once at full tide, furled around the globe 'like the folds of a bright girdle'. 'But now I only hear/Its melancholy, long, withdrawing roar'. Humanity now stood on the 'naked shingles of the world', and there was no longer 'joy, nor love, nor light, nor certitude, nor peace, nor help for pain'.

Gauguin, as an adult, was caustically anticlerical. Towards the end of his life, in the South Pacific, he wrote a long essay entitled 'Catholicism and the Modern Mind' in which he tore into the 'oppressive, debasing, stultifying, theocratic priestly class', but he still felt that some deep truth could be extracted from Christ's parables. And, as he put it in some notes written at that low point of his life, when he split from his wife in Copenhagen, he was still looking for an art that would, with a single glance, 'engulf the soul in the most profound memories'.

To Vincent, too, after a period of fervent piety, it came to seem that conventional Christianity was dead. 'Within ten or fifteen years,' he wrote to his sister, 'the whole edifice of the national religion collapsed.' He continued, however, to believe that art could make up for some of that gap, that it could – to use a favourite word of Vincent's – console.

There were many artists, writers and poets who were struggling with this same challenge. Essentially, there were two possible strategies. One was to create an art of new symbols to replace the old. This was a path followed by many French writers. A new movement named Symbolism had been launched by a poet, Jean Moréas, in the newspaper *Le Figaro* two years before. It was an approach that grew out of the work of Parisian poets such as Stéphane Mallarmé.

'Poetry,' according to Mallarmé, 'endows our stay on earth and constitutes the only spiritual path.' But half the pleasure in poetry lay in its ambiguity. 'To *name* an object is to suppress three-quarters of the enjoyment to be found in a poem . . . *suggestion*, that is the dream.'

Temperamentally, and by Bishop Dupanloup's training, Gauguin was inclined towards this new movement of Symbolism, which was allegorical, dreamy, poetic, vague and, to use his favoured term, 'abstract'. In a year or two, he would be taken up by the Symbolists and invited to the Tuesday gatherings at Mallarmé's apartment. But he had not yet joined; most of his work to date had been a depiction, more or less rearranged, of what he saw before him. Only his *Vision*, not more than two months old, could be called a Symbolist work. His painting of the vineyard took him a step further in that direction.

Vincent's religious training had been the opposite of Gauguin's. His boyhood had been spent in the village of Zundert in Southern Brabant, a rustic parish in which his father was pastor to the few local adherents of the Dutch Reformed Church (the neighbourhood was predominantly Catholic). Pastor Theodorus van Gogh followed a reforming theological movement known as the Groningen School, which was comparable to the ethos known in Britain as 'muscular Christianity'.

He consequently encouraged an active faith: doing good, not examining the soul. 'Dare to live!' exhorted one of his favourite poets, Reverend Petrus A. de Genestet. 'Devoted and happy, fresh and early/Awake with the sun, stretch your hands to the plough in the great field!'

God's nature was revealed by the beauties of the world: an attitude similar to that of John Ruskin (Vincent's mother, like the great critic, was a keen watercolourist). 'The view of the starry sky,' sang the Reverend Bernard ter Haar, also avidly read by the Revd van Gogh, 'reminds the Christian of the dwellings of the house of the father,/ The sprouting of the grain of his Resurrection/The rising sun of his immortality.'

Later, after he lost his faith, Vincent retained a passionate love of what he actually saw. This was the second possible response to the painful disappearance of supernatural belief. It was a northern and Protestant answer. Ruskin, like some Dutch theologians, found the signs of God in the wonderful structure of nature: the leaves of a flower, the strata in a rock. Vincent believed that you could find the infinite in a blade of grass.

The Scottish philosopher Thomas Carlyle went one further and propounded a creed he dubbed 'natural supernaturalism'. What existed, he argued, was itself miraculous, with or without religious sanction. In his book *Sartor Resartus* (or *The Tailor Reclothed*), Carlyle proposed that all beliefs and symbols, like old clothes, wore out and must be discarded. But the new beliefs for the new world should be derived from the real world, not from the outworn iconography of Madonnas and martyrdoms. Vincent read Carlyle's works with enthusiasm.

Temperamentally, and by his upbringing, Vincent inclined

towards Carlyle's natural supernaturalism. Eventually, he was to declare that, 'If I am at all capable of spiritual ecstasy, then I feel exalted in the face of truth, of what is possible.' The night sky put Vincent in mind of eternity. Sunset, too, was a moment of the day that filled him with feeling and which he had often painted.

But, for the time being, Vincent was eager to paint symbolic paintings – such as the *Sower* – and to attempt biblical scenes such as Christ in the Garden of Gethsemane, which he had twice attempted in Arles and twice abandoned. His next picture was a compromise. It looked real but was full of hidden symbolism.

'We are working hard,' Vincent told Theo, 'and our life together goes very well.' The work in the studio was intense. For the moment, though the rain had let up, both painters had indoor projects to pursue. Contrary to his prediction that it would take him a long time to settle down in Arles, Gauguin had two major paintings in hand. One was the *Night Café*, with Madame Ginoux in the foreground, the other a new painting inspired by the sight of the sunset in the vineyard.

Vincent thought this picture, done 'altogether from memory', would be 'very fine and very unusual' if Gauguin did not spoil it or leave it unfinished (as he presumably had that first Arles picture of the negress). Vincent himself was also working, from memory, on a painting of the field of vines, 'all purple and yellow' in the dying sun. The two artists responded to this revelatory spectacle in entirely different ways.

Vincent painted the *Red Vineyard* over the next few days, peopling the field with figures from his memory and imagination (for instance the woman on the right looks like Madame Ginoux, unsuitably dressed for grape-picking in her Arlésienne costume). He was working in the way that Gauguin called *de tête* – from imagination – or *peintre de chic*.

That he should do this had always been part of Vincent's plan for the time after Gauguin arrived, just like the shared expenses and the communal cooking. It was another aspect of the sharing of ideas: *collaboration*. But the question of working from memory was vexed for him. On the one hand, his natural tendency was to paint from what he saw in front of him, often very rapidly in one exhilarating rush. As he was well aware, that was often how he produced his best work. On the other hand, he also knew that it was not the way that painting should be produced.

The accepted academic procedure was as follows. First, one should produce a sketch, or *esquisse* – possibly preceded by an even rougher preliminary sketch, or *ébauche*. Studies, or *études*, of particular aspects of the intended picture would probably be required. Only then was it possible to attempt the final work, the painting itself, or *tableau*. The evolution of a picture, then, was an orderly, highly intellectual affair. In fact, even when he painted at the highest speed, Vincent generally followed a carefully thought-out strategy. But he did not follow the 'proper' stages.

It was true that these rules had been breached frequently by avant-garde painters. Much of the rage that poured down on the Impressionists was provoked by the fact that they exhibited as finished *tableaux* works that had the informal air and rough lack of finish appropriate to *études*. But some, even among the radicals, still preferred this methodical manner of working. Georges Seurat, for example, the most successful of the experimental young painters in Paris and Gauguin's enemy and rival, always set about things in this way. He developed his works from beginning to end with intellectual rigour.

Vincent was unsettled by the issue. In his letters to Theo

he constantly classified his paintings into studies and pictures – the *Bedroom*, for example, he counted as a *tableau*, and also the *Night Café* – but there were always far more of the former than the latter. Most of what he did, he sadly concluded, were only *études* – at best, stepping stones towards the proper, finished works that he might achieve in a few years' time, if his health held up. The problem, obviously, was that it was what he actually saw before his eyes that Vincent found most inspiring and exciting.

In this picture of the *Red Vineyard*, though, he worked *de tête*; he kept close to what he and Gauguin had actually seen on Sunday evening. The place was one that he knew well; it was the same field that he had depicted for the picture at the end of September – the most intense point of the grape harvest – which now hung in the Yellow House. This earlier picture was now renamed the *Green Vineyard* to distinguish it from the new *Red Vineyard*. Yet there was still more collaboration hidden here. One of Émile Bernard's best pictures of the early autumn, which Vincent had not seen but had surely heard about, showed the buckwheat harvest, with workers labouring in a field of deep red and gold.

In his imagination Vincent populated the scene with workers who were no longer actually there (the grape harvest had ended weeks ago) and gave it the red and gold of the sunset. The waterlogged road down which he and Gauguin had tramped to Arles became a river of light. A traveller stands upon it, gazing at the distant towers of the city of Arles.

Although it might pass for a work from nature, the *Red Vineyard* had a visionary mood about it. It could be read as a post-Protestant parable. The workers in the vineyard toil virtuously; all around them pours down the glory of the light. One among them, a traveller on the road, stares up at the transfigured sky: eternity.

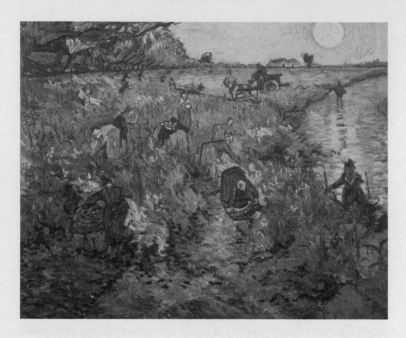

The painting recalled a sermon Vincent had preached twelve years before. When he rejected his first career as a trainee art dealer – and his employers rejected him – Vincent at first did not know what to do. He was grateful to get an unpaid post as assistant master at a miserable boys' school in Ramsgate (he had lived in London while he worked for Goupil's and his English was good). After a term, he got a better job at another school in Isleworth, west of London, run by the Revd T. Slade Jones. Vincent also helped the Revd Jones as a lay preacher, and preached his first sermon on 29 October 1876, in the Wesleyan Chapel, Richmond.

Vincent had told the congregation of a pilgrim who met a woman dressed in black. The pilgrim asked this woman – an angel – how far it was to the city of the distant hill bathed in the golden rays of the setting sun. It was far, she replied. The journey took from morn to night. And the pilgrim carried on, 'sorrowful yet always rejoicing' – a favourite saying of Vincent's. It summed up his whole life – blighted, bedevilled but touched with glory.

But in the *Red Vineyard* this meaning was only hinted at, almost hidden in a real sunset landscape outside Arles. It was very difficult for Vincent to violate the truth of what he saw. That was at the root of his difficulty with his imagined figure, the *Sower*. But that sober truthfulness was also a very Dutch, and a very Protestant, thing about him.

He laboured slowly and carefully on his *Red Vineyard*, smoothing the thick paint over the coarse fabric. He spent days on it – he who could paint a portrait in an hour. When he finished it, he was satisfied. 'I think,' he boasted to Theo, 'that you will be able to put this canvas beside some of Monticelli's landscapes.'

Monticelli was an eccentric painter from Marseilles – dead since the year before last – whom Vincent revered and with whom he closely identified. Many others thought the man had been a crazed alcoholic who daubed canvases with absurdly thick layers of pigment. There was indeed a resemblance between some of Monticelli's later work and the *Red Vineyard*, but Vincent's colour – in fact, everything about his painting – was far richer and stronger.

Meanwhile, on the other side of the studio, Gauguin was at work on a picture that departed much more radically from the view they had both seen. From the actual sight of the vineyard, Gauguin took little more than rich colour harmony – the gold of the setting sun, the purple-red, 'like wine', of the autumnal leaves, the grey-white chalk of the earth turned pinkish in the dying light. The background of his picture was solid gold, like the burnished setting of a medieval altarpiece. Against this rose a pyramid of dark bluish-red, divided by a lower curved mound.

Vincent had cautiously placed some small figures, half

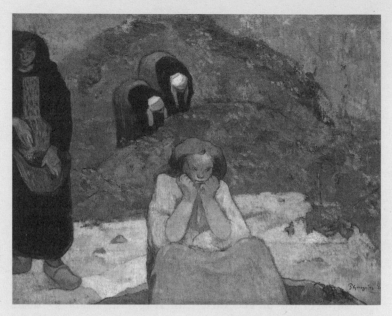

remembered, half invented, in his picture. Gauguin was much more daring. In the background he placed two women dressed as Breton peasants (and Brittany is not even a wine-growing region). Gauguin was highly pleased with this cavalier treatment of the facts. 'It's an effect of vines that I saw at Arles,' he chortled to Bernard, 'but I've put Breton women in it – so much the worse for *exactitude*.'

These women, so arbitrarily transplanted from the north-west, were bent over, picking grapes. In the foreground was seated the brooding figure of a young woman, head in hands; she had long red hair and slanting, cat-like eyes. To the left was a woman in black wearing enormous Breton clogs, a figure from Vincent's imagination transferred to a painting by Gauguin. She had come from Vincent's reading of a poem by the romantic poet Alfred de Musset, '*La Nuit de Décembre*' or 'December Night'.

In it the writer complained that, from childhood, wherever

he had wandered on the face of the earth, he had been accompanied by a figure clad in black. 'Who are you?' he at last demands. 'Our fathers were the same,' the figure replies. 'I am your brother. I am neither god nor demon. When you are suffering, come to me without fear. I am solitude.'

The young Vincent had been taken by this poem and copied it into a scrapbook he kept, perhaps because it dramatized the lonely course his life was already taking. But as he did so he made some unconscious changes. The poet had written of a figure dressed in black who resembled – '*ressemblait*' – him like a brother; Vincent altered that to '*regardait*', 'looked at'.

Obviously, he quoted the poem to Gauguin – it was one of his favourite texts – because Gauguin later wrote of a man dressed in black who *looked at* him in this way. The change in wording was like a tracer dye revealing Vincent as the source. Gauguin, too, found the poem a poignant metaphor for the state of the outcast. But in his picture, as Vincent often did, he changed the sex of the silent companion. The figure became a woman in black.

The coarse jute, combined, as Vincent noted, with much thicker paint than usual, gave the image a texture like rich medieval embroideries such as the ones described in Zola's *The Dream*. And the encrustations of pigment were more like Vincent's technique than Gauguin's, so here was more collaboration – Vincent's paintwork on Gauguin's jute. As a painting it was a bold step – like Gauguin's *Vision* – into the realm of abstraction.

The whole effect was of symbolism, an allegory, but an elusive one. Gauguin later gave the picture various titles, as he often did: first, *Grape Harvest*, *Poverty* or *Human Miseries* – the last perhaps echoing the name of a Balzac novel, *Splendours and Miseries of Courtesans*.

So this was some sort of allegory of humanity. There was also an archaic, ecclesiastical feeling about the painting. Was there a slight resemblance in the arch of the purple vineyard to a Romanesque portal, like the one of St Trophime at Arles, with a standing saint to one side and angels bending over above?

And what was the meaning of this strange image? Gauguin preferred not to spell it out. His favourite method of concocting a painting was 'following my fancy, following the moon, and finding the title long afterwards'. Eventually he gave an explanation of sorts to Schuffenecker: The seated woman was 'a poor desolate person' (Gauguin described her to Theo as 'bewitched'). She was not 'privileged with intelligence, grace and all the gifts of nature'. She was thinking 'of little' but felt 'the consolation of this earth (nothing but the earth)'. The sun flooded down on the red triangle of the vineyard, and a woman dressed in black looked at her 'like a sister'.

So – one might gloss this characteristically obscure interpretation – the seated woman stands for poor, suffering humanity. Her own satisfactions come from the physical world, the earth and the sun. She sat, to quote Matthew Arnold, on the 'naked shingles of the world'. Her only companion is solitude. This was a religious painting for the irreligious, an altarpiece by a lapsed Catholic.

Both Vincent and Gauguin were highly pleased with this new picture. When Gauguin had only just begun it, Vincent was already hopeful that it was going to be an important work. Later, he thought the brothers Van Gogh – that is, Theo – should buy it: 'It is as beautiful as the Negresses, and if you paid say the same price as for the Negresses (400, I think) it would be well worth it.' Gauguin himself was extremely satisfied. This was, he reported to Bernard, his best painting of the year – better even than the *Vision of the Sermon*. As soon as it was dry he would send it to Paris.

On Tuesday 6 November the newspapers were full of reports of the sensational murder trial which had begun the previous day in Paris. It was one of those cases that gripped the attention of the nation, including the two painters in the Yellow House. The accused, who went under the name of Prado, was a fascinating figure, dapper, good-looking, cunning in disguise, multilingual and a ladies' man. But the crime of which he was accused was nasty. He had, it was said, cut the throat of a prostitute and made off with her jewels.

This case was of special interest in the Yellow House. Vincent believed that this murder, and another similarly sensational case the previous year featuring a criminal named Pranzini, had been hatched in a place he knew very well: the Café du Tambourin on Boulevard de Clichy.

A good deal of Vincent's life in Paris had revolved around this bar. He had organized an exhibition of Japanese prints there, and had had – it seemed – an affair with the owner, a middle-aged Italian woman named Agostina Segatori. In her heyday she had posed for Corot and Manet and, according to Gauguin, she was 'still beautiful' at forty-six. Vincent had been 'very much in love with her'. Instead of real flowers, according to Bernard, Vincent had presented her with painted bouquets.

As Gauguin told the story, Agostina Segatori had a man with her to help run the café. This manager wanted to keep Agostina's favours for himself alone. One day he suddenly threw a glass of beer at Vincent, who was immediately thrown out in the street, where a passing gendarme told him to move along.

A lot of Vincent's canvases remained in the café, which

moved him to fury. But that was that. The affair, until then one of Vincent's less disastrous amorous adventures, ended in humiliation. But, evidently, with Agostina Segatori, Vincent had had something he had not otherwise enjoyed – a guiltless physical liaison.

Before they quarrelled, Segatori – or *La Siccatori*, as Gauguin called her, with his usual inability to get names straight – had apparently told Vincent all sorts of secrets about the Pranzini and Prado cases, which had been plotted in her café, and he passed them on to Gauguin. Unfortunately, Gauguin couldn't recall any of the details. Indeed, he couldn't remember Pranzini's name correctly either (he finally settled for 'Pausini'). But of one thing he was sure, both trials had been fixed. Prado and Pranzini were doubtless innocent. But what did that matter? 'The police were bound to have the last word.' As always, Gauguin sympathized with the criminal, outcast and victim.

It was very wet. *L'Homme de bronze* reported that 'tempests and downpours were unleashed all day long over our town on Tuesday, Friday and Saturday.' Even during the day it might have been necessary to light the gas in the studio. The room in which the two men were confined was less than 16 feet across, and its longest wall measured 24 feet. But, because of its irregular shape, it narrowed to 9½ feet on the other side. It was not a tiny space, but neither was it large enough to avoid another occupant.

There were three windows, two in the front wall facing the public gardens in Place Lamartine and another at the side, looking out into the Avenue de Montmajour. It was a goldfish bowl. These windows were at adult head-height; curious children could climb up and peer in.

Quite apart from the question of privacy, there was also

the matter of light. Vincent loved the sun streaming in through the south-west-facing windows. But most artists preferred a northern aspect, because of the colder, less brilliant illumination that resulted.

Into the studio was packed all the equipment – brushes, paints, easels, stretchers, half-completed canvases – necessary for two painters working at full stretch. Their completed works hung on the walls alongside the prints by Daumier, Delacroix and Japanese artists. The fug of oil paint and pipe smoke must have been overpowering, especially on cold days when the windows could not be opened. Vincent's untidiness – the chaos of half-squeezed paint tubes, never properly sealed – was disquieting to Gauguin.

This was the room into which the two painters were now cooped up for virtually all of their waking hours. Even when they left the studio, it was probably together: to go to the café or the brothel. Now they had given up having their meals in the Restaurant Venissat, so cooking and eating took place in the room next door to the studio. This claustrophobic pattern of life would have put a strain on the most phlegmatic pair of friends. But Vincent and Gauguin were both highly neurotic, in diverse ways.

The divergence was psychological and also physiological – one could almost have said chemical. They worked, thought and created at dissimilar rates; as a result, Gauguin produced over a painting career of thirty years roughly as many pictures as Vincent did in the space of less than ten. This was reflected in the amazing speed with which Vincent sometimes turned out a picture – gathering up the paint 'as if with a shovel', as a witness described it, so that 'the globs of paint, covering the length of the paintbrush, stuck to his fingers'. He must have displayed just such a bravura, if messy style of execution when slashing paint on *L'Arlésienne* in an hour or less: a creative frenzy which might well be distracting in a room 15 feet across.

Vincent did not always proceed at that frantic rate, and all his work – no matter how rapidly flung on the canvas – was carefully thought out. But even Vincent in more measured mode might be off-putting. He would get up, a witness recalled, pace three steps one way, then three another. He would stare at the canvas, hands folded on chest, for a long time. 'Suddenly he would leap up as if to attack the canvas, paint two or three strokes quickly, then scramble back to his chair, narrow his eyes, wipe his forehead and rub his hands.'

Vincent's whole bodily rhythm was like that; Gauguin recalled his 'short, quick, irregular' steps. Vincent himself admitted he was sometimes 'nervous and flurried in speech and manner'. He found talking while he worked helped him to concentrate; it may not, however, have helped his companion.

Gauguin was much more contained. According to Judith Molard, a teenage girl who observed him in his studio, Gauguin 'did not appear to be in the throes of inspiration when he was painting. His mouth would be slightly open, his eyes steadily focused as he applied his paint quietly and steadily.'

According to another acquaintance, 'his slow gait, his sober gestures, his severe facial gestures gave him much natural dignity.' That demeanour kept people at a distance, but 'behind this mask of impassive coldness were concealed ardent senses and a sensuous temperament always in search of new sensations.'

As Gauguin saw, looking back on those days in Arles, a conflict was inevitable in that studio: 'Between two such beings as he and I, the one a perfect volcano, the other boiling inwardly, some sort of struggle was preparing.' On the other hand, what they were producing was prodigious. 'Though the public had no suspicion of it, two men were performing there a colossal labour that was useful to them both. Perhaps to others? There are some things that bear fruit.'

Vincent's disorderly habits were mitigated to some extent by an unexpected addition to this bohemian household. Vincent had a devoted cleaning lady. It had been part of his original invitation to Gauguin at the end of May that they should engage a sort of housekeeper to come in for a few hours a day. During the summer, when he was only using the house as a studio, he found a suitable person, a woman whose husband worked around the corner at the station (probably she was recommended by Roulin, who worked there too).

She was middle-aged or elderly and had, as Vincent put it, 'many and varied off-spring'. Rapidly she became devoted to Vincent and he dependent on her. He would not have had the confidence to move into the Yellow House properly in September if he had not had her to make his bed and keep his floor tiles clean and red.

At first she had come in twice a week, charging one franc a time, but by the late autumn, after Gauguin's arrival, she was coming in five days a week. Presumably it was she who did the washing up after they started eating at home. Poor and unconventional though he might be, Vincent still required a servant, at least a part-time one, to live. She, with Roulin, was the most faithful of his friends in Arles. Later, after the crisis, his behaviour grew so strange it made her nervous. But even then she offered to take a message to Theo in Paris if she could get a free rail pass. Vincent never mentioned her name.

It was probably also the cleaning lady who washed and looked after Vincent and Gauguin's clothes. In both cases, their attire needed a good deal of attention. Gauguin's smart Paris business attire, now at least five years old, was rapidly wearing out.

Vincent, too, mentioned several times to Theo that his clothes were becoming worn, although not long after arriving in Arles he had bought 'two pairs of shoes, which cost me 26 Frs., and three shirts, which cost 27 Frs.'. Towards the end of August he had bought a black velvet jacket and new hat with the idea of going to Marseilles with Gauguin – when he arrived – and strolling down the boulevard dressed as his hero, Monticelli, was dressed in a portrait, 'with an enormous yellow hat, a black velvet jacket, white trousers, yellow gloves, a bamboo cane, and with a grand southern air'.

Gauguin, with his Breton fisherman's get-up, was not the only one who was dressed in costume as an artist. But Vincent never got to Marseilles. His hat hung on one of the hooks at the end of his bed, with his work clothes. The rest of his outfit was stored in his chest of drawers.

In addition to the painting inspired by the sunset over the vineyard, Gauguin was continuing with his *Night Café*. It was a familiar scene to the painters. This, a few seconds' walk away, was the first calling point if the two painters wanted to get out of the house in the evening.

Unlike Vincent, who had painted his *Night Café* on the spot, Gauguin carefully assembled his in the studio from sketches, memory and imagination. In the picture, his viewpoint was different from the one that Vincent had taken up. While Vincent had positioned his easel near the door, looking down the length of the oblong room, Gauguin took up an imaginary seat at one of the marble-topped tables that lined the walls. On the other side of the table he placed Madame Ginoux, posed as in his drawing of the previous weekend.

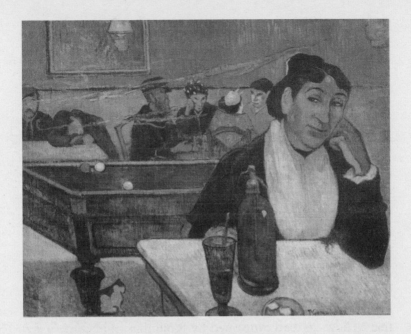

But Gauguin's Madame Ginoux was almost unrecognizably different from *L'Arlésienne* whom Vincent had painted with such amazing brio. In Gauguin's drawing, she was almost blank in expression. But in the painting, through a few small adjustments – an increased twist of the lips which stops just short of a leer, a more sidelong look of the eyes – she had become slyly knowing. In front of her on the table are a soda siphon, a glass of absinthe and the invariable accompaniment of that bitter drink, a couple of sugar lumps on a plate.

The practice of absinthe drinkers was to dribble the absinthe, a liqueur including wormwood, through a sugar lump into a glass of water. The sugar was placed on a spoon such as the one protruding from the glass in Gauguin's picture. When the absinthe reached the water, minute particles of vegetable matter within it became suspended, and the drink turned from clear to a beautiful, cloudy green. When

Toulouse-Lautrec had drawn a pastel portrait of Vincent in Paris he placed just such an opalescent aperitif before him.

Absinthe was the preferred drink of the poor, particularly in Southern France. It was also popular with writers and artists, who were positively attracted by its sinister reputation. Medical researchers had become convinced that absinthe contained a hallucinogen – so, quite apart from its alcoholic content, it might cause convulsions, madness and death. Creative people believed, or imagined, that this same property might give them wonderful new ideas. Absinthe was the natural drink for a lowlife picture such as this, intended not exactly as a brothel scene but with 'figures seen in the brothels', as Vincent noted.

In preparation Gauguin had done drawings in his sketch-book of brutish-looking women, two of whom appear in the background. One, unseductively, has curling-papers in her hair. They were accompanied by Roulin.

Since this was not a legally tolerated brothel, the whores must be *insoumises* or streetwalkers – a different category of the profession – who did indeed use the café, as Vincent assured Bernard. It is not clear whether Madame Ginoux was intended to be another of these streetwalkers herself, making an arrangement with the spectator across that marble table, but her expression suggests that she is.

At another sits a man who has fallen asleep or passed out cold, and the Zouave – a model Vincent had painted and drawn in the summer. Gauguin had obviously borrowed, or been lent, the figure – a perfect example of collaboration. In fact, here was a scene from Vincent's life, populated with figures from his raggle-taggle circle. The whole effect is far more sardonic than erotic.

Gauguin had attempted, or nearly, a subject – the brothels – which obsessed Bernard. He had included those incidents from contemporary life, in the manner of Daumier and Zola, which Vincent had included so successfully in the *Falling Leaves* diptych. This *Night Café* was an admirable example of collaboration – except that Gauguin didn't like it.

Around the end of the week or the beginning of the next, he told Bernard he had done:

a café that Vincent likes a lot and that I like less. At bottom it's not my sort of thing and local low life doesn't work for me. I like it well enough when others do it but it always makes me uneasy. It's a matter of education and one can't remake oneself.

He put his finger on the main weakness of his picture: the fact that Madame Ginoux didn't seem integrated with the rest of the composition. She seems to have been cut out and pasted in, which in a way she was. 'The main figure,' Gauguin concluded, 'is much too stiff and formal.' Vincent's picture of the *Night Café* was real, and hellish. This one was more of an amiable caricature and, as Gauguin noted, that wasn't really *him*.

Around this time, Vincent, with the example of Gauguin's *Night Café* in front of him, also made an effort to produce an elaborate brothel picture. This also showed that collaboration had its limits.

Brothel-painting was something that he and Bernard had been discussing by post for months. Prostitution was part of Vincent's life, and long had been. The only women he ever went with, he remarked rather bitterly to Theo, were whores at 2 francs intended for the Zouaves. At one time Vincent had lived with a reformed prostitute; now in Arles his only sexual relations were bought with small sums of money. His feelings on the subject were deep and raw.

By contrast, brothels were a subject with which the pious,

twenty-year-old Bernard had developed a literary, artistic and probably entirely theoretical obsession. Throughout the summer and autumn he had bombarded Vincent with bundles of drawings of brothel scenes done from imagination, and also poems in the manner of Baudelaire on the squalor and shame of prostitution. Some of the drawings and most of the poems were extremely bad – as Vincent bluntly pointed out. Typically, he only admired those which seemed to have some reality.

Bernard was insistent that when and if he came to Arles they should all work in the brothel and that in the meantime Vincent should make a start. It was an idea which was half-appealing to him. The subject of brothels was in the air. Toulouse-Lautrec – friend and fellow student of Vincent and Bernard – later made it his own. In Paris, Vincent had done some nude paintings of startlingly animal sensuality. According to Bernard, the model was a prostitute of the lowest grade – dubbed *pierreuse*, or gritty (though others believed she was Agostina Segatori).

When it came down to it, however, Vincent shied away from the brothel project. One problem was that he only really liked to paint people from life. He felt he was too unattractive to persuade the loose women of the Rue du Bout d'Arles to pose for free, and he could not afford to pay them. To please Bernard, he did a little picture from memory of a whore quarrelling with her pimp in the Café de la Gare, but it disappeared (or he destroyed it, as he felt it was not real enough).

Perhaps Vincent also had an unexpressed reservation: this was really Bernard's dream, not his. What he really wanted to do was portraits. Now he attempted the brothel theme one more time. Quite clearly, this time he portrayed not the Café de la Gare, but a *maison de tolérance* such as the one he had described to Bernard. In the foreground a woman in yellow

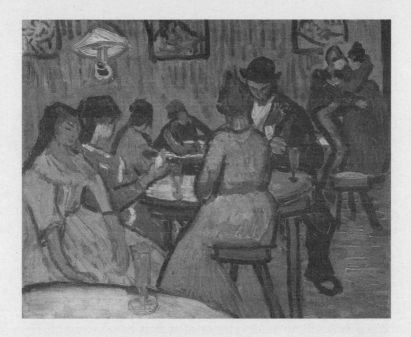

sits alone at a round table, a glass of absinthe in front of her. Behind, two of her companions play cards with a man wearing a bowler hat – more absinthe glasses at their sides. In the distance, a Zouave sits alone, and to the right a man and a woman in a red dress are dancing.

The mood is quiet, almost domestic – very different from the satire and squalor of Bernard's drawings or the ironic humour of Gauguin's. Only the erotic pictures on the walls – suggested by a few quick squiggles – reveal the character of the place. This painting was very small, not even a study but a *pochade* – no more than a first idea jotted down in paint. But, though tiny, the sketch that Vincent produced was a work of remarkable ambition. The arrangement he had worked out involved eight figures, some large, some small, in different interlocking positions.

By then Vincent had looked hard and long at Bernard's

painting *Breton Women in the Meadow*, which Gauguin had brought with him and was hanging on the wall of the Yellow House. Evidently, he wanted to see what he could learn from it. This, too, was a complicated arrangement of numerous figures ranging from the foreground into the middle distance. At some point Vincent made a careful watercolour copy of this painting. There are similarities with some of Bernard's drawings too.

The only previous occasion on which he had attempted a large, complicated figure composition of this kind was over three years before at Nuenen in the Netherlands. He had worked there on the *Potato Eaters*, in the orthodox manner, producing first studies of individual figures from live sitters, next a rough sketch of the composition, then a more detailed one, and finally the finished picture. Although it was entirely painted in gloomy shades of blue-grey and dun, the *Potato Eaters* was still an achievement of which he was proud. His current *pochade* was intended as the start of something similar.

'I have done a rough sketch of the brothel,' Vincent reported to Theo, 'and I quite intend to do a brothel picture.' But for some reason – perhaps because of the difficulty of finding models, perhaps because other ideas distracted him and in the last resort it was not his scheme but Bernard's – the *Brothel* by Vincent van Gogh remained an unrealized masterpiece.

5. Perilous Memories
11–14 November

In the post Vincent received an invitation to exhibit in Paris. Monsieur Edouard Dujardin – writer, editor of *La revue indépendante* and owner of a gallery and bookshop at 11 Rue de la Chaussée d'Antin – invited him to take part in the next exhibition he was organizing. This was a distinct sign of recognition. *La revue indépendante* was an influential literary magazine which strongly supported the work of Georges Seurat and his followers, notably Vincent's good friend Paul Signac. The exhibitions organized by *La revue indépendante* were a valuable shopwindow for the radical painters of Paris. A chance to exhibit in Paris, and perhaps sell some work, was exactly what Vincent had been yearning for a few weeks earlier, just before Gauguin arrived.

In September he had agreed happily enough to Theo's suggestion of showing his pictures in this very place. Now he rejected the resulting offer with fury. He had no intention of exhibiting in that 'black hole'. And he was 'disgusted' by the proposal that he should present Dujardin with a painting in exchange for the honour of exhibiting. Vincent wrote a rude refusal, which he enclosed in his letter to Theo, but only so that Theo should appreciate the strength of his feelings. He presumed his brother would decline politely on his behalf.

Vincent, full of confidence for a month, had suffered a collapse of morale. Perhaps now he was painting side by side with Gauguin *de tête*, Vincent felt his work was developing;

therefore, most of what he had achieved up to now amounted merely to studies. He was not a master, only an apprentice. But, pleased with the finished *Red Vineyard*, as he told Theo, he was going to paint more pictures in that manner:

I am going to set myself to work from memory often, and the canvases from memory are always less awkward, and have a more artistic look than studies from nature, especially when one works in mistral weather. We are having wind and rain here, and I am very glad not to be alone. I work from memory on bad days, and that would not do if I were alone.

That last remark hinted at the fragility of his condition: only with company did he dare confront his feelings about the past.

Meanwhile, he had rather Theo just kept storing up his pictures as they arrived from Arles. As was usual with Vincent when he was excited about something, he went on and on, repeating the same point in different ways. Meeting him in person, people often found this wearing. It could be tiresome even on paper. Vincent reiterated at length, with increasing emphasis, that he now wasn't much interested in exhibiting at all, especially with *La revue indépendante*. 'I boldly venture to think,' he added, 'that Gauguin is also of this opinion. In any case he is making no attempt to persuade me to do it.'

There was a history to this. Gauguin had long been on bad terms with *La revue indépendante*. One reason was that he had fallen out with the favourite painter of the magazine and its circle – Georges Seurat – both personally and artistically.

Seurat – much younger than Gauguin, and even than Vincent – was the most successful of the young, radical painters in Paris. His innovatory method of painting with dots – pointillism – had converted Gauguin's mentor, the Impressionist Camille Pissarro.

Two years before, Gauguin and Seurat had had a stupid quarrel. While he was away for the summer of 1886, Signac had offered the use of his studio to Gauguin. Unfortunately, Seurat, who worked along the corridor and was looking after the key, didn't know about the arrangement. Consequently, when Gauguin arrived, Seurat rudely refused to let him in, perhaps suspecting that Gauguin wanted to steal a look at some new pictures which were stored inside. Angry words were exchanged; later that year Gauguin cut Seurat and Signac dead.

Gauguin sarcastically described pointillism as *petit-point*, a meticulous form of embroidery on canvas, mainly used for cushion covers. Beyond the personal vexation, there was a deeper divide. Pointillism seemed to Gauguin all too rational, scientific and external. He was searching for an art that dealt not with appearances but with dreams.

In January 1888 a review had appeared in *La revue indépendante* of Gauguin's pictures, which were on show at Theo's gallery. The reviewer, Félix Fénéon, was a journalist, anarchist and passionate supporter of Seurat. His opinion of Gauguin, while not completely negative, included several jibes and praise laced with irony:

Of a character barbarous and atrabilious, with little atmosphere, coloured by diagonal strokes driving across the canvas like torrential rain, these haughty pictures would typify the work of M. Paul Gauguin, if that *grièche* artist were not above all a potter.

Gauguin was half angry, half pleased by the barbaric image of himself that was summoned up. In particular, he was taken with the unusual word, '*grièche*', that Fénéon had picked to describe him. It meant 'bitter, irritable, discontented' and might be more readily applied to a fishwife than a painter.

Gauguin repeated it, jokingly, as if to remind anyone who might have forgotten that he was a formidable character. In fact, Fénéon was a fan of Gauguin's. The teasingly rude review was his critic's way of expressing an interest. But Gauguin was riled. It was not surprising that he did not encourage Vincent to exhibit with *La revue indépendante*.

In the Yellow House both painters were trying out an unorthodox priming to use on the jute. Generally, canvases were coated with animal glue, boiled up from some material such as rabbit skin, which prevented the paint from rotting the threads of the fabric. This was then covered with gesso, or fine chalk, mixed with white paint. Most artists, including Vincent, usually bought their canvases ready-primed and cut to size.

But, partly for economy, partly for artistic reasons, the painters of the Yellow House did much of this work themselves. They were cutting the jute sackcloth to the dimensions they wanted for a picture and tacking it over the wooden frame that kept it taut. They then applied a very unusual ground – not smooth, white gesso but liquid barium sulphate, which was thinner and light-brown in colour.

The effect of this was to accentuate the rough weave of the jute, which now showed clearly through Gauguin's pictures and gave them the strong, 'primitive' texture that he wanted. Vincent painted in his usual broad manner across the fibres of the sackcloth, which also gave his pictures an earthy quality akin to the earthenware he so liked. The only question was, would the barium-sulphate ground work or would these new pictures flake?

Another innovation concerned frames. These were a significant cost – the bill for the walnut and pine frames he had ordered for his *décorations* had led Vincent to run out of money while he was preparing the Yellow House – but they were important and, like so many aspects of painting, it suddenly seemed possible to think of them in a brand-new way.

Traditional frames were heavy things of carved wood, often gilded. But Seurat had, among his other new ideas, pioneered an unprecedented approach to frames. He painted the surroundings of the picture – the border and frame – with dots of colour just like the paintings themselves. These responded to every nuance of colour and tone in the painting itself.

Vincent had often used newly fashionable white frames – for the *Bedroom*, for example, or the fruit trees in blossom he had painted in the spring (Gauguin announced that this had been 'partly' his idea). Now, the two painters thought up an entirely new type – as rustic, radical and inexpensive as the sackcloth canvases.

Theo's new lodger, de Haan, had apparently paid 2,000 francs for an especially elaborate carved picture surround; Vincent had been paying 20 francs to a carpenter in Arles for each frame. The homemade frames cost just 5 centimes, the price of a copy of *L'Homme de bronze*. Vincent mentioned it to Theo. 'We find it very easy to make frames with plain strips of wood nailed on the stretcher and *painted*, and I have begun doing this.' This radical simplicity pleased Vincent. He sent Theo a drawing of the new sort of frame, around the *Red Vineyard*.

However, Gauguin wasn't happy with the stretchers Vincent had in the Yellow House. He wanted Theo to purchase a different variety, which could be tightened with screws rather than wooden wedges. The tightness of a canvas was a highly personal matter, as it affected the feel of the brush. This new sackcloth surface required careful tightening. Nor did Gauguin like the paints that Vincent had. He asked Theo to buy him an adjustable stretcher, with screws; and requested

Bernard to get some paints from Père Tanguy and send them south.

Evidently, Gauguin intended to stay in Arles for a while. He also wrote to Schuffenecker, his dogsbody, asking for another parcel of oddments, including his Degas etchings and his linen, to be sent to Arles. 'I'm going to annoy you again,' he announced jovially. 'Would you be good enough to look in my things? There must be one or two pairs of sheets there. We have need of them here.'

Every day that week was wet, and on Wednesday there was a positive deluge. The Rhône was dangerously close to the top of its embankment on the other side of the Place Lamartine. If it had gone over, the ground-floor studio of the Yellow House would have flooded.

These floods, along with the mistral, were the curse of Provence. There had been a disastrous inundation two years before, at just the same time of year. A huge amount of rain had fallen on Mediterranean Europe in October 1886 and the rivers Rhône and Durance had burst their banks. In a roundabout way, this catastrophe was one of the things that had drawn Vincent's attention to the area.

There was a festival – the *fête du soleil*, or fair of the sun – held in Paris after Christmas that year. A huge electric light, 8 metres across, was suspended from the ceiling of the Palais de l'industrie, imitating the scorching radiance of the South.

At the stand of *Le Courrier français* – a racy magazine which brought out a special issue dedicated to the floods – customers were greeted by a 'charming little Arlésienne'. Altogether, there was a great deal to attract a light-hungry Dutch painter who had moved to Paris only to find himself still in a chilly, northern, wintry city.

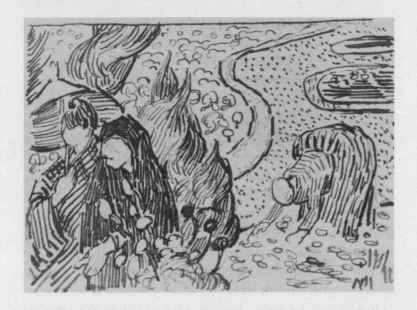

This time there was no flood. Thursday 15 November was overcast but dry. It remained so for most of the rest of the month.

Inside the Yellow House, Vincent plunged deep into his own past. It was a perilous thing to do, but with Gauguin's company he felt emboldened. His new painting was of two women – one old and grey-haired, one much younger and carrying a red parasol – walking in a garden. In the background, a female gardener bends over to tend the plants. The angle of vision is extremely steep.

This mental image was airless and claustrophobic. The beds and paths reared up behind the walkers like the painted backcloth of a play. But it was, for a garden, alarmingly dynamic. A path swirled around a couple of island beds. Cypresses twisted violently just to the rear of the women.

It was hard – most uncharacteristically for one of Vincent's pictures – to work out exactly what was where. Were the women walking? Were they on the path or on the flower bed? There didn't seem enough room for them to stand between the flowers and the nearest cypress. It was also quite unclear where the scene was supposed to be and who those women were. To Theo, Vincent gave two differing accounts of the location. First, he said it was a memory of the garden at a place called Etten.

Theodorus van Gogh, Vincent's father, had been pastor in this village from 1875 until 1882. It held powerful memories for Vincent, although he had only actually lived there for a few months, from April to December 1881. But this had been a pivotal moment in his life: he had abandoned his efforts to become a preacher and was embarking on an equally quixotic attempt to become a painter.

In Etten that summer he had fallen violently in love with his widowed cousin, daughter of his mother's older sister, Kee Vos-Stricker. He was twenty-eight when he fell for Kee, and she was older by seven years and had an eight-year-old son. They spent the summer months of 1881 talking and walking around Etten. Eventually, Vincent proposed: she answered, 'Never, no, never.'

Final though that seemed, at the end of November Vincent travelled to Amsterdam to plead his cause again. At her house, he was told that when he arrived, she had left. 'Your persistence,' said her family, 'is *disgusting*.' Vincent then put his hand in the flame of the lamp and said, 'Let me see her for as long as I can keep my hand in the flame.' But they blew out the lamp and said, '*You shall not see her.*'

Afterwards, Kee's brother took Vincent to one side and pointed out that only money would make a difference in this matter. 'When I left Amsterdam,' Vincent remembered, 'I had a feeling as if I had been on a slave market.' Whatever Kee's feelings might have been, it was clear that the fundamental objection to Vincent was his lack of cash.

This no doubt made sense to her family – Vincent, after all, had no income and no prospects – but to him the verdict was unbearable. To kill his love was like killing himself. The sanctimonious hypocrisy of Kee's family gave him a feeling of physical chill (Vincent loathed cold). He had a feeling 'as if I had been standing too long against a cold, hard, whitewashed church wall'.

Vincent's response to the rebuff over Kee was to go out and find a prostitute. He had fought 'a great battle' and his urge for an ordinary sexual life came out on top. 'One cannot forgo a woman for too long with impunity. And I do not believe that what some call God and others the Supreme Being and others nature is unreasonable and pitiless.' That December Vincent had a furious row with his father, who threw him out of the house. Such were the memories that Etten held for Vincent.

But was this painting actually of the garden at Etten? Vincent later called it a memory not of Etten but of Nuenen, a completely different Dutch village, where his father had moved in 1882. It had been his last parish.

This place held another set of associations for Vincent, some of them bitter. In the dark and cold of December 1883, unsure that Theo could continue to support him, he returned to the family home. He was then thirty and still had no means of support. The eccentricity of his dress and behaviour embarrassed his parents; their failure to support him in his determination to become an artist irritated Vincent. Nonetheless, his father made an attempt at making the peace. His family put up with the ridicule that he attracted.

But matters were not improved by another love affair, less serious on his part, with Margot Begemann, the daughter of

an elder of the church. She was twelve years older than him,
emotionally unstable and plain. When her family insisted that
she must not marry Vincent – mocking her and saying she
was too old – Margot took a large dose of strychnine and
would have died had Vincent not made her throw up. He
carried her to her house, where her brother made her more
thoroughly sick.

What, Vincent cried out, should we think of such a religion, which drives people to acts of mania? 'Oh, they are
perfectly absurd, making society a kind of lunatic asylum, a
perfectly topsy-turvy world.' He made a series of drawings of
the garden at Nuenen, with a solitary female figure; under
one he wrote the word 'melancholy'.

It was at Nuenen, not at Etten, that Vincent might have
expected to find the two women who were actually in his picture: his widowed mother and his youngest sister, Wilhelmina.
Wil – who suffered from 'melancholy' and pains in her
stomach just as he did – was the only one of his three sisters
to whom Vincent was close. She had ambitions to write; he
fondly hoped that she might marry a painter. Touchingly, he
was also keen that she should see his work, and hoped she
might come to visit him in the Yellow House. The truth was
that Wil, now in her mid twenties, was stuck at home with
her aged parents, her life passing by.

Vincent ignored his two other sisters, Anna and Lies, but
he sent beautiful letters to Wil, simpler and more tender than
those to Theo, Bernard or Gauguin, and full of his hopes and
thoughts. Later in the week, he described his garden picture
to her, detailing the colours and the plants, and drew a little
sketch.

It was, he explained, intended to be like a 'comforting'
piece of music: not a realistic depiction of the garden but
something like a poem, in which the colours and curving,

meandering lines brought the subject to mind but, as in a dream, 'stranger' than it was in reality.

'I know this is hardly what one might call a likeness,' he wrote, 'but for me it renders the poetic character and the style of the garden as I feel it.' Vincent did not claim that the two women had a realistic or, as he put it, 'a vulgar and fatuous' resemblance to his sister and mother. Nonetheless, the harmonies of colour somehow evoked them. 'The sombre violet with the blotch of violent citron yellow of the dahlias' suggested his mother's personality; the orange and green checks against the sombre green of the cypress summoned up a 'vaguely representative' impression of Wil. There was indeed little 'vulgar resemblance' between the woman in the painting and photographs of Wil, who had an oval face and less prominent brows. The features in the picture belonged less to her than to Kee Vos-Stricker.

Wil and Kee and, for that matter, Margot Begemann, were all trapped. Perhaps they merged into one another in his imagination, as did the various gardens Vincent had known. The one in the painting looked more like the grounds of the parsonage at Nuenen than it did Etten, but it looked even more like one of the public parks in the Place Lamartine.

If this picture was a dream, as Vincent wrote to Wil, it was a jangling, jarring one: an amalgam of painful memories. It was intended, Vincent told Wil, to hang in his own bedroom. But unlike the *Red Vineyard*, Vincent's garden picture wasn't a great success – which didn't bode well for the new method of working from memory.

Vincent continued to tinker with it until the paint was piled up on it like icing on a cake. It ended up amazingly slathered with pigment – more so than anything else he, or Monticelli, ever painted: an index of his determination to get the picture right. In the end, though, he felt that he had spoilt

it. 'I think,' he reflected, 'that you also need practice for work
from the imagination'.

Gauguin's new picture also concerned his feelings about
women. He took a new piece of jute and began a scene of
farmyard life with an unexpectedly sensual edge. In the middle
of the composition was a peasant woman with her dress
pulled down to her waist so her torso was naked, white and
vulnerable. She had collapsed on to a mound of pale grey
material, presumably hay, with one arm – reddened from
working in the sun – extended on the mound in front of her,
and her head resting on the other.

    At the summit of the haystack are a couple of gentle bulges
resembling breasts or buttocks. Her pitchfork is lying to one
side of her and her blue dress is piled up on the other. In the
left foreground and top right of the painting are the most
unexpected ingredients: two large, yellow pigs. The nearest
of these creatures is cut off by the frame, its ear flopping down
in a closely observed piggy fashion; the second is ambling
round the back of the haystack, its curly tail waving jauntily
in the air.

    It was evident that Gauguin had made every effort to
suggest a visual link between the pigs and the woman. Her
white cap, which she is still wearing, flops in precisely the
manner that the closer pig's ear lists on the side of its face.
The sleeve of her white chemise, folded over and trailing
behind her, mirrors the curvature of the other animal's tail,
thus making a witty but lewd analogy between her bottom
and the animal's rump.

    The woman lolls forward, overcome by heat, or weari-
ness, or desire; she looks like a voluptuous, swooning slave
in a sadomasochistic masterpiece of Delacroix, the *Death of
Sardanapalus*. This was a masculine fantasy of female surrender,

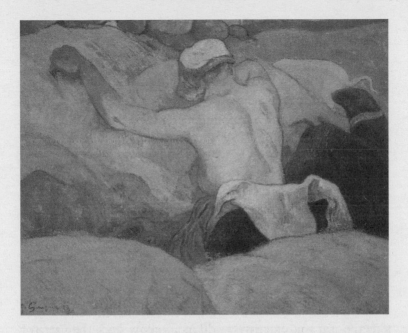

set not on the bed of an ancient potentate but amid the muck and mess of a farmyard.

The figure had been studied from a living model in Brittany, where they were more familiar with artists and their strange demands and it was easier to persuade the locals to pose than it was in Arles. He had brought with him a coloured drawing of the woman, holding on to the back of a chair. It was natural therefore that in the painting she was wearing Breton costume, as were three of the women in Gauguin's vineyard painting. The pigs, however, were less easy to explain.

It was true that Gauguin – unlike Vincent – was fond of including animals of all kinds in his work. Rooting pigs were to be found on the back of the little ceramic with a nude figure of Cleopatra that he had asked Schuffenecker to send from Paris to add to the decorations of the Yellow House.

There were also not just one but two texts – both piggy and sexy – stored away in Vincent's literary archive.

A month and a half before, in mid September, Theo had sent him a copy of a Parisian weekly, *Le Courrier français* – the very same one that had been the special issue about the Rhône floods. It was aimed at young men about town. Its staple subject-matter was the nightlife of the capital, and a common theme was sexual liaisons between middle-class men – such as the readers – and available, working-class women. The illustrations were outrageously lascivious; two had been the subject of prosecution for obscenity that year.

Vincent's eye had been caught by a short story, '*La Truie bleue*', by a young writer named Charles Morice. He recommended it to Theo as 'very good' and added, 'it just makes one think of Segatori.' This tale was a standard *Courrier français* item in one way, in that it concerned a pick-up on a Parisian street, but it was extremely odd in another, since the narrator met up not with a woman but with a pig. Translated, its title was 'The Blue Sow'.

The man telling the story is wandering aimlessly one day when he encounters the beast. 'I noticed, lounging in front of me and walking almost at my pace, all alone and with the determined walk of one who knows where she is going . . . a SOW.' The creature is smartly dressed in blue silk, suitably let out to contain her girth, and her little corkscrew tail is 'decorated with a knot of bright blue of a grace that was quite impertinent'.

Rapidly, and wordlessly, the narrator falls in love with this creature. She exudes an aura of sensuality, undiluted by tiresome bourgeois social conventions, which he finds intoxicating. He is charmed by her gait, her look, her grunt. Their eyes meet for an instant, reflected in a shop window, hers seeming to contain 'a depth of malicious experience, the science – all the science of life'.

It was likely that Vincent recommended 'The Blue Sow' to Gauguin as he had done to Theo. Perhaps Agostina Segatori came up in conversation when they were talking about the Prado trial and that reminded Vincent of the story.

Certainly, there were passages in Gauguin's picture that recalled 'The Blue Sow'. For example, the gentle curves of the hay echoed feminine anatomy. A little to the left of the woman's naked breast, a second bosom seems to rise from the surface of the stack. Equally, the upper contours of the haystacks rhyme with the pigs' backs.

Exactly thus in 'The Blue Sow', the 'soft milky clouds' were seen by the narrator as 'essentially soft, feminine things'. 'Nothing will persuade me that those vague, rounded forms which make my senses dream are not the shapes of caresses, kisses, and voluptuousness.' René Magritte was yet to be born but Gauguin's exercise in rustic eroticism had a suggestion – thirty years before the word was invented – of the surreal.

But there was nothing of the farmyard in the porcine Parisian fable, nor of the intense summer heat that had caused the woman in the painting to strip to the waist. Those, and more pigs, were described in another text which Vincent admired: Émile Zola's *The Sin of Father Mouret*. This was one of Zola's strangest works, not realist at all but highly fantastic, but its theme, like that of 'The Blue Sow', was close to Vincent's own experience.

It deals with a devout priest, Serge Mouret, who has a sister, Désirée – 'desire' – who is physically blooming but mentally childlike. Her great interest in life is her farm animals – which cause her brother intense nausea. Waves of disgust go through him as she shows off her pets in the manure-strewn yard which swarms with rabbits and hens and other beasts. The whole scene is charged with heat, the word '*chaleur*' is repeated again and again.

Désirée's new addition to her menagerie is a little pig. When it appears, the priest is overwhelmed by the gross physicality of the animals:

He smelled in one reeking breath the fetid warmth of the rabbits and poultry, the lewd odour of the goat, the jejune fat of the pig. It was as if the air were filled with fecundity, and it weighed too heavily on his virgin shoulders.

As Gauguin said, he liked to follow his fancy when painting and only find the title later. At first he called his new picture simply the *Pigs*, a description that covered the two animals and also the half-naked woman. Later on, Gauguin had a different idea. He exhibited the painting as *En Pleine Chaleur* or *In the Heat*. The first title seemed to refer to Charles Morice's story; the second recalled the Zola novel.

The picture was filled with Gauguin's own intimate feelings of sexual attraction and repulsion. In his mind pigs stood for guiltless carnality – that was why he liked them. 'For a long time,' he wrote years later, 'I had virtue dinned into me; I know all about that but I do not like it.'

If Gauguin's painting of the grape harvest was marked by his religious boyhood, so, paradoxically, was this: it was an exercise in pure, poetic, almost cerebral lechery. 'I should like to have been born a pig,' Gauguin reflected at the end of his life. 'Man alone can be ridiculous.'

When Gauguin later dispatched his new work to Theo, he expressed particular satisfaction with two paintings: the *Pigs*, and *Human Misery*. Gauguin believed them to be 'fairly bold' and also 'a little coarse'. That coarseness was both a matter of style – the abstracted forms, the loose brushwork – and also, especially with the pigs, the sexuality of the subject matter. 'Is that,' Gauguin wondered, 'because the Southern sun puts us on heat? If they should alarm the customers don't hesitate to put them on one side, but personally I like them.'

One diversion that Arles offered, even on a rainy day, was its museums. Vincent had visited them shortly after he had arrived the previous February. There was the Musée Réattu, the local museum of paintings – mainly academic works by artists with Provençal connections. This Vincent thought 'a horror and a humbug' that ought to be in Tarascon (that is, it belonged with Tartarin and his fellow cap-hunters, in the realm of farce). There was also a museum of Roman and Early Christian antiquities, on Place de la République, which Vincent deemed 'genuine'. These would be of interest to Gauguin, who liked classical art.

Opposite was one of the great early medieval churches of Southern France, the Cathedral of Saint-Trophime. This, Vincent had mixed feelings about. He thought its carved porch 'admirable', but he was ill at ease with the serried figures of saints, Christ in judgement above the door, the damned being led to eternal torment, others to heavenly bliss:

It is so cruel, so monstrous, like a Chinese nightmare, that even this beautiful monument of so grand a style seems to me of another world, and I am as glad not to belong to it as to that glorious world of the Roman Nero.

By that he meant that the world of Dante's inferno, depicted here, seemed as remote as the horrors and tortures that had taken place in the Roman arena a few hundred yards away.

He preferred the here and now: 'the Zouaves, the brothels,

the adorable little Arlésiennes going to their First Communion, the priest in his surplice, who looks like a dangerous rhinoceros, the absinthe drinkers' – but he felt cut off from them, too: they were like beings in another world.

Medieval architecture – and antiquities generally, apart from certain paintings – gave Vincent the creeps. He was depressed by the medieval church – much like Saint-Trophime – in Zola's *The Dream*; later, when he was incarcerated in ecclesiastical cloisters for the good of his health, he thought these gloomy surroundings contributed to the hallucinations and fears that assailed him.

Gauguin did not agree. He thought the carvings of Saint-Trophime an excellent example of art that was stylized and unnaturalistic, 'with *proportions* very far from nature', and yet Vincent had in fact admired the sculptures, without suffering any nightmare. Art, the carvings of Saint-Trophime showed, was not realism but an expression of what one felt in a certain 'state of soul'.

Gauguin prided himself on being immune from religious superstition: 'A sceptic, I look at all these saints, but to me they are not alive. In the niches of a cathedral they have meaning – there only.' He was not terrified by the 'childish grotesqueries' of the gargoyles.

Walking inside up the wide steps to investigate the interior – the 'cross above', and 'the great transept' – Gauguin was not impressed by the priest in his pulpit 'babbling' about hell. 'In their seats the ladies talk about fashion. I like this better.'

Everything, Gauguin believed, was both serious and ridiculous. The castle, the cottage, the cathedral and the brothel were all aspects of life. What was one to do about it? Nothing. 'The earth still turns round; everyone defecates; only Zola bothers about it.'

Nonetheless, the sculptures of Saint-Trophime got into both Vincent's and Gauguin's minds. Vincent, as one might expect from someone with so powerful a visual sense, was led into associations by what he saw. The obelisk in the square outside St Trophime, a relic of the ancient hippodrome at Arles, suggested comparisons to him. A cypress tree, for example, was as beautiful in its way as an Egyptian obelisk.

The Christ in judgement above the portal of the cathedral made him think how little he liked most portrayals of Jesus; only Rembrandt and Delacroix, he thought, had really been able to paint this subject. Then it made him think how Christ himself was the greatest of all artists – an artist not in paint or stone but in human beings. Just by speaking his parables – the sower, for example – he had created a new life for mankind (this was a theme of certain Dutch theologians).

Below Christ on the portal was the symbol of St Luke, the patron saint of painters – a castrated ox. This made Vincent think what a humble, dirty, physical affair painting was; and yet it was in some way connected with what Christ had done: a means of making new ways of living and feeling. He wrote all this to Bernard, and Gauguin had read these letters in Brittany and pondered them.

Gauguin, for his part, was struck, for all his urbane scepticism, by the hellish 'grotesqueries' of Saint-Trophime. As an eleven-year-old boy, after all, he had chanted the words of Bishop Dupanloup: the child who gave way to the siren call of fleshly demons would become prey to a terrible fiend.

That was exactly what one of the most arresting carvings on the cathedral showed: the punishment of lust by a goggle-eyed devil. Gauguin said nothing about this, but the following year he made a carving in which a demon, with his own features, reaches down to grasp a naked woman while gnawing his thumb in torment. It seemed to echo the scenes of damnation and salvation in Arles. He gave it a title of bitter irony: *Be in Love and You Will Be Happy*.

On Tuesday 13 November Theo wrote Gauguin a letter from his office in Paris. Unlike his communications with Vincent, this was businesslike, brisk and written on his firm's headed writing paper, but it brought more excellent news for the painter when it arrived on Wednesday. Theo wrote that Gauguin's new paintings were having a great success in Paris:

Degas is so enthusiastic about your works that he is speaking about them to a lot of people, and he is going to buy the canvas representing a spring landscape, with a meadow with two female figures in the foreground, the one sitting and the other standing.

Two others were definitely sold – 'the upright landscape with two dogs in a meadow, the other one a pool by the side of the road' – for which Theo suggested Gauguin should receive 375 francs and 225 francs respectively. Another, the *Ring of Breton Girls*, could also be sold for 500 francs, provided Gauguin made a small change. As it was, one of the girl's hands seemed to touch the frame in distracting fashion.

This was exciting news for Gauguin on two counts. One was that his sales through Theo's gallery now began to look as if they were bringing in a steady income. Here were three pictures sold or virtually sold, plus the one that Degas wanted to buy. But the fact that Degas was not only buying a painting but enthusing about Gauguin's work all over Paris was yet more exhilarating.

Gauguin admired Degas most among all living artists. On occasion he took compositions of Degas's as models for his own, translating the latter's cast of ballet dancers and other Parisiennes into Breton peasants. Degas's emphasis on drawing and his slow, cerebral method of building up pictures in the studio were examples to Gauguin.

Now, this same Degas was buying his paintings and singing his praises. As he explained to Bernard:

That is the greatest possible compliment to me: I have as you know the greatest possible confidence in the judgement of Degas – moreover it's a very good starting point commercially speaking. All the friends of Degas have confidence in him.

Gauguin's optimism increased exponentially. There was only one puzzling aspect of Theo's letter: he wrote of having sold a picture of two dogs in a meadow. As far as he could remember, Gauguin had never painted such a canvas. It was some time before the explanation dawned on him. Then he sat down to reply:

You can imagine that I searched in my memory for a long time to recall what picture could have two dogs in it and I realized that the 2 black and red calves had been taken for carnivores. It came to me eventually and I'm glad to clear up the confusion.

He agreed it was necessary to adjust the *Ring of Breton Girls*.

Gauguin then went on to describe the atmosphere in the Yellow House, where everything was proceeding well: 'Good Vincent and *grièche* Gauguin are still living happily together and eat at home – simple cooking that they make themselves. But My Gawd (as they saaay) this damn rain is impeding them terribly for open air work.' Here Gauguin tried to imitate the accent of the South of France, which he found absurd.

Gauguin wrote in triumph to Bernard, describing these successes. He predicted that in ten years or so Bernard, too, would be a great success (it had taken Gauguin about that amount of time to gain this success from the period in the late 1870s when he began to take painting more seriously). But, despite the good news, his mind was full of suspicions concerning machinations in the Paris art world.

Theo had written to Vincent with some gossip he had heard about his rivals, Signac and Seurat:

They are to start a campaign (having *La revue indépendante* as the organ for their propaganda) against us others. They are going to represent Degas *Gauguin above all* Bernard etc . . . as worse than devils and to be avoided like carriers of a plague.

Bernard was not to breathe a word of this important information: 'Keep it to yourself and *don't say anything to Van Gogh* otherwise you'll make me seem indiscreet.'

Gauguin sent his regards to Bernard's charming sister, with whom he was perhaps a little in love. He was still dreaming of founding a studio in Martinique, but for the time being he was happy to invite Bernard to Arles, now that he – Gauguin – had put the Yellow House in order. It seemed that Bernard might not have to join Milliet in the army, as he was claiming to be unfit. 'If you don't do your military service after all,' Gauguin assured him, 'you can come here with no fears. I have now arranged a way of life which would be economical for three, so if you had nothing because your father cut off your allowance you would find a secure existence here.' Gauguin seemed to have taken over the household.

Meanwhile, Vincent was engaged on another picture painted from memory and imagination. It depicted a young woman intently reading at night in a book-lined room. Behind her was the glowing sphere of a large lamp spreading light. In her hands was a book bound in the distinctive yellow

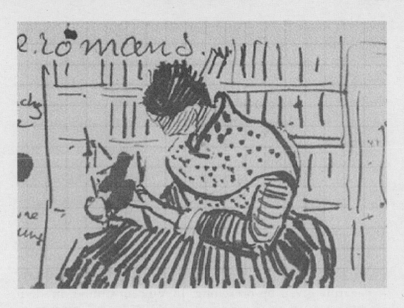

wrapping of a cheap French novel. The reader was wide-eyed with fascination.

Vincent clearly painted this with his sister Wil (to whom he described it) in mind. He was keen to recommend books to Wil, as he did to everyone he cared about. To him, this was much more than simply passing on tips about entertaining reading. When Vincent had lost his faith in orthodox Christianity, he had gained a new belief – homemade, quixotic and paradoxical – in modern literature. It had happened, characteristically, with great rapidity. During his most exalted religious phase he had instructed Theo to put aside all books except for the Bible and pious texts. Then came his loss of faith, his new career as an artist and the stormy love affair with Kee Vos-Stricker. Suddenly, he developed an enormous appetite for the contemporary novel.

The year after his affair with Kee, Vincent was living with a reformed prostitute, Sien Hoornik, and devouring the

works of Emile Zola. That writer remained one of the corner-
stones of Vincent's mental world – in some ways a replace-
ment for holy writ. So, too, were Zola's followers Guy de
Maupassant, Alphonse Daudet, Jean Richepin, Huysmans,
Flaubert and the brothers Edmond and Jules de Goncourt
(whose collaboration reminded Vincent of the one between
himself and Theo).

He had recommended all these to Wil the year before.
'One can scarcely be said to belong to one's time,' he insisted,
'if one is not acquainted with them.' He hoped to find a copy
for her of Maupassant's *Bel-Ami* – the writer's masterpiece, in
Vincent's view.

In presenting his sister with this reading list, Vincent was
giving her the key to life as he understood it. He had evidently
never truly given up preaching. In Vincent's mind, modern
novels, with their close descriptions of modern life, love,
suffering and labour, were more than a substitute for the Bible
– they were its successor. He felt that Christ himself would
agree with him on that point.

This concentration on the here-and-now quieted Vincent's
churning emotions; he felt that comic literature – Daudet's
Tartarin, for example – was a cure for the 'melancholy' that
afflicted him, Theo and Wil:

The diseases from which we civilized people suffer most are melancholy and pessimism. So I, for instance, who can count so many
years of my life during which I lost any inclination to laugh –
leaving aside whether or not this was my own fault – I, for one,
feel the need for a really good laugh above all else.

Vincent read the English novelists, too – Dickens and
George Eliot. Just hearing that a fellow student at the *Atelier*
Cormon in Paris was a reader of Balzac made Vincent feel

that this stranger was someone to esteem. He read constantly in three languages – English, French and Dutch.

Scenes from novels were constantly coming into his mind, as when poor Margot Begemann tried to poison herself. 'Do you remember,' he asked Theo then, 'the first Mrs Bovary who died in a nervous attack?' The obscurity and accuracy of this reference were typical; he compared Margot Begemann not with Emma, second wife of Charles Bovary and heroine of Flaubert's novel but with his first wife, of whom the reader was told little except that she died after hearing bad news about her fortune.

A few months after his father died, Vincent painted a still life that showed his father's Bible – massive and ancient – with, beside it, an extinguished candle. This stood for the ending of Theodorus van Gogh's life and the lost power of the holy book. Beside it was the new source of truth, a yellow paperback novel of Vincent's coming apart at the spine through constant reading. Its title was legible: *La joie de vivre* by Émile Zola.

Vincent dreamt of painting a bookshop in the evening, with its front yellow and pink. This was, he felt, a truly 'modern subject' because books were 'such a rich source of light to the imagination'. This picture might hang as the central panel in a triptych, a modern altarpiece, between a wheatfield and an olive grove. The bookshop would represent the sowing season of the mind, 'like a light in the midst of darkness'.

The painting Vincent now did was in a similar spirit. The books on the shelves behind the young woman were spreading light just as much as the lamp in the background. She was a person trapped by cold conventionality – as his sister Wil now was and he himself had been. But, through the book, she was receiving the message that would save her.

The picture echoed another that had, to his mind, a similar message – a Rembrandt showing Mary reading by lamplight beside the cradle of the infant Christ.

But, crammed though it was with Vincent's deepest feelings and beliefs, the painting as a picture was not a great success. Compared to the portraits he produced with a sitter before his eyes, the young reader was insubstantial and unconvincing – a ghostly creature of ectoplasm rather than living flesh. The hands holding the books seem to lack bones, like the tentacles of an octopus. This way of working – in which Gauguin was encouraging him – was not producing the expected results. Up to now the atmosphere in the Yellow House had been harmonious. Now, that was about to change.

6. Divisions
15–23 November

On Thursday 15 November, the newspapers were full of the final day of the Prado case. It had been very much like a scene from a novel. Prado presented himself as if he were a hero from Balzac, and his use of language resembled the prose of Zola, mingling sexuality and horticulture in a heady metaphorical brew. His mistress, Eugénie Forestier, was for him 'the wind that carries off from a man his ripest desires, as it removes the exuberance of scent from a flower'.

This rhetoric would have appealed to someone of Vincent's literary tastes, while his own experience of life had some points of similarity with Prado's. He too could say, with the accused murderer:

Who am I first of all? What does it matter? I am unfortunate. An adventurer, isn't that right? My God, hurled on to this vast stage of human life, I yielded, a bit by chance, to everything I felt beat in my heart and boil in my brain.

Prado played the part of victim brilliantly. Nonetheless, he was found guilty with no extenuating circumstances. When the death sentence was pronounced against him, he inclined his head and said nothing.

In the studio, the painters continued to work so closely together that their projects intertwined. But the results were mixed. Around this time Vincent made a picture of a bullfight.

The priming of the canvas was exactly the same as that for the *Memory of the Garden*, suggesting that it was produced not long afterwards.

Now, bullfighting was a subject that Gauguin himself had always intended to attempt when he arrived in the South. He had written as much to Vincent in July: 'I always had a fancy to interpret the bullfights in my own way, according to my own ideas.' But he arrived in Arles after the last fight of the season had taken place so, for Gauguin, this project was to remain forever unrealized. He was still hoping to do a bullfight painting fifteen years later, on the other side of the world.

Vincent, on the other hand, had witnessed – and described – some of the bullfights in the Roman Arena soon after he had arrived in Arles. These were, he felt, a 'sham', 'seeing that the bulls were numerous but there was nobody to fight them'. What he'd seen was not the Spanish-style *corrida* in which the bull is finally killed by a matador with a sword but the local Provençal sport which was, strictly speaking, not a fight at all, but a race – *la Course Camarguaise*.

In this, the objective was to seize various tassels, rosettes and ribbons from the horns of the animal, then take refuge quickly behind the barrier around the arena. The men who tried to do this were known as *razeteurs*. The best *razeteur* was one who managed to tweak off the most awkwardly placed of these cockades. This process was not dangerous at all to the bulls, which were herded away afterwards, but highly risky for the *razeteurs* (Vincent saw one who crushed a testicle while leaping the barrier). These events took place regularly in Arles. There had been one on 30 September, featuring five bulls from the Camargue and one Spanish-cross cow, and one on both 7 and 14 October.

The *Course Camarguaise* was one of the most ancient rituals of Provence – akin to the bull games of ancient Crete and the

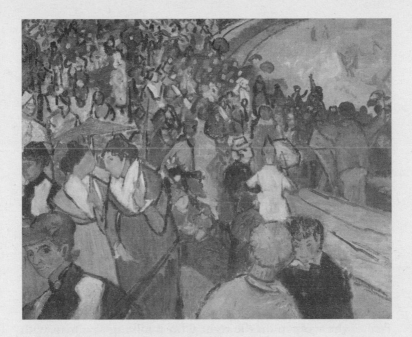

wild-beast games that had been staged by the Romans in the arena. However, it was not the spectacle itself that interested Vincent but the spectators. 'The crowd,' he told Bernard, 'was magnificent, those great colourful multitudes piled up one above the other on two or three galleries, with the effect of sun and shade and the shadow cast by the enormous ring.'

And this was what he now set about painting from memory. His mental viewpoint is from the upper tiers of seats in the great open, oval structure on a hot day. Many of the Arlésiennes have opened their red parasols even though – from the predominately blue tone of the audience – this seems to be the shady side of the auditorium. Below, a man stands and waves both his arms, hat held in one hand, as if something exciting has just happened.

The sandy floor of the arena itself is visible only in the

distance, but it is just possible to make out a bull, a huge cockade still dangling from one horn, and a running figure. In the centre of the picture there is a woman in Arlésienne costume with the distinctive profile of Madame Ginoux, talking with another woman beneath a parasol. Seated behind them are Roulin the postal supervisor, with his wife, Augustine, holding their baby daughter, Marcelle. In the bottom left another woman turns away from the spectacle in the arena. She has a specific, clearly remembered face – thin, with a sharp chin and prominent eyebrows. But who is she?

Taken as a whole, the picture is only a partial success. Most of the crowd are unrealized, no more than black outlines against the blue-green shade. These blend uneasily with the few faces that Vincent knows better. Though a large and ambitious picture on a piece of jute, this was, for Vincent, extremely thinly painted. In many places – for example, the face of the woman on the right who is talking to a man with bristling blond hair – bare textile is visible. It looks very much as if, for one reason or another – perhaps lack of suitable models or vivid memories – Vincent simply gave up this painting half-way through. He never described or mentioned it. On the other hand, he didn't destroy his bullfight either.

Gauguin was now working, according to Vincent, on 'a large still life of an orange-coloured pumpkin and apples and white linen on a yellow background and foreground'. In subject, this was not so different from the picture proudly displayed that week in the window of Bompard fils, the local art dealers in Place de la République.

The paintings exhibited there were regularly boosted by paragraphs in *L'Homme de bronze*. In this case, the writer was full of admiration for a picture set in September of ripe grey and black figs tumbling from a basket set upon the ground. It is unlikely that Gauguin and Vincent thought much of it, though they could hardly avoid seeing it, since the Place de la République was the central square of Arles.

Gauguin's picture belonged to the same artistic family, but it had the exact, daring colour harmony of Vincent's *Sunflowers* – translated into an autumnal still life of fruit and vegetables from Marguèrite Favier's shop next door. The *Sunflowers* were the paintings of Vincent's that Gauguin most admired. He had said something extremely flattering about them that very week, which Vincent relayed to Theo. 'Gauguin was telling me the other day that he had seen a picture by Claude Monet of sunflowers in a large Japanese vase, very fine, but – he likes mine better.' Ominously, however, Gauguin's *Pumpkin and Apples* was never heard of again, perhaps because he abandoned or destroyed it.

The other painting Gauguin was undertaking at this point was a subject that Vincent had treated much earlier in the year: the washerwomen. Laundresses and washerwomen were one of the staple themes of contemporary painting – either Degas's slatternly Parisian creatures, engaged in activities much more strenuously physical than those of respectable ladies, or more wholesome peasant women at rural washing-places such as were depicted by Pissarro and Gauguin himself.

Earlier in the year Vincent had also painted women washing both at the laundry platform on the Roubine du Roi canal near the Yellow House and at another spot to the south of town. Vincent had represented the women as small figures in the distance, but he had also thought of painting them from up close – like Gauguin's women in Martinique – with their colourful costumes.

Vincent did not paint this subject, the laundresses at close quarters, possibly because to do so he felt he would have had to carry out studies from models, which were almost impossible for him to find. But Gauguin now did. So the

origin of his new picture was complex indeed: he was execut-
ing a picture that Vincent had imagined on the basis of an
earlier painting of Gauguin's own.

In preparation, Gauguin drew the outline of a local woman
muffled up against the cold in her shawl, viewed from behind.
Then, on a piece of jute, he began a picture of two women
at the Roubine du Roi canal. It was, just as Vincent had
envisaged, a partial rerun of the Caribbean landscape owned
by the brothers Van Gogh.

Like his picture of Martinique, this new one had a standing
figure seen from behind in the foreground and another bending over further back. The earlier landscape was scattered
with browsing dogs and goats; one large beast thrust its head
into this Arlésienne composition, nibbling at a tuft of vegetation right at the front of the picture. In both pictures there
was water in the background. But the new painting was very
far from the idyllic mood of the black women gathering
mangoes in Martinique.

It was harder to decipher than anything Gauguin had ever
produced: a bewildering picture in which many of the forms
were teasingly ambiguous. Gauguin had chosen a viewpoint
at the top of the steep bank of the little canal, looking vertigin-
ously down. The waters of the canal swirl like a mountain
torrent, cresting into a small white wave (could even the
recent rains have produced such an effect in a placid back-
water?). Behind the hunched figure of the standing woman,
an autumnal bush flares in orange and red so vivid it looks
like flame.

A second bush flickers in front of her; again, it seems like fire.
The green foliage to her right reads at first, or even second
look, like a shadow cast by this phantom blaze. Gauguin's
picture was a bizarre blend of the rustic and the hellish.

It was true that the Roubine du Roi canal washing-place

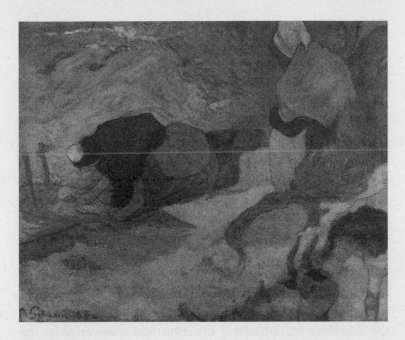

was not a particularly savoury spot. A stone's throw away
were the brothels of the Rue du Bout d'Arles – just over the
railway and behind the gasworks. This was the place where
the women from the *maison de tolérance* at No. 1 would do
their laundry; so, too, would the other women of the district,
such as Marguèrite Favier from the grocer's shop next door.

Gauguin had harboured dark suspicions of the women in
Martinique. They put magical charms on the fruit they sold, he
had been warned, in order to ensnare you. Perhaps Gauguin
was also wary of the Arlésiennes, despite those hygienic visits
to the brothels. After all, they too had a reputation for exerting
a fatal attraction. This painting, in contrast to the lyrical
landscapes of the Alyscamps, suggested that Gauguin felt far
from comfortable in Arles.

★

On Sunday the eighteenth the fog was so dense that work would have been difficult in the Yellow House without the gaslight on, even during the day. Vincent felt that the foundations of southern houses were inadequate, so one felt the damp more in the Midi, but with the fire lit the house was quite cosy: there were fireplaces in the kitchen and Vincent's bedroom. Lighting and tending the blaze was now a regular daily chore and the purchase of coal and wood a regular monthly expense: another 4 francs. So the odour of coal smoke was added to the other smells of the Yellow House.

Over the next few days it brightened up, though it continued to get colder. As the weather outside improved, however, the atmosphere within was deteriorating. Around the middle of the week, Gauguin wrote to Bernard. It was clear that since his previous letter, things had started to go wrong. Then, he had recommended that Bernard come and stay in the comfortable household Gauguin had established in the Yellow House. This time he poured out complaints about his new place of residence, its inhabitants, its surroundings and – above all – Vincent:

I feel completely disorientated in Arles, I find everything so small and mean, both the landscape and the people. In general Vincent and I are very little in agreement, especially on painting. He admires Daudet, Daubigny, Ziem and the great Rousseau, all of whom I feel nothing for. And he hates Ingres, Raphael, Degas, all of whom I admire; I reply, 'Corporal, you're right,' to get some peace.

'Corporal, you're right' was the refrain of a popular song. It was a witty way of ending a conversation, which Gauguin used from time to time when dealing with tiresome officials. But it probably only inflamed Vincent's desire to expound his convictions.

Gauguin both muddled and exaggerated Vincent's ideas. His list of his housemate's great artistic loves is an odd one. He added Alphonse Daudet to the list, who was one of Vincent's favourite writers, not a painter. Did he muddle Daudet with Daumier — typically getting a name wrong — another painter Vincent loved? Or was he just getting tired of hearing so much about what Vincent did and didn't like?

It was perfectly normal for artists to have differing personal pantheons that reflected their ideals and aspirations. There was no need to quarrel about it. But when two people are cooped up together day and night, small discrepancies of temperament become points of friction. Tact and diplomacy are required; but it is an understatement to say that Vincent was short on those qualities. He was unable to leave a point of disagreement alone.

Years later, when he wrote down his memories of his stay in Arles, Gauguin was still grumbling about Vincent's idiosyncratic views:

Despite all my efforts to disentangle from that disordered brain a logical reasoning behind his critical opinions, I could not explain to myself the complete contradiction between his paintings and his views.

This was unfair, but it was perfectly true that Vincent's tastes were different from Gauguin's — and sometimes unconventional for an avant-garde artist. For his part, Vincent, as his hero-worship faded, ended up finding Gauguin's opinions always 'a little vague and obscure'. Patience was slipping away.

Gauguin complained that his companion had 'an unlimited admiration for Meissonier and a profound hatred for Ingres. Degas was his despair and Cézanne was nothing but a fraud. When thinking of Monticelli, he wept.'

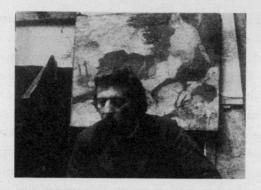

Ernest Meissonier, the most commercially successful painter in Paris at the time, was an academic hack as far as most advanced artists were concerned, but Vincent found much merit in his work (a point on which posterity, on the whole, has agreed with Gauguin). 'Now,' Vincent insisted, 'if you looked at a Meissonier for a year, there would still be something in it to look at next year, you may be sure of that. Not to mention his lucky days, when he had perfect flashes of genius.'

One would have to be blind, Vincent believed, to think that Meissonier was not a real artist 'and a first-rate one'. Gauguin declared, with his military scenes in mind, that Meissonier was 'the painter of those armoured hordes where everything looked like iron – except the armour.'

As so often, Vincent's passionate advocacy was caused by the feeling that Meissonier's paintings gave him. He was particularly fond of a picture called the *Reader* which he had known for many years and wanted an etching of for the Yellow House. It showed a long-haired, bearded man wearing seventeenth-century costume intently perusing a manuscript in a tall, shuttered room. It was the kind of Meissonier that reminded him of the old Dutch masters, but more – obviously – it reminded him of himself. Meissonier's reader was the brother of Vincent's own *Reader*, his young woman reading in a book-lined room.

Vincent connected Meissonier, who was born in 1815, with other painters of the mid century, several of whom Gauguin listed with irritation: Charles-François Daubigny, Félix Ziem, Théodore Rousseau. Vincent called them 'the generation of '48' – the year of Republican revolution – and persisted in believing that their work was compatible with Impressionism.

Vincent had loved their paintings long before he had ever come to Paris and discovered Impressionism. He loved them still, because he found emotion in their work. Looking at a dawn landscape, lit by the morning star, he was reminded of them: 'Daubigny and Rousseau have depicted just that, expressing all that it has of intimacy, all that vast peace and majesty, but adding as well a feeling so individual, so heart-breaking.'

Many a time Vincent reminded Gauguin that others had already achieved what they set out to do: that was, made paintings that were *consoling*. He himself could not forget 'all those lovely canvases' of Rousseau and the others. 'It seems hardly probable that anyone will do better than that, and unnecessary besides.'

Of those outdated painters whom Vincent defended, Adolphe Monticelli was the oddest. Monticelli was regarded as hopelessly eccentric by contemporaries and had little support from posterity, but Vincent was convinced he was a great painter. Monticelli's wild use of thick paint and flurried brush strokes suggested ways in which he could develop his own art.

Vincent had a Dutch feeling for earthy, physical paint in which anyone could trace the movement of the artist's hand. He revered Rembrandt and Frans Hals and saw possibilities in paint that were seen by no one else in France at the time, and certainly not by Gauguin.

Gauguin summarized the difference between them well to Bernard:

He is romantic and me, I incline more to a primitive state. From the point of view of colour, he likes the chance effects of impasto in the manner of Monticelli, whereas I detest all that messing about with brushwork and that kind of thing.

Vincent was indeed romantic. He wanted a passionate engagement with what he painted, whether a person, place or thing. He smeared and slashed tubes of pigment on the canvas like a man who relished the feel and smell of the stuff. Gauguin, on the other hand, inclined 'to a primitive state'. He wanted the simplicity and poetry of an earlier age; he loved Botticelli, Ancient Greece, Persia, the Middle Ages, the exotic arts of hot countries, and he admired methodical, classically inspired painters – Degas, who idolized Ingres, who in turn worshipped Raphael. This cool, lineal manner, expressing warmly erotic feelings, was of little interest to Vincent. Nor was the rather different formal discipline of Cézanne. Gauguin overstated or misremembered some of his housemate's aversions: Vincent revered Degas, although he could be sharp about Cézanne.

Gauguin was not the only one to find Vincent hard to live with. Shortly after he had arrived in Theo's apartment in Paris two years before, trouble started. Theo's great friend Andries Bonger reported that Vincent hadn't the slightest idea of how to behave in society. 'He is always quarrelling with everybody. Consequently Theo has a lot of trouble getting along with him.' Bonger described how Vincent began 'interminable discussions which were sparked off by impressionism and in which he touched on all conceivable subjects'. Gauguin would have recognized that description.

Theo later told his fiancée, Jo, how, when he came home tired from a day at the gallery, Vincent would begin to expound his own views about art and art-dealing, which always led to the conclusion that Theo must leave Boussod et Valadon (still generally known, from its founder, as Goupil's) and set up on his own. This went on far into the night; sometimes Vincent would sit down on a chair beside Theo's bed and carry on talking while his brother tried to sleep.

After a year, even Theo had had enough. 'There was a time when I loved Vincent a lot and he was my best friend,' he wrote to Wil:

but that is over now. It seems to be even worse from his side, for he never loses an opportunity to show me that he despises me and that I revolt him. That makes the situation at home almost unbearable. Nobody wants to come and see me, for that always leads to reproaches and he is also so dirty and untidy that the household looks far from attractive. All I hope is that he will go and live by himself, and he has talked about this for a long time, but if I told him to leave that would only give him a reason to stay on.

In Theo's eyes, Vincent was a divided personality:

It appears as if there are two different beings in him, the one marvellously gifted, fine and delicate, and the other selfish and heartless. They appear alternately so that one hears him talk now this way and then that way and always with arguments to prove pro and contra. It is a pity he is his own enemy, for he makes life difficult not only for others but also for himself.

Others found the same division between a lovable and an unbearable Vincent. Bonger found him, despite his impossible behaviour, 'frank, open, alive to possibilities, with a certain humorous edge of malice.' He told his parents that 'when Vincent was on form he was gay and jovial, relating jokes and stories, showing himself to be charming and an excellent mimic.' On the other hand, Bernard – much as he loved him – recalled Vincent 'vehement in discourse, interminably explaining and developing his ideas'.

Vincent was neurotically incapable of tolerating disagreement. And the more nervous opposition made him, the more compulsively verbose he became. The same pattern could be traced in his letters. At one especially tense moment he wrote two letters on one day, the second running to sixteen pages. Sometimes Theo's response to this sort of bombardment was simply not to reply. Silence drove Vincent to ever more frantic verbosity. Gauguin no doubt found the same.

There were several reasons why Gauguin may have been getting restive. In Paris his work was making an impact on important people such as Degas; meanwhile, he was cooped up in a remote provincial town with a compulsively articulate, opinionated and tactless companion. And Gauguin, like Vincent, was sensitive to criticism. 'He likes my paintings very much, but when I do them he always finds that I've gone wrong about this, and that.'

Vincent's next letter to Theo, written a couple of days later, contained an example of the kind of thing Gauguin had been hearing. He reported that Gauguin's canvas *Ring of Breton Girls* had arrived. This was the picture which was almost sold but needed a slight modification, since when it was put in a frame, one of the dancer's hands seemed to touch the edge in an awkward fashion.

It was the first of Gauguin's pictures from his long stay in Brittany earlier in the year that Vincent had actually seen, and he was not particularly impressed. Gauguin, he informed Theo, 'has altered it very well. But though I quite like this canvas, it is all to the good that it is sold.'

It was completely overshadowed by the best paintings Gauguin had done in Arles: 'The two he is about to send you from here are thirty times better. I am speaking of the "*Women Gathering Grapes*" and the "*Woman with the Pigs*". Vincent imagined – typically – that the reason for this improvement was that Gauguin's digestion was improving. Vincent had a tendency to relate any raised quality in his own painting to lack of intestinal troubles (and vice versa).

Gauguin would have had mixed feelings when he heard this judgement – which he doubtless received from Vincent in person. It was good, of course, to hear that his work had got so much better; but it was not so pleasing that Vincent was dismissive of one of the best pieces from his preceding eight months' work. It had always been a risk to bring together two such powerful artistic personalities – both touchy and each entirely reliant on the faith he had in himself. Now the strains were showing.

Officially speaking, Gauguin was the head of the studio, older, more experienced and more distinguished as a painter. Vincent reiterated as much in the same letter: 'It does me a tremendous amount of good to have such intelligent company as Gauguin's, and to see him work.' But, in practice, the hierarchy was much more complicated and unstable.

Each was learning from the other but had inner doubts as to whether the lessons were truly useful. Gauguin had tried out Vincent's yellow-on-yellow colour harmony and had been experimenting with thicker paint in Vincent's manner, especially in the grape harvest picture and that of the woman with the pigs. Vincent particularly approved of these pictures, partly because of their piled-on paint, as he told Theo:

His last two canvases, which you will soon be seeing, are very firm in the impasto, there is even some work with the palette knife. And they will throw his Breton canvases a little in the shade – not all, but some.

Gauguin, for his part, continued to hand out technical tips to Vincent. The latest was a method for reducing the thick, oily look of Vincent's trowelled-on paint surface. The answer was, Gauguin suggested, to rinse the pictures in water and leave them to dry. Eventually a more pleasingly matt surface would result.

This was one reason why, although Gauguin had an impressive batch of work to send off to Theo after his first month in Arles, Vincent wasn't sending anything, despite having his room 'full of canvases'. They were still drying; also, none seemed quite finished. When they were dry he would retouch them again.

As Gauguin's star rose, Vincent's spirits had plunged. He was undergoing a crisis of confidence in his work. The paintings from earlier in the year consisted almost entirely of visual responses to what he had seen in front of him. But Gauguin's arrival had temporarily persuaded Vincent that he had been on the wrong track. His excitement in September and early October, when he was producing his *décorations* for the Yellow House, had evaporated.

Now, he felt, it would be years before he became a mature artist such as Gauguin. Vincent was more than a little averse to success; he generally reacted to praise with anguished self-deprecation. In a novel by Daudet, he found a line he liked: 'to achieve fame is something like ramming the lighted end

of your cigar into your mouth when you are smoking.' As
Vincent now saw it, most of his work from the first eight
months in Arles was valuable mainly as raw material. It consti-
tuted a series of studies for proper, carefully planned pictures
he might do in the future:

Gauguin, in spite of himself and in spite of me, has more or less
proved to me that it is time I was varying my work a little. I am
beginning to compose from memory, and all my studies will still
be useful for that sort of work recalling to me things I have seen.

But that formulation, 'in spite of himself and in spite of me',
broadly hints at doubts on Vincent's part. And Gauguin, after
all, had just awarded the *Sunflowers* the highest praise.

This conflict helped make Vincent anxious, and that, in
turn, made him go on and on, repeating the points he wanted
to establish. In a letter, Theo had suggested that he frame
one of the series of orchards in blossom that Vincent had
painted in the spring. Brooding on this suggestion, Vincent
had concluded that Theo intended then to show the picture
to his senior colleagues at Boussod et Valadon. This imagined
possibility made Vincent nervous in several ways at once.

For one thing he had extremely sore feelings about Theo's
employers. After all, he had once worked for the firm himself
and had been sacked, leaving on 31 March 1876, the day after
his twenty-third birthday, to become an unpaid junior master
at a seedy private school in Ramsgate. It was the second in the
series of career disasters that had punctuated his life before he
became a painter. Habitually, he referred to the senior partners
in Boussod et Valadon as '*ces messieurs*' – those gentlemen.

Now that he himself was having doubts about the quality
of all those studies he had sent from Arles, he did not want *ces
messieurs* to have the chance to administer another humiliating

rejection. He suggested Theo keep what paintings he wanted for the apartment in Paris; the rest should be sent back so that Vincent could rework them or use them as the basis for further, more thoroughly conceived paintings. Success lay years in the future: 'But be sure of this, if we can stand the siege, my time will come.' Meanwhile, he would work quietly in obscurity.

Vincent continued on about this for some time, hinting at the kind of verbal onslaught that Gauguin was withstanding in person, before ending the letter on a workmanlike note – 'A handshake – we need some more paints.' Then he must have put the paper down and taken it up again some hours – or days – later to add disjointed snippets of news and observation. When he did so, his tone had changed: the whole document now vibrated with suppressed competitiveness. Vincent's mood had swung, his spirits had rallied.

Despite being smitten with self-doubt – an endemic problem for most creative people – Vincent felt the strength of his abilities. This came out as a vague prediction that in the future he would rival any artist alive. 'If, by the time I am forty, I have done a picture of figures like the flowers Gauguin was speaking of, I shall have a position in art equal to that of anyone, no matter who. So, perseverance.' He would be forty in five years; Gauguin was forty now. So, decoded, this passage was a claim that, in time, he would be the equal of his new friend and housemate.

When he had asked Theo to return his studies to Arles, he now emphasized, he meant only 'the bad ones'. He acknowledged that an unspecific 'they' 'all think what I have sent too hastily done. I do not contradict it, and I will make some alterations.' Who were 'they'? Painters who had seen the pictures at Theo's apartment? De Haan and Isaacson? Bernard and Gauguin? Degas, Seurat, Signac?

In the past, Vincent had alternated between defending his velocity of execution and admitting that, since everybody thought it was wrong, it might be a fault. There were times when he thought that speed was a positive virtue, allowing an artist to seize the essence of a subject in an instant, as he imagined the Japanese did. And he was inclined to be defiant now: 'Fortunately for me, I know well enough what I want, and am basically utterly indifferent to the criticism that I work too hurriedly. In answer to that, I have done some things *even more* hurriedly these last few days.'

Perhaps it was the excitement of producing those paintings '*even more* hurriedly' that had lifted his morale. They seemed to have been finished between the two halves of the letter. Out of a mixture of modesty and insecurity, Vincent wasn't prepared to say how good he thought these paintings were. Instead, he edged towards the subject. First, he related Gauguin's flattering remark about the *Sunflowers*; next he added that perhaps in five years' time he might have produced a picture of those flowers truly good enough to deserve that praise. Only then did he slip in a self-deprecating description of the two new pictures:

Meanwhile I can at all events tell you that the last two studies are odd enough. Size 30 canvases, a wooden rush-bottomed chair all yellow on red tiles against a wall (daytime). Then Gauguin's arm-chair, red and green night effect, wall and floor red and green again, on the seat two novels and a candle, on thin canvas with a thick impasto.

What he didn't say in this almost telegraphic account was that the first chair he had painted was his own. Of course he couldn't know that these two paintings he had just turned out so rapidly were to become among the most celebrated in

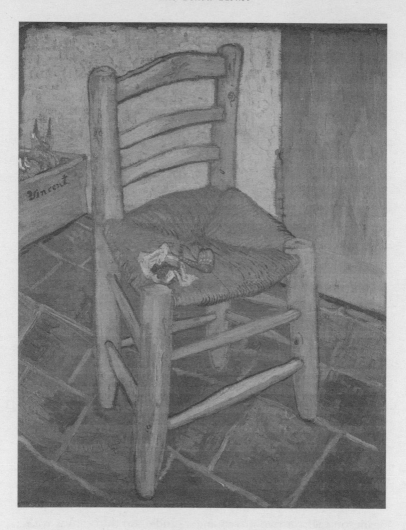

the whole of art. But, deep down, he must have felt that they were powerful; enough, at any rate, to cause a rise in morale. The pictures were not just remarkable, they were almost unprecedented.

From Wednesday on, the skies outside the Yellow House had cleared and light levels increased in the studio. It had stopped raining. But it was sufficiently chilly to deter someone who hated winter, such as Vincent, from venturing out to paint. Instead, he had remained indoors and painted a radically novel type of still life: he had had the idea of painting his furniture. While paintings of foodstuffs – such as Gauguin's *Pumpkin and Apples* – had been a staple of western art since the days of the Ancient Greeks, depictions of empty seats had not. Vincent, however, had long had intense feelings about chairs.

In February 1878, while he was in Amsterdam, unsuccessfully attempting to improve his classical languages to the point where he could enter university and study to become a clergyman, his father had visited him. The two of them went on many walks together. For once, father and son were in harmony. After Pastor Theodorus departed, Vincent was deeply moved by the sight of his father's unoccupied chair. He cried 'like a child'.

Furniture was part of having a home – a nest like the bird's nests he painted and drew many times while he was working at Nuenen. A domestic nest was something which Vincent strove to attain, and had finally achieved in the Yellow House. On the other hand, *empty* chairs suggested absent companionship, the loneliness that had often been his lot.

There was one precedent for depicting an empty chair: a drawing of Charles Dickens's study done after the novelist's death in 1870 by the English artist Luke Fildes. It showed the room without the great man and spirit that had filled it with energy. Vincent owned and prized this print, which was done for a magazine called the *Graphic*. He tried to get another copy for Theo. It was more to him than just a memorial to a writer he revered.

Then, in 1882, Vincent foresaw the death of the artist Fildes himself and his contemporaries – English illustrators whose work he collected: 'Empty chairs – there are many of them, there will be even more.' Perhaps now, he envisioned an empty chair in the Yellow House. After nearly a month of harmonious coexistence, the new tensions between Vincent and Gauguin raised the question of whether he would stay. There had been a hint of this in Vincent's most recent letter to Theo:

I hope we shall always remain friends with Gauguin and doing business with him, and if he could succeed in founding a studio in the tropics, it would be magnificent. However, it requires more money according to my calculations than it does according to him.

This was another point of friction. Gauguin estimated that he could set off for Martinique with 2,000 francs in hand; Vincent felt it would require more than twice as much. The underlying issue was clear: the more money Gauguin needed, the longer he would have to stay in Arles to accumulate it.

There were still more feelings embedded in the two chair pictures. They were an encapsulation of all Vincent's ideas and emotions about the *décoration* of the Yellow House. The rush-bottomed chair in particular – his own – was exactly the kind of unpretentious object that set the tone of monastic simplicity Vincent had aimed for in the house. It had been all that he could afford: rough and rustic. But it was also a good example of the kind of 'crude thing', like earthenware and the paintings of Monticelli, which he felt Parisians lost out by not appreciating.

Like the *Bedroom*, another portrait of furniture, these two pictures were hymns to the Yellow House and also – as the house itself was – manifestos of what Vincent stood for. The painting of his own simple straw-bottomed chair – just the kind of thing you sat on in the Café de la Gare and the local

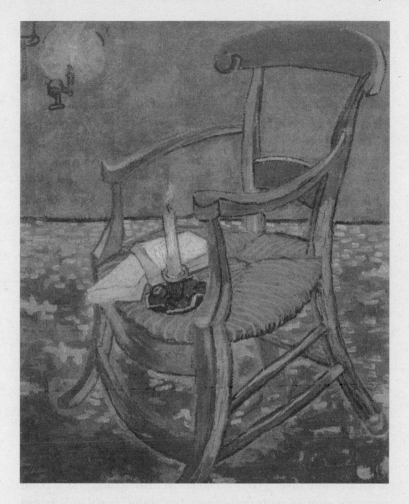

restaurant – is built of straight lines and lozenge shapes as sturdily as a house or the chair itself was made. Its basic colour chord of sunny yellow against the blue of the studio door and the bluish plaster of the wall was one of Vincent's favourite combinations from that year in Arles. It was the same contrast as the fields of wheat against the summer sky.

Gauguin's Chair, on the other hand, is mainly made up of

shallow curves, in the key (to pursue the musical analogy) of red and green. Its effect is more subdued and mysterious. In the picture of Vincent's chair one can clearly see the red terracotta tiles of the studio floor. In the other, the whole surface has become a mass of glittering reflections from the gas lamp on the wall.

Thus the two paintings contrasted the two conditions of light in which Vincent and Gauguin were now working – daylight, when the skies above Arles cleared and the sun shone, and darkness, when the gaslight in the studio was turned on. This was the fundamental division of Vincent and Gauguin's days, as it would be for any painter, because working by daylight and by artificial light are two very different activities.

These two sources of illumination differed in their coldness or warmth, the manner in which they made reflections, and their angle of direction. All those factors affected the way the two artists saw what was on their canvases and what was in front of them – and nothing could be more important for a painter than the way he saw.

Finally, of course, in these two paintings, Vincent symbolized the two ways of painting that were then under such tense discussion in the Yellow House. His own chair has on its seat his pipe and tobacco. In the background, he added – perhaps later in January when he worked again on this picture at a time when he was much in need of solace – a box of sprouting onions, a symbol of new life of the kind that Vincent hoped would grow from his new art.

On the seat of Gauguin's chair he placed 'two novels' and a candle, which stood for another kind of solace and inspiration – the kind that came from reading and the imagination. The lighted candle was not only necessary upstairs in the Yellow House, where the gas had not been put in, but also showed that books provided spiritual and intellectual light.

The two volumes were covered in yellow paper, showing that they were modern French fiction of the sort written by Flaubert, the Goncourts, Zola and Daudet.

So, the two chairs hint at two opposed methods of making art – the first spontaneous and from life, the other from imagination and memory, *de tête*. One approach was more instinctive with Vincent, and the other suited Gauguin. But both were employed by each artist: they were the two methods used for making pictures in the Yellow Studio, complementary like night and day. The slightly more comfortable chair was Gauguin's, as befitted his position as head of the studio – it was also generally used by sitters when they came to the studio to pose for their portraits – and the modest, simple, four-square one was Vincent's. That humble chair of Vincent's, though, made the better picture, so vigorously and directly painted you felt you could reach out and pick it up, so simple that anyone could comprehend it.

In these two strange studies of cheap furniture, Vincent had summarized a great deal that was being debated in the Yellow House and in his own mind. In doing so – on the evidence of the letter – he had made himself feel better. Dangerously worked up though he was becoming, Vincent had just hit his top form again – for the second time since Gauguin had knocked on his door. In the next few weeks he would produce a stream of masterpieces, though none better than the two chairs. As far as anyone outside the Yellow House could see, however, it was Gauguin who was forging ahead.

On Thursday 22 November Gauguin dispatched his first month's work to Theo in Paris. He didn't send everything – the *Washerwomen* was probably still too wet; the first landscape of the farm and the Alyscamps picture with the falling leaves he evidently thought of as just trial pieces. Apart from the *Ring of Breton Girls*, which he had retouched, there were four new pictures in his consignment, which Gauguin listed by title: first, *Night Café*; second, *Landscape* or *Three Graces at the Temple of Venus* (this was his first Alyscamps picture); third, the *Pigs*, fourth, *Human Misery*. The last two, especially, he thought 'quite bold'.

Gauguin's accompanying letter was businesslike but filled with understated self-satisfaction: he was pleased with his work. Gauguin's only doubts concerned not the quality of the pictures but the experimental jute canvas. It was more awkward to handle, and he was worried about the paint flaking off when the pictures were unrolled in Paris and stretched again on wooden frames. At this point, probably because of this concern, he and Vincent stopped priming their canvases with the highly unusual barium sulphate and began using lead white instead. Tactfully, Gauguin went through the proper procedure with Theo, explaining the advantages of the new support. After all, Theo was paying 300 francs a month for these pictures, and the jute was Gauguin's own idea. It would be unfortunate if, as a result, the paint fell off when they got to his gallery.

If it proved difficult to tighten them on their stretchers, Gauguin advised wetting them all over, allowing them to dry and trying again. He was anxious to know if they arrived in good condition. A lot of his hopes were resting on these four new pictures from Arles.

Vincent had received a letter from his friend Eugène Boch. A Belgian painter, Boch had been one of Vincent's best friends in Arles during the summer. His portrait hung, with that of Milliet, in Vincent's bedroom. Vincent had said fare-well to him on the morning of 4 September, when he departed, on Vincent's suggestion, for the coalfields of southern Belgium, an area known as the Borinage.

This landscape was the opposite of Provence in many ways – sombre, Northern, industrial; 'dismal', as Vincent put it – yet it was dear to his heart. He toyed with the idea of travelling north to work there when he returned to Paris the following year, then alternating between painting in the coal mines and Arles – 'the land of the oleander and the sulphur sun'. This was, he explained to Boch, the place where he had first begun to work from nature.

That was true. In 1878, after giving up the attempt to qualify for university entrance so that he could become a pastor like his father, Vincent had gone south to Brussels.

His parents were in despair about his career, or lack of one. Their eldest son was now twenty-five. Vincent hoped to find some kind of lowly ecclesiastical post for which a degree was not necessary. Eventually, it was arranged that he would be provisionally accepted on a training course for evangelists in Belgium. But after the initial three months he was not given a grant. So, not wanting to be a burden on his father any longer, Vincent found a temporary job as a preacher in the Borinage.

This area – south of the city of Mons and just north of the French border – was one of the grimmest areas in Europe. Its misery and bleakness gave a foretaste of the First World War, fought a few decades later across this same landscape.

Vincent had travelled into the world of Dickens's *Hard Times* and Zola's *Germinal*. As it happened, Zola was at work on the latter novel – set in the French mining district a little further south – at the exact time that Vincent was in the Borinage.

'It is a gloomy spot,' he wrote of Marcasse, a mine near which he lived for a while:

and at first everything around looks dreary and desolate. Most of the miners are thin and pale from fever; they looked tired and emaciated, weatherbeaten and aged before their time. On the whole the women are faded and worn. Around the mine are the poor miners' huts, a few dead leaves black from smoke, thorn hedges, dunghills, ash dumps, heaps of useless coal, etc.

But Vincent looked back on the place with an artist's eye, telling Boch about subjects – including the mine of Marcasse – which he would have liked to paint. 'The tip girls in their pit rags especially are superb.'

He still dreamt of painting such subjects: the shift going to the pits, and the factories, 'their red roofs and their black chimneys against a delicate grey sky'. All of this had not yet been done but should be painted: 'One ought to go down into the mine and paint the light effects.'

These mines were extraordinarily dangerous places. During the winter gas built up and would explode during the spring and summer. Miners were continually dying as a result, in tens, even in hundreds. One such explosion took place in the area in which Vincent was preaching on 16 April 1879. It was powerful enough to reach up the shaft, demolish the buildings around and set the pit wheel alight. Vincent did his best to help the wounded after this disaster.

However, while some members of the mining community appreciated Vincent's efforts to help them, others thought he was a lunatic. Children threw things at him as he walked down the street. Added to his odd behaviour, Vincent did not have the most essential skill for a preacher – he could not speak in public. This seemed strange in view of his compelling eloquence on paper, but it was his fate to be able to project his thoughts only at a distance – through painting and writing. It was suspected at the Protestant church in

Petit-Wasmes that he was 'losing his mind and becoming a burden'.

Therefore, reasonably enough from their point of view, his superiors did not reappoint him after the probationary six months. Once again, Vincent had failed. But he remained in the Borinage. It was at this low point – in the summer of 1879 – that Vincent transformed himself from a would-be preacher into an artist. He began to draw more and more; how he lived is not clear. A meeting with Theo was acrimonious. Not only his parents but also his siblings were now thoroughly alarmed that Vincent would never find employment and instead become a layabout.

Their job suggestions, relayed by Theo, only infuriated Vincent. Theo's own idea was that Vincent might become 'an engraver of bill headings and visiting cards, or a book-keeper or a carpenter's apprentice'. His sister Anna suggested baking. Then, Vincent went on a strange artistic pilgrimage. In the early spring of 1880 he went to Courrières in northern France to visit Jules Breton, a painter of heroic peasants whose work he much admired at the time.

It was a typically impractical project. He had not bothered to check that the artist was in residence; probably, Breton was in Paris at the time. But it did not matter because, discouraged by the sight of Breton's high, regular 'Methodist' wall, Vincent returned without finding out whether he was there or not. He walked eighty-five miles with only 10 francs in his pocket, sleeping in a haystack and an abandoned coach which was covered in frost and bartering drawings for food. He returned from this apparently disastrous expedition strangely encouraged.

He was starting to find his own direction in life. Up to now, all his suppressed talents, sympathies and tastes for art and literature had been struggling to sprout like bulbs in

darkness. The psychic discomfort this caused explained some
– though perhaps not all – of his odd behaviour. Now the
first green shoots of his life as an artist started to appear.

His relations with his parents became more and more tense.
On a previous visit home, Vincent had spent all day reading
Dickens and would only answer when spoken to, sometimes
giving 'correct' answers, according to his mother, sometimes
'strange ones'. He then sent his parents a copy of *Les Misérables*,
which again caused outrage. Victor Hugo, complained his
mother, 'takes the side of criminals and doesn't call bad what
is really bad. What would the world look like if one called
the evil good? Even with the best of intentions that cannot
be accepted.' Vincent was on a collision course – no doubt
deliberately – with everything his father and mother believed.
It was an extremely thorough, if belated, act of rebellion.

Later that spring of 1880, Vincent's father suggested that
he be sent to a well-known mental hospital at Gheel, in
Belgium. And, probably at the same time, Vincent's parents
urged him to consult Doctor Johannes Nicolas Ramaer, a
respected psychiatrist in The Hague. Vincent agreed to see
him and ask for medicine but, at the last moment, he refused
to leave. His father went anyway and was told that his son
evidently had a malfunctioning cerebellum.

'What will become of him?' wailed Pastor van Gogh, 'Isn't
it insane to choose a life of poverty and let time pass by
without looking for an occasion of earning one's bread?' But
the plan to send Vincent to Gheel was fiercely resisted, by
Vincent himself and, according to Gauguin, by Theo. (The
name 'Gheel', coincidentally, sounded exactly the same as the
Dutch word for 'yellow', Vincent's favourite colour of that
summer and autumn in Arles. For all that time, looking back,
he felt he had maintained a 'high yellow note'.)

Rather than going to Gheel, Vincent had returned to his

new study of drawing in Belgium. By July, his religious beliefs had started to merge into a faith in art. 'I think,' he wrote to Theo, 'that everything which is really good and beautiful – of inner spiritual and sublime beauty – in men and their works comes from God.' If, he continued, 'someone loves Rembrandt, and seriously' – meaning *he*, Vincent, loved Rembrandt seriously – 'that man will know there is a God.'

At the end of the next year, 1881, at the height of the row about his love for Kee Vos-Stricker, he went further in an argument with his father:

I had such a temper, one I cannot remember having had in all my life, and I bluntly told Pa that I thought this whole religious thing horrible, and that exactly because I had studied these things closely during a most miserable episode in my life, I wanted no more to do with it at all and will have to avoid it like a fatal thing.

His faith in the Christianity of his father had been transformed into a belief in the religion of art.

Very likely, it was when Boch's most recent letter arrived that Vincent told Gauguin about his time in the Borinage, his father's plan to send him to Gheel and the explosion in the mine. Gauguin stored those stories up, turned them over in his mind and transformed them into a poetic parable: a portrait of Vincent in words.

Gauguin received an extremely exciting communication, forwarded by Theo, from a man called Octave Maus. A Belgian lawyer, critic and writer, Maus had been one of the founders five years before of a society called *Les XX* – the Twenty. Like the Impressionists and Independents in Paris, *Les XX* were dissatisfied with the official art of the *salon*. From 1884 they had organized annual exhibitions in Brussels of work by forward-looking Belgian artists. Selected foreigners were also invited to show.

Whistler, Monet, Cézanne and Seurat had all received this accolade, and so had such junior pointillists as Signac. But, until now, Gauguin had not. This invitation was, therefore, like his sale to Degas, an exhilarating sign that he was suddenly gaining acceptance.

He wrote in triumph to tell his friend Schuffenecker. Poor old Schuff's hopes to exhibit with *La revue indépendante*, on the other hand, had been rebuffed. So Gauguin's glee was tempered with commiseration and laced with thanks. He had at last received the ceramics, linen and Degas prints he had asked Schuffenecker to send.

Gauguin wanted Schuff's opinion about his new work, especially the two pictures he believed were the most successful, the *Pigs* and *Human Miseries*. He asked him to take a look at them in Theo's gallery and, if he had a spare moment, to send his critical impressions to Arles. Gauguin was highly conscious that he had tried for something new – paintings 'simply painted on coarse canvas thickly with imperceptible divisions of colour seeking for a broad sense of form'. He felt he was moving so fast he couldn't assess the results himself. Life was whirling past as if seen from a fast-moving train, 'and like the driver I'm looking forward towards the destination – but there's rather a risk of being derailed . . .'

He then went on to expound how hopeful he felt. This was just the beginning. Gauguin felt full of artistic power and optimism – though not, he emphasized, necessarily about his financial prospects. He wanted to rush forward into the unknown future of his art: to 'attack'. 'I sense untapped forces in myself and I say proudly: We shall see!' He signed this euphoric missive, 'from a great big madman who loves you all,' and added, 'P. Go'.

That signature, which he had used occasionally before and now did more frequently, was a private, rather rude pun. Pronounced in the French manner, 'P. Go' came out as '*pego*', which was naval slang for penis, so he was signing himself 'the cock'.

Barely had Gauguin received the invitation to exhibit with *Les XX* in Brussels than another arrived from – of all people – Edouard Dujardin of *La revue indépendante*. They, too, wanted him to exhibit, in the same show to which Vincent had previously been invited to send pictures. Here was an opportunity for revenge. His enemies were delivered into his hands!

Gauguin might be bad at remembering names, but he certainly hadn't forgotten the sneering remarks in Félix Fénéon's review in that publication almost a year before in which he had been described as '*grièche*'. Nonetheless, Fénéon was an admirer of Gauguin's work and had probably suggested this invitation.

If Gauguin had surmised this, he didn't care. He lost no time in composing an elaborately ironic letter of refusal to Dujardin. It was intended to sting. He was, he wrote, confused by the honour that they had done him by this invitation. His powers as an artist did not allow him to rival the extraordinary progress made by the pointillists, his work lacked 'clarity and luminosity' – a recollection of past slighting criticisms. Therefore, he had decided to avoid all 'publicity got up by groups'.

In contrast, Gauguin wrote a short, polite letter of acceptance to Octave Maus, whose organization hadn't insulted him and whose invitation was extremely welcome. Then he wrote in glee to Schuffenecker again, forgetting, in his excitement, that he had already told Schuff all about the invitation from *Les XX* in his previous letter. He enclosed a copy of his refusal to exhibit with *La revue indépendante*.

'I would like to see those gentlemen's faces when they read my letter,' Gauguin gloated, unthinkingly reminding Schuffenecker of the insult he had suffered. 'They once wrote in their revue that I was a *grièche* artist, and I want at least to deserve that description.'

Now that Gauguin's career as an artist was rapidly gathering pace, his thoughts turned to the women in his life: his sister and his wife. He hoped that they would at last understand that he had been right all along.

'I don't know whether my success,' Gauguin mused, 'has come to the ears of my charming sister.' He imagined Marie Gauguin, with whom he had long ago fallen out, might be in Peru, attempting to get money out of their rich relations, the Tristán y Moscoso clan. In reality, poor Marie was in Germany making a slender income as a seamstress – an occupation to which Gauguin's mother had briefly been reduced, considered only one step above prostitution.

The other individual Gauguin ardently wished to know of his success was, of course, his Danish wife, Mette. Estranged though they were, he and Mette could not quite let go of each other, in part because Gauguin greatly loved his children, especially his daughter Aline. He and Mette exchanged letters, bristling with hurt feelings, with which they usually managed to offend each other, but even this irritable correspondence had now slowed to a trickle. And yet, Gauguin still imagined that his family might be reunited, with Mette admitting he had been wise all along. 'My wife has not sent any news,' he complained to Schuffenecker:

For 3 months I have had not a word from her. As soon as I have a little money from Van Gogh I will send it to her. And if as I hope one day I reach the point of supporting my family by painting we will see perhaps that I am right. In any case what does it matter? I get pleasure from plenty of other things, and it is into my art that all the warmth goes.

In that last thought, once again, he seemed to echo Vincent, who felt that, to an artist, ecstasy was visual not sexual. 'We painters,' he had written to Bernard, 'must get our orgasms from the eye.' This was an aspect of the artist's monastic life, an aesthetic compensation for the deprivation of physical love and comfort: 'Anything complete and perfect renders infinity tangible, and the enjoyment of any beautiful thing is, like coitus, a moment of infinity.'

Gauguin had learnt this lesson. On a studio window in Paris in 1894, he wrote, '*Ici faruru*', 'Here we make love'. And in the remote Marquesas Islands, on the portal of his last house Gauguin carved the words '*Maison du Jouir*', which meant House of Pleasure but could also mean that it was a 'House of Orgasm'.

Until he arrived in Arles, Gauguin's sexual life had been far from flamboyant. Nobody really knew what he had got up to as a youthful sailor; much, much later he boasted of a romance with an opera singer in Rio de Janeiro on his first voyage at seventeen. But this had a fictional ring to it. Throughout the later 1870s and earlier 1880s, despite the frictions with Mette, he had apparently been a faithful husband and devoted father.

Even after he had left his family in Copenhagen, his behaviour had been surprisingly chaste. There were those rumours of an affair with Schuffenecker's wife, Louise – but in Brittany the Scottish artist Archibald Hartrick related that Gauguin's one cry then was, 'Pas de femmes', 'No women'.

He could be caustic about the *amours* of others, describing the fatter mistress of a fat painter as his 'slop-bucket'.

However, Gauguin was taking enthusiastically to those brothel visits. In doing so – as with the cooking and the homemade canvases – he was following Vincent's script. All three plans – culinary, practical and amatory – were in the letters written to Bernard which Gauguin himself had read attentively while still in Brittany.

In a sense, to Vincent, all three were part of the household economy. Fundamentally, he thought of sexual intercourse and painting pictures as two competing ways in which energy could be directed: an occasional brothel visit kept the expenditure of energy on women to a frugal minimum. 'Don't fuck too much,' he exhorted Bernard in his direct Dutch way. 'Your painting will be all the more spermatic.' He gave examples from the private lives of celebrated artists:

If we want to be really potent males in our work, we must sometimes resign ourselves to not fuck much, and for the rest be monks or soldiers, according to the needs of our temperament. The Dutch, once more, had peaceful habits and a peaceful life, calm, well regulated.

This was exactly the advice Gauguin passed on to Schuffenecker: 'Hygiene and coition – with that well regulated and independent work a man can manage.' Gauguin's formula for a productive life – 'Calm down, eat well, fuck well, work ditto and you will die happy' – was an echo of Vincent's to Bernard.

Vincent sometimes advocated a degree of sexual moderation verging on abstention. Delacroix, for example, that master whom Vincent and Gauguin idolized, 'did not fuck much, and only had easy love affairs, so as not to curtail the

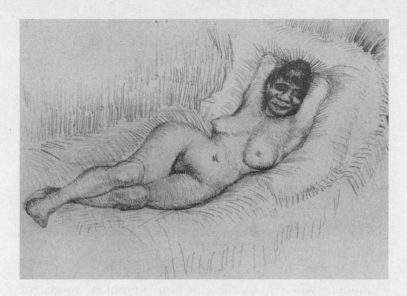

time devoted to his work'. It was precisely Degas's detach-
ment from sexual life that made his work 'virile and
impersonal'.

There were, however, exceptions to this austere rule: painters who had such robust life-force that they could exert
themselves in this way. '*Rubens!* Ah, that one! He was a
handsome man and a good fucker, Courbet too. Their health
permitted them to drink, eat, fuck . . .' And it seemed that
Gauguin was one of this vigorous group.

After all, he had fathered a family of five already. 'He is
physically stronger than we are,' Vincent informed Theo, 'so
his passions must be much stronger than ours.' But it was a
different matter for those such as Vincent, Theo and Bernard
whose health was more precarious and whose blood did not
circulate so freely. Sexual intercourse was in any case an
activity at which, as Vincent put it, 'professional pimps and
ordinary fools' excelled.

There was a hint of defensive insecurity in that. In the

summer Vincent had almost become impotent, he confessed, through exhaustion (though that seemed to pass). Was there also a touch of jealousy and disapproval in Vincent's attitude to Gauguin's feats in the brothel? He certainly seemed to disapprove of the extravagance involved.

This, Vincent decided, was the one deficiency in Gauguin's management of the domestic finances: a tendency to blow it all on 'hygienic expenses':

While I am often absent-minded, preoccupied with aiming at *the goal*, he has far more money sense for each separate day than I have. But his weakness is that by a sudden freak or animal impulse he upsets everything he has arranged.

So here was yet another, perhaps unspoken source of tension between the painters.

Despite his energy-conservation theory of sexuality, Vincent felt sympathy for prostitutes as people. They were fellow misfits – just like painters, 'exiled, outcast from society'. The whore, he preached to Bernard, 'is certainly our friend and sister'.

Gauguin came to agree. At the end of his life he wrote an essay, *Against Marriage*, in which he proclaimed that '"woman" who is after all our mother, our daughter, our sister, has the right to earn her living.' A woman, in Gauguin's critique, was faced with three choices: she could marry, remain a virgin or she was forced to become 'what is known as a fallen woman'. In that case, she was 'brought down in the world and penned up in specially designated districts' – just like the women in Rue du Bout d'Arles.

He had tried hard to make his own marriage work but it had proved incompatible with his urge to become a painter;

Vincent had been told by Kee Vos-Stricker's brother that his proposal of marriage would get nowhere without money. They were not the only ones for whom marriage had proved too difficult: many writers and artists of their generation – bohemians – experimented with unconventional relationships. Some of them were happy, some not.

If the institution of marriage, Gauguin argued:

which is nothing other than a sale, is the only one declared to be moral and acceptable for the copulation of the sexes, it follows that all those who do not want to or who cannot marry are excluded from that morality. There is no room left for love.

Although brothels and prostitutes hadn't played an important part in Gauguin's life to date, they had in Vincent's. For him, too, it was a question of either having a wife, children and happy domestic life or following the vocation of the artist. To be a painter was similar to being a priest or monk, with the exception that every couple of weeks you might go to the brothel in order to live a well-regulated, calm existence.

This strange and contradictory pattern of reasoning – a rationalization of his own lonely state – did not prevent Vincent from having intense feelings of longing and regret for the wife and children he had never had. Many of the paintings of the next few weeks would concern this very matter: he was soon to depict a family.

7. Musicians in Colour
23 November–4 December

Towards the end of the week, the two painters went on another evening walk and saw a striking sunset. It was perhaps on Friday 23 November, a cool day on which the sky was almost clear. Once more they had walked over towards the Alpilles, on the road to Montmajour, but now the air was distinctly wintry as the two painters looked at the darkening heavens above them. It was a little before ten past five in the afternoon when the sun dipped behind the horizon.

Again, Vincent described the sight to Theo: 'Yesterday evening an extraordinarily beautiful sunset of a mysterious, sickly citron colour – Prussian blue cypresses against trees with dead leaves in all sorts of broken tones without any speckling with bright greens.' And once more, both painters were given an idea for a picture.

Later, Vincent looked back nostalgically on these shared evening strolls with Gauguin. Eighteen months on, shortly before he left Provence, he painted a picture, from memory, of two figures ambling along a road together in the gathering dusk. The moon has risen, there are stars in the sky, a cypress looms above them. A light was visible in a cottage window.

On the afternoon of Sunday the twenty-fifth, in the large public gardens on the other side of Arles, the *Société Philharmonique* gave an open-air concert. The third piece performed was the march from Wagner's *Tannhäuser*. It was chilly that

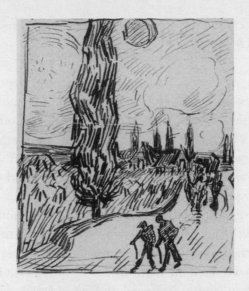

day, and Vincent and Gauguin were too busy to attend, despite Vincent's great interest in Wagner.

He and Theo had been to several concerts of music by the German composer in Paris. This was of course by no means an unusual taste. The music of Wagner, who had died five years previously in Venice, had long been causing intense excitement and controversy. A movement known as Wagnerism had swept the artistic world, affecting not only other musicians but writers and even painters. During the summer Vincent had read an introduction, by Camille Benoit, to the life and thought of the great composer.

Vincent was greatly struck by Wagner's daring identification of music with religious faith, which the composer put in almost blasphemous terms, using the language of Christian worship:

I believe in God, in Mozart and in Beethoven; I also believe in their disciples and apostles. I also believe in the sanctity of the spirit and in artistic truth whole and indivisible. I believe this art has a divine source, and that it lives in the heart of all men illuminated by celestial light.

Wagner cast himself as a musical John the Baptist; others, he prophesied, would come afterwards and create the works of art of the future. Vincent felt the same about his own painting. There would be a future artist, he predicted, who would do with colour what Wagner had done in sound: mix it in new and beautiful combinations that would soothe the mind and speak to the soul: 'It *will come.*'

The comparison of music and painting was more than just an analogy; many artists and writers believed it to be a profound truth. Indeed, they went further and believed that all the senses vibrated in harmony. The poet Baudelaire had written that 'scents, colours and sounds all correspond.' Huysmans, an author Vincent revered, extended his musical feelings even to tastes. He had written in his novel *Against Nature* of a collection of liqueurs that was also a 'mouth organ'. Each liqueur 'corresponded with the sound of a particular instrument'. Dry curaçao, for instance, was like 'the clarinet with its piercing, velvety note'.

Vincent had discovered the laws of colour while he was living in Nuenen and found them 'unutterably beautiful'. Around the same time, excited by the analogies he now understood between painting and Wagner's music, he took lessons from the organist of St Catherine's Church in Eindhoven, a man called Vandersanden. These were not a success: Vincent continually compared musical chords with Prussian blue or cadmium yellow, so that the organist concluded that he was dealing with a madman.

It is true that synaesthesia, experiencing one sensation in terms of another, can be found in those suffering from mental problems and those under the influence of hallucinogens. But if Vincent was mad in this respect, so were many other artists and musicians. Gauguin claimed that when he looked at a Delacroix, he had 'the same feelings as after reading something'. When he heard a Beethoven quartet, 'I leave the hall with coloured images that vibrate in the depths of my soul.'

Cézanne, Gauguin declared, seemed to be a pupil of César Franck: 'He is always playing the organ.' His work wasn't just polychromatic, it was polyphonic.

In Arles, enthusiasts for the new sport of velocipede-riding were increasing day by day, the two-wheel bicycle proving more popular than the tricycle. The town had its own velocipede shop – Fabre in Rue de Grand-Clar – which sold and rented the machines. Free lessons were offered. There was talk of starting a velocipede club.

Meanwhile, in Paris there was another visible sign of the rapid modernization of the world. Every day that Theo looked out over Paris from his apartment in Montmartre, the Eiffel Tower was a little taller. Soon it would be completed for the great Paris World Fair that was to be held the following year, 1889. Theo wrote about this amazing futuristic structure to the youngest Van Gogh brother, Cornelius.

Earlier Vincent had thought of showing fifty radiant paintings from Arles at the Great Exhibition. Gauguin was actually to exhibit there. When Gauguin looked at Eiffel's massive structure, he saw the future, 'a sort of gothic lacework of iron'. 'This exhibition,' he proclaimed, 'is the triumph of iron, not only with regard to machines but also with regard to architecture.' But where was the art to match it?

Of course both Gauguin and Vincent were working to create just that: the painting of the future. In his book *Sartor Resartus*, Carlyle had a beautiful image for this process. As old beliefs and images crumbled and vanished, 'organic filaments of the New mysteriously spun themselves into being'. That was precisely what was happening in the Yellow House: new images, novel ways of seeing the world were emerging out of nothingness.

Now Vincent made a fresh attempt to paint the subject that stood in his mind for the planting of a new world: the *Sower*. Its meaning derived from one of the parables of Christ. The sower cast his seed on the land. Some was eaten by birds; some fell on stony ground; but some fell on good ground and that 'brought forth fruit: some a hundredfold, some sixtyfold, some thirtyfold'.

The notion of the possibility of transformation, both artistic and personal, still lay at the centre of Vincent's thought and effort. It could be thought of as growth from a seed. He had written about this very analogy the previous year to his sister Wil, paraphrasing the parable: 'In nature many flowers are trampled underfoot, frozen or scorched, and for that matter not every grain of corn returns to the soil after ripening to germinate and grow into a blade of corn.' But people were like grains of corn:

In every human being who is healthy and natural there is a *germinating force*, just as there is in a grain of corn. And so natural life is *germination*. What the germinating force is to the grain, love is to us.

Some people, some ideas, fell on fertile ground; Vincent was never to know to what an amazing extent that was true of his own work.

The metaphor of germination meant an enormous amount to Vincent, perhaps partly because of the extraordinary, still unfolding, transformations of his own life from art dealer into preacher into painter. He also hoped for the remaking of human life into something which would escape the bitter suffering that seemed too often to be the lot of mortal men and certainly of Vincent van Gogh. Art was a way of imagining a future world. The *Sower* was a symbol of resurrection.

Vincent had painted and drawn sowers again and again in the years when he was working in Holland. But even when he drew them from life, these labourers casting seed on the turned ground were all derived from one original: the *Sower* painted by Jean-François Millet in 1850. This heroic figure strode across a darkening field, with a gleam of perhaps transcendental illumination on the horizon.

The idea had returned to him while he was painting the harvests in June. He had, he wrote then to Bernard, 'a hankering after the eternal, of which the sower and the sheaf of corn are the symbols'. (And even more of a symbol, he added, was the starry sky above, which he dreamed of one day painting.)

The extra element Vincent could now add, he felt, to the masterpiece of his hero Millet was his own new, exaggerated, intense colour: a visual vocabulary he hoped and believed would communicate to the heart as music does. 'Millet's Sower,' he noted 'is a colourless *grey*.' Now, could you paint the *Sower* in colour, with a simultaneous contrast of, for instance, yellow and violet? He presented himself with this challenge: was it possible, yes or no? 'Well, do it then.' And, thus psyching himself up, he did.

He made a sketch for the *Sower*, then yearned to turn it into a real picture, a masterpiece, a *tableau*. 'My lord, I do want to do it. But I keep asking myself if I have vigour enough to carry it through.' It had been a terrific struggle, which made him feel like 'a sleepwalker'. He had started it outdoors in the fields and carried on with it indoors in the studio of the Yellow House. He changed the figure, altered the colours, painted and over-painted.

As it finally emerged, the *Sower* was a vision more than an

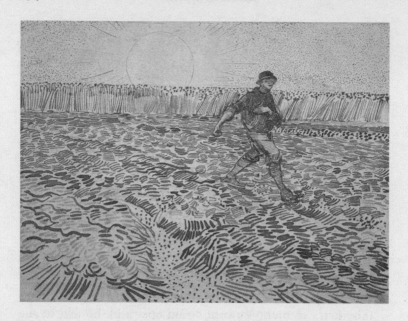

everyday landscape. A huge yellow sun in the background fills the sky with radiance; in front, there is a turned field, purple and orange. The sower himself, violet in the low sun, throws his grain on the earth. Some is eaten by the black birds behind him, but some would grow a hundredfold.

This picture was one of Vincent's greatest efforts of the year. But in the end, he deemed it a failure (even so, he didn't destroy it as he had another big, difficult project he had attempted in July and again in early autumn, *Christ in the Garden of Gethsemane*). The idea of painting a second, more successful *Sower* continued to excite him.

Now, the sunset he and Gauguin had seen together, combined with the lessons he had learnt from watching Gauguin at work, suggested a new approach. The summer *Sower* had been gloriously filled with hope – expressed by the yellow and violet. But the figure was striding in the middle distance.

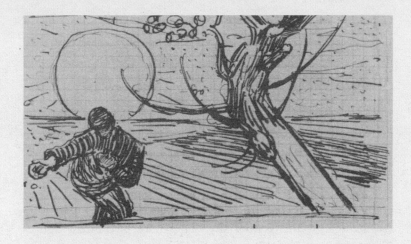

As a composition, therefore, it lacked force – which might have been why Vincent judged it less than successful.

His next attempt was more dramatic than his last. Very near to us, a sower walks past: a dark figure, silhouetted against the orb of the sun. Beside him, a tree juts diagonally across the painting, its branches bearing a few dead leaves. (A similar curving tree was also prominent in a print by the Japanese artist Hiroshige, of which Vincent had painted a copy the previous year.)

This was more crepuscular than the June *Sower*; the light is dying, not dawning. A massive sun is dipping down low in the extraordinary yellow-green sky – just as Vincent had described it – with a few streaks of pink cloud.

To create this image, Vincent drew on Gauguin's habits of composition. Gauguin liked to place figures close to the viewer: there was just such a tree as this one twisting across his masterpiece of the early autumn, the *Vision of the Sermon*. Gauguin was fond of diagonals cutting across his compositions: he had used one in the *Washerwomen*, where the river bank runs from bottom left to upper right.

Vincent's summer *Sower* was ecstatic; this was almost melancholic, with a mood of late autumn moving into winter. The earth was bare, the light was fading, but still there was hope. Seeds were being planted which would germinate in time.

Vincent was so pleased by this new *Sower* that he immediately made a second version on a smaller piece of jute in which the figure was even larger and closer, the sun yet lower. After that, Vincent never made another effort to paint his *Sower*. He was content.

In his sunset picture, Gauguin placed dark blue-violet trunks against the yellow sky. There are two small figures half-obscured behind one of the trees – a woman in Arlésienne costume and a man. They have turned away from each other. When he exhibited it the next year, Gauguin added a line of conversation to the title, *Blue Trees*. 'Your turn will come, pretty one.' Was this a variation on the age-old *memento mori* – a reminder of death? Was it a promise – or a threat? As so often with Gauguin, the message was ambiguous. But the sickly yellow sky and the gathering dusk gave the picture a sinister air.

Another letter arrived from Theo, containing, as so often, a 100-franc note. Vincent thanked him, then immediately broached once again a subject that was on his mind, namely, how large a bank roll Gauguin would require to set off for Martinique. Always the financier, as Theo had gently mocked him – Vincent had decided on a figure of 5,000 francs. That meant, assuming Gauguin continued to sell a couple of paintings a month and saved almost everything, he would still have to stay in Arles for a year. Gauguin himself felt 2,000 francs would be enough – in which case he might be off much sooner.

Vincent did not want that. He hoped Gauguin would wait for at least twelve months, then go with 'another man or with other men, and would found a studio there for good and all'. Perhaps he secretly imagined the other man might be him. In any case, a year was a long time, 'a lot of water will flow under the bridge before then.'

There was therefore something a little unconvincing about Vincent's declaration, 'I am very glad of Gauguin's success in the matter of the continuous sales.' It would, in fact, have suited Vincent well if Gauguin had sold a little less. This was evidently a matter that was causing Vincent anxiety; Gauguin no doubt heard that figure of 5,000 francs over and over again.

Vincent, his own isolation relieved, rejoiced again that Theo was not alone in Paris:

You cannot imagine how much it pleases me that you have painters staying with you, and that you are not living all alone in your apartment, just as it pleases me very much to have such good company as Gauguin's.

From having been suspicious of Isaacson and de Haan, Vincent had come to see them as artistic pilgrims treading the same path as he himself had. De Haan, as it happened – though Vincent probably did not know it – was uncannily similar to him in many ways. He was almost exactly a year older than Vincent, short, red-haired, in poor health, well-read in English literature and in revolt against his bourgeois family in Amsterdam who bankrolled him.

In the future, the parallels would multiply: de Haan became the companion of Gauguin, collaborated with him in the decoration of their lodgings in Brittany and planned to depart with him to found a studio in the tropics. Either because of this wild scheme, or because of an unsuitable love affair with a Breton landlady, his family threatened to cut off his allowance and recalled him to Holland, where he died. De Haan was as close to being Vincent's *doppelgänger* as anyone could be. The two men were never to meet.

Vincent had been impressed by the drawings de Haan had sent him. Here was another painter and draughtsman who had looked hard at the Dutch masters of the seventeenth century, Rembrandt in particular, and was now faced with the startling revelation of Impressionist colour. So, too, was Isaacson.

Vincent wanted to know if they had read two of his favourite texts on colour, Silvestre's book on Delacroix and the article on the subject in the *Grammaire des arts du dessin* by Charles Blanc. 'And if they have not read them, let them do so now.' By making this proposal, Vincent was giving Isaacson and de Haan the clue that had led him to understand the language of shade and hue.

Four years before, Vincent had already turned himself into one of the most forceful draughtsmen alive, though few had seen or admired his drawings. But he had only been painting for two years, and he still struggled with colour. Then, he discovered a map of that mysterious world. It was provided by Blanc's *Grammaire* of 1867, which had a neat diagram that presented the entire complicated realm of colour as a six-pointed star. It was a triumph of rational French analysis. The points of the star represented the three primary colours – red, blue and yellow – and three mixtures of them: orange, green and violet.

The mixed shades were placed between the primary from which they were derived; so orange had yellow on one side and red on the other. Opposite each primary, indicated by a dotted line on the diagram, was its complement – which was, in turn, the result of mixing the other two primaries. So the complement to yellow was violet. To red it was green, and to orange, blue.

It was a wonderfully orderly system. Any painter of course knew that the real world of colour was much more complicated than this. There was an infinite range of possible combinations, just as there was an endless array of possible musical sounds. But the star was like the musical scale; starting from it, you could plan harmonic effects resembling musical chords.

Then there was the question of simultaneous contrast: a colour could look quite different according to the other hues and tones around it. The quantity mattered too. Gauguin was fond of telling the story of Cézanne saying, 'in his accent of the Midi – "A kilo of green is greener than half a kilo." Everyone laughed. "He's crazy."' But, Gauguin pointed out, the crazy one was not Cézanne: 'Because your canvas is smaller than nature, you have to use a greener green. That is the truth of falsehood.'

Once, Vincent broke off a letter to his sister Wil to repaint a red, orange and yellow sky. While he was writing, it had struck him that it was not quite right. 'Then I took a colour that was there on the palette, a dull dirty white, which you get by mixing white, green and a little carmine. I daubed this greenish tone all over the sky.' And behold! The picture was in harmony. There was a lot of experimentation involved in using colour.

Few people alive cared as much about colour as Vincent and Gauguin. 'Me,' Gauguin recalled, 'I loved the colour red. Where to find a perfect vermilion?' When Vincent touched his yellow brush on the white wall, the plaster seemed to turn violet: an example of simultaneous contrast.

Gauguin later claimed that, in the matter of colour, he had been the teacher and Vincent the pupil. 'When I arrived in Arles, Vincent was trying to find himself, while I who was a good deal older, was a mature man.' But from the day of Gauguin's arrival, Vincent – he felt – had made 'astonishing progress': 'I undertook the task of enlightening him – an easy matter, for I found a rich and fertile soil.'

'Every day,' according to Gauguin, 'he thanked me for it.' Very probably, Vincent did thank him for hints and tips. But Gauguin was muddled about what lessons he had imparted. Looking back, he recalled that Vincent was mired in Seurat's pointillism, which, Gauguin felt, 'did not correspond to his nature, which was so far from patient and so independent'. Under his tutelage Vincent had quickly progressed to do the yellow-on-yellow masterpieces that Gauguin so admired.

But this was nonsense. Vincent had painted the *Sunflowers* in August, months before Gauguin had arrived.

When Vincent went to Paris in 1886 he had encountered the full brilliance of Impressionist colour. In the two years he spent there, he found ways to incorporate those shockingly bright hues into the direct Dutch drawing that had come naturally to him. Then he became fascinated by the idea of colour as a 'symbolic language'. Vincent imagined that this might be a communication of the heart: 'I am always in hope of making a discovery there, to express the love of two lovers by a marriage of two complementary colours, their mingling and their opposition, the mysterious vibrations of kindred tones.' He hoped 'to express hope by some star, the eagerness of a soul by a sunset radiance'.

There was a fundamental problem with this project of Vincent's. There was no such language of colour. It was not possible to express the complex emotions Vincent had in mind – the affinity of lovers, the thoughts within a head – through reds, blues, yellows or their myriad derivatives.

Colours remained just colours, though his researches led Vincent to create new and beautiful combinations.

Vincent's use of colour was carefully worked out. The viewer, he explained to Theo, should 'understand that I am in the midst of a complicated calculation long *beforehand*. So now, when anyone says that such and such is done too quickly, you can reply that they have looked at it too quickly.'

Indeed, it was just this calculation that often put him in 'a feverish condition' which he had to soothe with tobacco and drink. As so often, he imagined that his predecessor in the South, Monticelli, had been just the same: 'the logical colourist, able to pursue the most complicated calculations, subdivided according to the scales of tones that he was balancing, certainly over-strained his brain at this work.' That was what had driven Monticelli to the bottle.

Vincent – as usual connecting everything in his mental world – added Wagner to Monticelli, Delacroix, the Dutch painter Jongkind and himself in a list of crazy drunks and heavy smokers. These had all hit the bottle or lit their pipes, Vincent presumed, because of the mental exhaustion of devising complex harmonies of notes or colours.

Among the most prominent of Vincent and Gauguin's neighbours were the police. The Gendarmerie was the largest building on Place Lamartine, and the officers of the law were always active. The previous Saturday a shepherd had been waylaid in the square, lured to the Alyscamps and robbed. The following Monday there was a nasty fight between two carpenters in the Rue du Bout d'Arles. Numerous streetwalkers were sentenced at the monthly tribunal on Wednesday.

All in all, the gendarmes were a noticeable presence in the neighbourhood. At some point, Gauguin made two caricatures of their chief, Joseph d'Ornano, the Central Commissioner

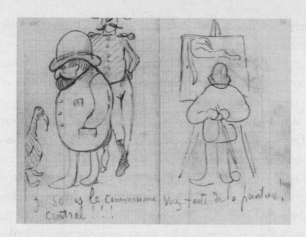

of Police. In the first, d'Ornano was shown as a short, pomp-
ous man in a bowler hat, bearded and with his hands in his
pockets. Behind him, in Gauguin's caricature, lounges a tall
gendarme. The commissioner looks down at a nervous-
looking turkey bearing a resemblance to Gauguin. 'Je souis
le Commissioner Central!!!' the commissioner announces in
his southern accent.

In the second caricature, he is inspecting a painting on an
easel. '*Vous faites de la peinture!*' he exclaims – 'You're doing
a painting!' On the canvas was an indecipherable squiggle.
Gauguin was inclined to have bizarre brushes with authority:
the following year he was mistaken for the fleeing conspirator
General Boulanger and arrested. Before too long he was to
be accused by d'Ornano of murdering his housemate, but
that was surely not the occasion recorded in this pair of
humorous drawings. More likely, the policeman came upon
the painter at work outside.

Unlike Vincent, Gauguin was braving the autumn chill.
Despite his disappointment with the Arles countryside, he
now produced a series of landscapes. Perhaps it was a way of
escaping the studio.

Gauguin still focused on the area around the washing-place on the Roubine du Roi canal. Having already painted a strange, stylized, almost nightmarish version of the subject, he now produced a much more normal everyday one. In the earlier picture the canal harboured alarming whirlpools and was flanked by bushes of fire; in this new work it shrank to its real — very modest — dimensions.

Four Arlésiennes are shown kneeling at their laundry, one of whom — wearing an orange skirt and yellow scarf — has Madame Ginoux's profile. The sky is overcast. Some of it could have been done outside, but it wasn't an exact depiction of what Gauguin could have seen in front of his eyes. The trees in the field across the canal were in full, light green leaf, and in late November they were certainly not. Gauguin did not have much regard for verisimilitude.

A second painting concentrated on the nondescript track on the other side of the canal. This more accurately records the sparse vegetation and bright wintry weather of that time in Arles. The sky is partly covered by white cloud, partly a light blue. A dog lounges on the path next to a long shadow thrown by a tree indicating the sun is low in the sky. In the background a little girl skips and a woman stands behind her. Laundry from the washing-place, invisible behind the bank, lies in the hedgerow.

A third Arles landscape depicts a farmhouse, with a medieval arch from the Alyscamps visible behind and a trio of cypresses. The soil in the foreground is the pinkish white of the chalky Crau; two dogs are wandering across it, one sniffing under the other one's tail. A couple of heads look over a hedge on the left, one of them that of an Arlésienne.

The composition is similar to a Breton landscape from earlier in the year which Theo especially admired. He compared it, following Vincent and Gauguin's musical analogies, to 'a beautiful symphony'. He rhapsodized over the rich harmonies of russet, red and green. There was nothing rich about this Arles landscape though. It was so thinly painted that it looked scratchy; the jute showed through in many places.

Gauguin was doing what Vincent had done in the months before he arrived – painting the scruffy urban fringe of Arles. But there was little suggestion that he loved this place as Vincent did. These pictures had an oddly desolate mood. As he had written to Bernard, he now found everything in Arles – the landscape, the people – 'small and mean'.

8. Painting a Family
23 November–4 December (continued)

Vincent, who could not bear the cold, stayed in the studio, where he started to work from life. His last few letters to Theo had been full of hints that he desperately wanted to paint people rather than landscapes. 'As for me,' he dropped into the last one, 'I am thinking more of Rembrandt than might appear from my studies.' And Rembrandt, to Vincent, was above all the master of the human face. He passionately admired the Dutch master's *Jewish Bride*. When he had gone to visit the museum in Amsterdam with his friend Anton Kerssemakers, he sat down in front of this picture and told his friend, 'You will find me here when you come back.' When Kerssemakers returned, Vincent looked up and declared:

Would you believe it – and I honestly mean what I say – I should be happy to give ten years of my life if I could go on sitting here in front of this picture for a fortnight, with only a crust of dry bread for food?

Vincent's problem with painting portraits was always persuading, or being able to afford to pay, someone to pose. He had underlined this difficulty again to Theo:

I regret – as always, how well you know – the scarcity of models and the thousand obstacles in overcoming that difficulty. If I were a different sort of man, and if I were better off, I could force the issue, but as it is I do not give in, but plod on quietly.

It was by portraits that he wished eventually to be judged: 'At the age of forty when I make a picture of figures or portraits in the way I feel it, I think this will be worth more than a more or less serious success at present.' Gauguin, of course, was now forty.

But, suddenly, Vincent started to paint a stream of pictures of people in rapid succession. He never explained what had changed or how he had managed it. But no fewer than five of the models came from the same family – the Roulins. He had already painted and drawn Joseph Roulin, the postal supervisor at the station, several times. Now he obtained sittings from Roulin's wife, two children and four-month-old baby.

One of these was another joint sitting, like the one with Madame Ginoux. Augustine-Alix Roulin came to the studio in the Yellow House and posed for both painters. Like her predecessor, Madame Roulin looked straight at Gauguin but did not make eye contact with Vincent. This was perhaps an indication that – even if Gauguin hadn't arranged the session – his presence was reassuring to her. She was nervous of Vincent, as her daughter later remembered. If the less alarming Gauguin hadn't been there too, perhaps she would have been reluctant to come to the studio alone.

She sat in a corner of the room. To her left was the glazed front door, now fixed shut, that faced Place Lamartine; to her right was the window that looked out on the Avenue de Montmajour. It was an evening sitting lit by the gas lamp on the wall; Gauguin's painting reproduces the shadows it threw behind the chair (it was the one in which Gauguin himself usually sat).

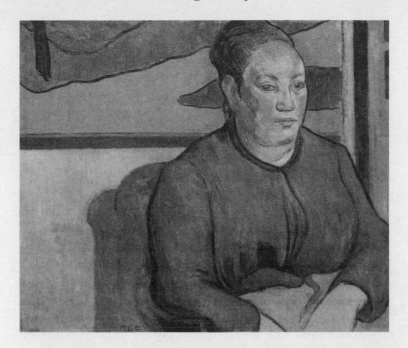

Both men produced paintings as a result of the sitting, and this time it was Gauguin, not Vincent, who depicted, more or less, what he saw in front of his eyes. His painting shows a stolid, dumpy woman. Behind her, his recently completed sunset picture, *Blue Trees*, hangs on the wall. But – it was the only modification he made – the canvas was greatly enlarged. The winding path and greenery of *Blue Trees* completely filled the upper left of Madame Roulin's portrait. Beside it was the window in the door, black with night.

Altogether, Vincent's picture was more thickly executed than Gauguin's and looked as if it had been more quickly done. He greatly admired the appearance of dashing speed in the portraits of the old Dutch master Frans Hals, in which heads, eyes, nose and mouth were 'done with a single stroke of the brush without any retouching whatever'. The yellow

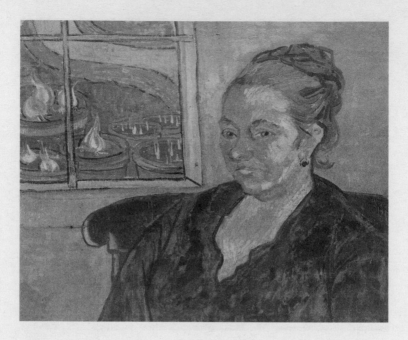

strokes indicating the fall of the gas light on the side of
Madame Roulin's head were slashed on in the manner of his
one-hour portrait of Madame Ginoux.

Vincent's painting also took more liberties with the facts
than Gauguin's. Unlike Gauguin, he didn't depict the darkness of the evening, nor Avenue de Montmajour, which lay
outside the window. Instead, he depicted the winding paths
of the gardens in Place Lamartine and, in front of them, giant
pots full of sprouting bulbs. Of course, even in Provence,
spring flowers do not grow in late November. Nor, though
he had once thought of putting tubs of oleander in front of
his door, was it likely that Vincent's window-boxes were so
well ordered. The sprouting bulbs were signs of new life.

Augustine Roulin had an earthy look that matched the
germinating bulbs in the pots outside. She resembled a human
tuber. To Vincent, though not apparently to Gauguin, the

woman in front of him was above all a mother. The golden and ochre colours that suffuse the picture were the result of the gas flame on the wall, but they also represented the glow of maternity.

On the evening she posed in the Yellow House, Augustine Roulin was about six weeks past her thirty-seventh birthday. She had been born in Lambesc, a little town between Aix and Marseilles, on 9 October 1851 (a year and a half before Vincent, and three years after Gauguin). She and her husband, Joseph, had had three children spread over two decades. The latest addition to the family had arrived only on 31 July.

It was likely that the four-month-old baby accompanied her mother to the sitting. The Roulins' house at 10 Rue de la Montagne des Cordes was a few minutes' walk from the Yellow House – the first turning on the right down Avenue de Montmajour. Gauguin made a couple of drawings of the infant, perhaps at this sitting. In one she was on her mother's knee, nestling against her left hand.

Even if Augustine had left the infant at home while she posed, it was obviously her motherhood that was uppermost in Vincent's mind while he painted her. Perhaps that gave him the idea for the brand-new painting project on which he now embarked with frantic energy. In the following days he painted all the Roulins, some more than once.

He gave an excited account of this unprecedented series to Theo when he next wrote, the following week:

I have made portraits of a *whole family*, that of the postman whose head I had done previously – the man, his wife, the baby, the young boy, and the son of sixteen, all of them real characters and very French, though they look like Russians. Size 15 canvases. You know how I feel about this, how I feel in my element, and that it consoles me up to a certain point for not being a doctor. I hope to get on with this and to be able to get more careful posing, paid for by portraits. And if I manage to do *this whole family* better still, at least I shall have done something to my liking and something individual.

This was a highly coded utterance, dependant on the fact that the brothers had talked and written to each other so much over the years that a single word was enough to sketch in a whole set of associations. Thus, when Vincent remarked that the Roulins 'look like Russians', he wished to remind Theo of a newspaper clipping from *L'Intransigeant* which Vincent had sent to him a couple of months before. It was from an article on the Russian novelist Dostoyevsky, published on 10 September, shortly after Vincent had moved into the Yellow House.

The author had described the great man: 'Dostoyevsky's face was that of a Russian peasant: flat nose, small flashing eyes, a broad forehead furrowed by scars and pimples, the temples dented as if shaped by a hammer.' He quoted a contemporary as saying, 'Never have I seen a similar expression of suffering on a human face.' That last statement in itself would have been enough to attract Vincent's attention.

The rest of this pen-portrait – the flat nose, the broad forehead – was reminiscent of the features of Joseph Roulin as painted and drawn by Vincent. Indeed, photographs of Dostoyevsky did resemble Roulin, down to the shape of the beard. And the great novelist himself, according to the newspaper piece, looked like a 'Russian peasant'.

That was part of the fascination of the Roulins as sitters: they were working class; not dirt poor, because Joseph had attained the rank of a minor functionary, but poor enough. The whole Roulin family lived on 135 francs a month, while Gauguin and Vincent in a miracle of economy were scraping

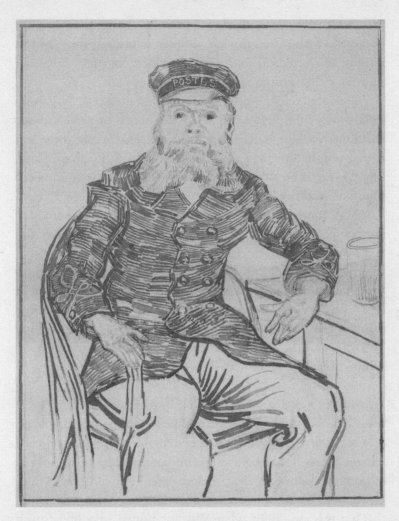

by on 150 each. Previously, Vincent had been spending 250 on his own and still ran out of cash.

Thus, in painting the Roulins, Vincent was studying an entire clan of ordinary people. That would have helped Theo to unpack the meanings compressed into the emphasis on painting a '*whole family*' and the apparently baffling statement that 'it consoles me up to a certain point for not being a doctor'. Vincent had not up to now expressed the slightest interest in a medical career, on paper at any rate. What he meant by this strange remark was complicated.

He wanted to help suffering mankind but also analyse those sufferers as Émile Zola did in his sequence of novels about the dynasty of the Rougon-Macquarts. The first of these had been published in 1871, and the series was not yet complete. *The Dream*, which Vincent had been reading at the end of October, was the eighteenth in the sequence.

Zola's fundamental notion was to follow the fortunes of the various members of this extended family through the years of the Second Empire. They were all descended from a woman named Adelaide Fouque, who came from a Provençal town called Plassans – Zola's name for his own native city of Aix – just as the Roulins both came from Lambesc, a few miles to the south-west of Aix.

In the novels, one of the characters Vincent found most sympathetic was Doctor Pascal Rougon:

He really proves that no matter how degenerate a race may be, it is always possible for energy and will-power to conquer fate. In his profession he found a force stronger than the temperament he had inherited from his family; instead of surrendering to his natural instincts, he followed a clear, straight path.

That was no doubt what Vincent hoped to achieve with his painting: to find in art a force stronger than his neurotic temperament. In a way, Zola's idea in his sequence of novels was diagnostic: he aimed to follow all the physical and mental permutations of an inherited flaw through several generations. 'Degeneration' was a fashionable term. There were theories circulating about the degeneration of nations and races. An

Italian theorist held that criminals were marked out by a certain physical type. Vincent was attracted by such ideas but frustrated by Gauguin's failure to fit into the schema: 'One thing that angered him,' the latter remembered, 'was to have to admit that I had plenty of intelligence, although my forehead was too small, a sign of imbecility.'

The ancestress of Zola's fictional clan, Adelaide Fouque, became deranged. In her descendants, mental instability took many forms – alcoholism in *L'Assommoir*; the self-destructive devotion to painting of Claude Lantier in *L'Oeuvre*; in *The Sin of Father Mouret*, religious fanaticism.

Vincent might well have felt a personal interest in all of these fictional disorders. He had read all the Rougon-Macquart novels and knew their contents intimately. They were often in his mind when he was working, in ways one might not guess unless he revealed what he was thinking.

Sketching at the Abbey of Montmajour in the summer with Milliet, Vincent saw an 'old, overgrown garden' and it made him think of the garden called *La Paradou* in *The Sin of Father Mouret*. As it happened, one of the farms up there was also called *Le Paradou* – 'paradise', in Provençal.

There were four other sitters in the Roulin family. Joseph was forty-seven, a decade older than his wife. Armand, the elder son, was seventeen and training as a blacksmith's apprentice in his parents' native town of Lambesc. The younger son, Camille, was eleven. And Marcelle, the baby, was just four months old. For these portraits, Vincent used an upright format, unlike the horizontal one that both he and Gauguin used for their pictures of Madame Roulin. This suggests that her sitting had come first, and then Vincent got the idea of painting the series.

The setting of her portrait was more specific, with the

window frame and the symbolic bulbs outside. All the others were shown against a plain colour. Behind Joseph was a lemon yellow, the complementary colour to the handsome dark blue of his *administration des postes* uniform. Armand was backed by mossy bluish-green. In the larger version of his portrait, Camille, whose shirt was a light blue, was backed by orange and red, divided by a line across the canvas. The backdrop to baby Marcelle, held up by her mother, was golden yellow. Thus, if the portraits had been hung together, they would have looked like a unified sequence – different colour chords, diverse personalities, but all harmonizing with each other.

It was hard to guess from their appearance at what time of day these portraits had been painted. But late afternoons, evenings or Sundays would have suited most of the Roulins best. During the day, Joseph was at work and Armand was in Lambesc, a train journey away. In the morning, Camille was at school (in France education was free and compulsory). The posing of the baby can only have been a rapid affair. The first picture that resulted – Madame Roulin holding the infant in her arms – looked like an action photograph, with little Marcelle vigorously waving her arms.

For the painting of Joseph, Vincent might not have needed a sitting at all, since he had given several sittings in the summer. Roulin, moreover, was bad at posing, awkward and self-conscious. 'He often has to carry loads you would call too heavy,' Vincent reported, with Roulin's family responsibilities in mind, 'but it doesn't prevent him, as he has the strong constitution of the peasant, from always looking well and even jolly.' The Roulins had been in financial straits when the baby was born.

Joseph must have agreed to have his family transformed into a cycle of paintings. That he did so, and accepted paintings in return, was testament to his friendship with Vincent. It also

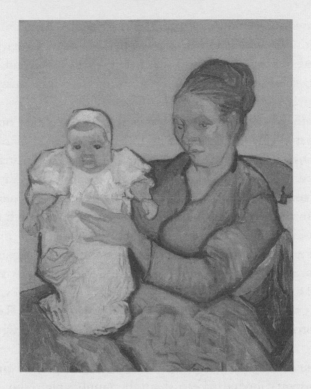

suggested that – like Second Lieutenant Milliet, Vincent's other improbable friend – he had become fired by his strange companion's passion for art.

Their bond, however, had other roots. Vincent's relationship with his father, Pastor Theodorus van Gogh, had been tense and several times had exploded into violent conflict. But Vincent had two of the most harmonious relationships of his life with older men of proletarian origin – Roulin, and the elderly Parisian dealer in paintings and artist's materials, Julien Tanguy, a simple man and ardent republican who had risen from humble origins and was still far from well-off.

Vincent painted Tanguy's portrait and compared him to

Socrates – ugly but wise – and his wife to the Greek philosopher's shrewish spouse, Xanthippe. Madame Tanguy regarded Vincent as a bad influence who took her husband off to the louche Café du Tambourin with its blousy and promiscuous *patronne*, Agostina Segatori.

With Roulin and Vincent it was much the same: he also compared this sitter repeatedly to Socrates – ugly as a satyr 'but such a good soul and so wise and so full of feeling and so trustful'. Vincent painted him and drank with him. Vincent reflected that Roulin was not quite old enough to be a father to him but nevertheless had 'a tenderness for me such as an old soldier might have for a younger one'.

Like Tanguy, Roulin had risen from working-class roots to a slightly more elevated position. As *entreposeur des postes*, he was in charge of unloading the sacks of mail at the station. It was a position of some authority and one of which Roulin was proud, carefully adding it to his name when he wrote a letter.

Vincent sometimes visited Roulin at his house, where the latter would invite him to share the family's soup, but they more often met elsewhere, because they had one other thing in common – Roulin, like Vincent, liked to drink. Roulin had refused payment for his sittings in the summer, but it cost Vincent to provide Roulin with food and drink while he sat (in one of the drawings he has a glass of beer to hand and looks more relaxed). But Vincent imagined that lingering and holding forth in cafés was more natural in the South. He believed Roulin was 'the reverse of a sot, his exaltation is so natural, so intelligent, and he argues with such sweep, in the style of Garibaldi'.

Roulin was one of those who believed that the present order favoured the bourgeoisie; the republic needed reform. Therefore, he would have encountered Camille Pelletan, the leader of the Radical Republican Party (whose programme was reform) and representative in the Chamber of Deputies for an area around Aix-en-Provence (his constituency included Roulin's hometown, Lambesc).

This younger Pelletan was a man after Roulin's heart, a believer in equality, fraternity and liberty. He even looked a little like the postal supervisor, with a wide face and spade-shaped thicket of beard. Pelletan loved bars and cafés and was never to be seen without his '*pipe prolétarienne*' (just like Roulin, Gauguin and Vincent). It seemed likely that young Camille Roulin was named after the younger Pelletan.

But, by 1888, Roulin was attracted by another political movement. He had become a supporter of General Georges Boulanger (the one whom Gauguin was later mistaken for). Boulanger appeared for the moment to be a new Napoleon: a military strong man and a reforming revolutionary. In retrospect, he looked like a potential fascist dictator; in 1888, he seemed the man of the hour.

In July, when the Roulins' new child was born, 'to the great indignation of this innocent baby's grandmother and some other members of the family', he named her after Boulanger's daughter, Marcelle. Moreover, anticlerical as he was republican, Roulin refused to have the child baptised and, when the family grumbled, held a feast anyway and performed the naming ceremony himself.

Vincent received a letter and 100 francs from Theo – for which Vincent sent thanks. 'It's rather more than time,' he began, 'for me to write you a collected letter for once.' Actually, it wasn't much more than a week since Vincent had written to his brother, but it was true that his letters of late had been far from collected.

'Our days pass in working,' he informed Theo:

working all the time, in the evening we are dead beat and go off
to the café, and after that, early to bed! Such is our life.

I think that we shall end up spending our evenings drawing and
writing, there is more work than we can manage. Of course it is
winter here with us too, though it's still very fine from time to
time. But I do not dislike trying to work from imagination, since
that allows me to stay in. It does not worry me to work in the heat
of a stove, but cold does not suit me, as you know.

Vincent's tone was calmer than it had been the week
before. Perhaps his luck in getting four new portrait models
had steadied him, temporarily at least. But anyone reading
Vincent's letters closely – as Theo did – would have noticed
a regular alternation of periods of despondency in which his
previous efforts seemed worthless to him with furious activity
and confidence.

After a period of tremendously hard work, there was a
phase of growing anxiety. At the moment he was painting
furiously – the *Sower*, the Roulins, one masterpiece after
another. In the weeks ahead his behaviour would become
alarmingly agitated. But, for the moment, his mood was
relatively steady:

If we can stand the siege, victory will come to us one day, in spite
of our not being among the people who are talked about. It is
rather a case that makes you think of the proverb – joy in public,
sorrow at home. What can you expect? Supposing that the fight is
still before us, we must just try to mature quietly.

But it was true that both artists were maintaining a
phenomenal rate of production. Gauguin was working a lot,
according to Vincent, and Vincent himself even more. Soon,
however, and despite Vincent's protestations that they never

did anything but paint, the two artists were about to make a couple of excursions, perhaps in an effort to get away from the studio in which they were constantly on top of one another. Besides, a circus had come to town.

On Sunday 2 December the Grand Menagerie of the Indies, under the direction of the brothers Pianet, was installed on the Boulevard de Lices, on the other side of Arles. It was open every day from 10 o'clock in the morning, and there was a performance every evening. Among the attractions were 'lions, lionesses, lion cubs, tigers, leopards, panthers, cougars, pumas, polar bears, hyenas, lamas, zebras, snakes, elephants and monkeys'.

The *Forum républicain* recommended its readers to go along to see the amazing evening shows: 'Messieurs Pianet are not content simply to present their animals, they have trained them.' On show were tigers presented in school desks; a lion playing leap-frog; a leopard pretending to be dead and a panther raising it up; and an elephant being served dinner by a monkey.

Gauguin filled twelve pages of his sketchbook with drawings of lions, lionesses and elephants, presumably during the day, when the animals were not being put through these preposterous routines. But the evening performances also left a deep impression on his memory.

He wrote of the circus three times, in his memoirs, *Avant et après*, in a newspaper he produced and wrote in Tahiti in 1899 (it never had more than 309 readers) and in a short story which mingled, as in a dream, all manner of events and people from Gauguin's life in Arles.

The first section of this story described the narrator's triumphant career in the army. Like Second Lieutenant Milliet, he served in Africa, where he hunted lions in the manner of Tartarin de Tarascon and eventually rose to the rank of

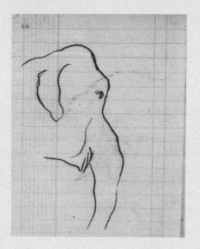 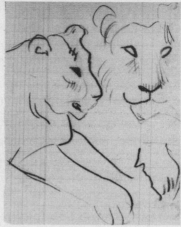

General. Then, leaving the army, the hero was transformed into a travelling-circus proprietor, just like the brothers Pianet and, after that, into 'Monsieur Louis', the brothel proprietor of Arles.

Gauguin's protagonist imagined wielding power over the savage animals in his menagerie, 'the most beautiful in the world'. Every evening he entered the lions' cage:

Cruelly, I harried them with the point of my goad to make them roar and spring, these terrible creatures who are called wild beasts, and I feasted myself on their smell. The beast in me was satiated and the crowd admired me.

As with the painting of *Woman with the Pigs*, sexuality and animality seemed linked in Gauguin's mind. This was, indeed, part of the fantasy life of the age. Art and literature abounded with animal and half-animal creatures – satyrs, fauns, mermaids, sirens – leading a more sensual and free existence than nineteenth-century Europeans. Gauguin's – and Loti's

– mirage of a tropical Eden full of dusky Eves was a similar daydream of escape.

In Gauguin's story, the narrator's relationship with the lordliest of all the beasts – 'the great royal tiger' – was positively erotic:

Nonchalantly he demands a caress, showing by movements of his beard and claws that he likes caresses. He loves me. I dare not strike him; I am afraid and he abuses my fear. In spite of myself I have to endure his disdain.

This intimacy was compared to that of the narrator and his spouse:

At night my wife seeks my caresses. She knows I am afraid of her and she abuses my fear. Both of us, wild creatures ourselves, lead a life full of fear and bravado, joy and grief, strength and weakness. At night, by the light of the oil lamps, half suffocated by the animal stenches, we watch the stupid, cowardly crowd.

So the menagerie was also 'an image of life and society' – the outcasts, wilder and freer, watched by the bovine public.

Vincent never described a visit to the menagerie but there are hints that he went there, too. Like the obelisk and the sculptures of St Trophime, the image of wild animals roaring in their cages got into his mind. His neighbours peered through his windows as if he were a 'curious beast'; when he entered an asylum, the noise of the other inmates struck him as 'terrible cries and howls like beasts in a menagerie'. Like Gauguin, he plainly identified with the captive creatures. But far from finding the spectacle erotic, Vincent seemed to have found the Grand Menagerie of the Indies horrifying.

★

It was now becoming uncharacteristically cold for Provence. On Tuesday there was a frost, and a much heavier one on Wednesday and Thursday. Gauguin got a message from Theo reporting that his package of work had arrived safely in Paris. He replied, remarking that he had been a bit worried the canvases might crack. Gauguin asked for Degas's address, which he had lost, so that he could write a letter in person thanking him for having been kind enough to buy a painting.

Meanwhile, Theo was extolling Gauguin's work to Wil. He felt that it was a good 'opportunity' for his brother to spend time in the company of such an artist as Gauguin. Degas himself 'greatly appreciated' Gauguin's new work and was even tempted to go down to see him at Arles. 'They're the lucky ones!' Degas had exclaimed to Theo, speaking of Vincent and Gauguin. 'That's the life!'

Of course, Degas was very wide of the mark in imagining that Gauguin and Vincent were living a rustic idyll. But if he had left his dusty studio on the slopes of Montmartre and gone south, it would have been intriguing. What would that crabby and caustic man, known for displays of acerbic wit at Parisian dinner parties, have made of the Yellow House?

Theo told Wil that it was in the 'depiction of the human figure' that Vincent found 'the best expression of his art' and that he seemed particularly pleased with the portraits he was currently doing. And well he might be. Vincent was in the middle of the most ambitious portrait-cycle of his career.

In a period of a week or two, he painted multiple images of all the Roulins except the father, Joseph, whose appearance he had already thoroughly explored. It seemed that he had at least two sittings each from the boys, Armand and Camille, as they appear in differing poses and clothes in several pictures. In the end there were two paintings of Armand and three of Camille. Madame Roulin appears in three and baby Marcelle in no fewer than five, two with her mother and three on her own.

The reason for this multiplication was partly to provide an extra picture to give to the Roulins. Giving the Roulins an oil painting in exchange for a few hours' work saved everybody's honour and was cheaper and easier for Vincent. In all, they ended up with six of Vincent's pictures – one of Joseph, one of his wife, one of each of their children and one of a magnificent bouquet of pink oleander. This had been painted in the summer, set in a majolica pot on the table in the Yellow House. Beside the flowers – the blooms that, to Vincent, 'spoke of love' – he had placed a couple of books, the uppermost being Zola's *La joie de vivre*.

These pictures – and others, a whole museum of modern art – decorated the Roulins' bedroom when they retired to Lambesc eight years later. But Joseph – afflicted by sciatica – soon accepted an offer from the Parisian dealer Ambrose Vollard for 450 francs a canvas. Had they waited a little longer, the Roulins would have got much more.

Vincent painted Armand Roulin on two large canvases – size 15, or 65 × 54cm – and, as with all the Roulin pictures, he reverted to ordinary canvas, not Gauguin's jute. For one thing, the jute was running out and, for another, in this special series of portraits, Vincent wanted to achieve delicacy and precision. The jute had never suited him as well as it did Gauguin.

The painting of Armand that his parents were given shows the seventeen-year-old in a smart get-up, probably his best clothes: a yellow jacket, black waistcoat, neck-tie, and hat at a jaunty angle. His features, however, are melancholy (or perhaps, as often with portrait sitters, just bored). A moustache grows with touching sparseness on his upper lip. This mood is stronger in the other picture, the one that Vincent kept.

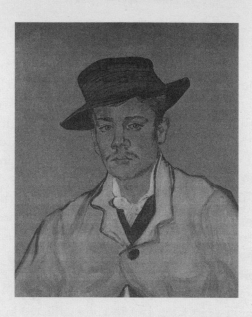

In this version, Armand seems younger. The green background is darker; his jacket and hat are black. Though the hat
looks the same – how many hats would a teenage Provençal
blacksmith's apprentice possess? – it was worn at a more
sober angle.

   Armand's younger brother, the eleven-year-old Camille,
is also lost in thought – or terrible tedium – in the biggest of
the paintings Vincent produced of him. He is sitting on one
of the rush-bottomed chairs, his arm over the back, his mouth
gaping open, staring into space.

   Camille looks much more alert in the other pose that
Vincent documented, producing two versions. This was on
a smaller canvas and shows only the boy's head and shoulders.
He is wearing a large blue cap and looking intently past the
painter. Behind him, yellow brush strokes radiate, as from the
sun. The sense of potential – the same quality symbolized by
those sprouting bulbs – is intense.

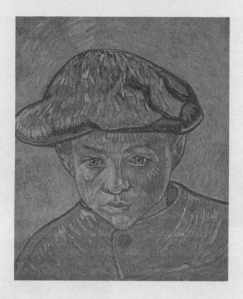

It was implicit in Vincent's idea of painting a whole family that he might portray the Roulins and their progeny at intervals through time. If he had lived out a full term, Vincent could have depicted Armand's transformation from a handsome if callow young fellow starting out in life to a heavy-jowelled police officer in colonial Tunisia. Armand died at the end of the Second World War. Camille's destiny was to become a shipping clerk for the Service des Messageries Maritimes, dying young, in 1922, as a result of war wounds. Madame Roulin lived until 1930, outliving her husband, Joseph, by twenty-eight years. She became a white-haired matriarch, still slightly resembling her portraits. But even if Vincent had had a normal lifespan, he could scarcely have chronicled the entire life of the baby, Marcelle, who lived to be ninety-two, not dying until 1980.

Vincent's pictures of this robust infant were even more packed with a sense of future possibilities than those of her

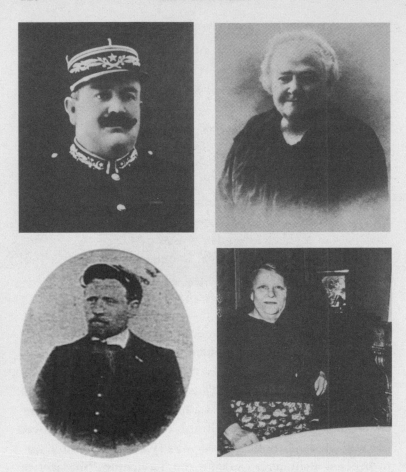

older brothers. He had planned to paint her as a newborn, close to 31 July: 'If I can get the mother and father to allow me to do a picture of it,' he had written to Wil, 'I am going to paint a baby in a cradle one of these days.'

The sight of this baby – and babies generally – moved Vincent greatly. It brought him up against the mystery of existence. 'A child in the cradle if you watch it at leisure,' he wrote after Marcelle was born, 'has the infinite in its eyes.'

That was in August, but it was not until now, at the onset of winter, that Vincent finally made his first painting of the youngest Roulin.

Once he started, he could hardly stop. First he painted, from life, little Marcelle – so ebullient she was almost springing out of Augustine's arms: a tiny parcel of compacted energy, just like a seed. From that he made another, larger painting of the mother and child, tracing the face of each from the first paintings.

Tracing was a technique used by Gauguin – for instance, to transfer his drawing of Madame Ginoux on to canvas for his *Night Café*. It was frequently used by Degas to construct his own paintings and pastels: 'People borrow a great deal from Degas,' Gauguin observed, 'and he does not complain. There is so much in his bag of tricks that one pebble more or less doesn't matter to him.' This particular device, it seemed, was passed from Degas to Gauguin to Vincent.

The result was a painting which was broader, less closely observed than either of the two studies from life on which it was based. But it was not, on the other hand, really done from memory. The subject matter was hallowed – and hackneyed – in Western art: mother and baby, which had blended over the centuries into the sacred theme of Madonna and Child.

Vincent then went on to paint three more pictures of Marcelle, head and shoulders only, documenting her solemn baby's stare and her admirably chubby cheeks and arms against a light-green backdrop. If her mother, Augustine, resembled a human tuber, here was the equivalent in flesh and blood of a seed. 'Young corn,' Vincent had reflected long before, 'has something inexpressibly pure and tender about it, which awakens the same emotion as the expression of a sleeping baby, for instance.'

★

When Vincent had written those words, he had had a humble home of his own with a woman and children for company. That was precisely what made the subject of the Roulins and baby Marcelle so emotionally perilous for him.

This family life had lasted for one and three-quarter years, from the day Vincent – shortly after his father had thrown him out of the family house in Etten – moved in with the prostitute Cristina or 'Sien' Hoornik in January 1882. They lived together in a small studio in The Hague.

Sien already had a four-year-old daughter named Maria, and from 2 July there was a fourth member of the household. On that day, Sien gave birth to a son after a difficult delivery which required forceps. He was named Willem. Vincent saw the infinite in his eyes, too (Willem grew up to become a railway employee, unpopular with his colleagues in the 1930s because of his fascist views).

Willem was another man's child, but that did not stop Vincent from being ecstatically excited by his birth. He sat next to Sien's hospital bed and thought of 'that eternal poetry of Christmas night with the infant in the stable, as the old Dutch painters conceived it'. Vincent thought of the child as radiance, like the sun, 'a light in the darkness, a brightness in the middle of a dark night'.

The family moved to a slightly larger apartment next door. This was in many ways the predecessor of the Yellow House – lovingly furnished with simple furniture and proudly described to Theo: 'The studio looks so much like the real thing, or so it seems to me, plain grey-brown wallpaper, scrubbed floorboards, muslin stretched on slats across the windows, everything bright.' Vincent's studies, prints and books lay all around.

There was 'a little living room with a table, a few kitchen

chairs, an oil stove, a large wicker armchair for the woman in the corner by the window'. Next to the mother's chair was placed a small iron cradle with a green cover – an object Vincent could not look at 'without emotion'.

This earlier studio in The Hague seemed 'a young home in full swing'. Vincent summed it up in a phrase: '*a studio with a cradle*'. A baby's potty was on the floor – there was no sense of 'stagnation'; everything seemed to bustle and stir with life. (The Yellow House, obviously, was a studio without a cradle.)

So it was then that Vincent experienced a life with a woman and children: what he had most yearned for:

I don't know if you've ever had that feeling which sometimes forces a sort of sigh or groan from one when one is alone: oh God, where is my wife, oh God, where is my child? Is being alone really living?

Fifteen months after writing those words, Vincent left his family and departed to work in the dismal northern Dutch heathland of Drenthe, where he again suffered 'that loneliness that a painter has to bear, whom everybody in such isolated areas regards as a lunatic, a murderer, a tramp, etc, etc'. Leaving Sien and the children was perhaps the hardest decision he had ever had to make. Such choices, he thought, made the heart 'shrivel with pain'.

From the beginning, all the forces of respectable society had been opposed to Vincent's liaison with Sien. When he had first arrived in The Hague, Vincent had had some useful lessons from his cousin by marriage, the painter Anton Mauve. As soon as he discovered Vincent's relationship with Sien, Mauve cut his ties with Vincent and his old employer,

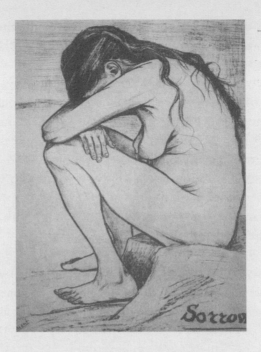

Tersteeg, and denounced Vincent violently in front of Sien
and the children.

Theo and their father, Theodorus, were appalled by Vincent's intention to marry her. As far as Theo was concerned,
a relationship with a woman from the lower orders was one
thing – he had one himself at this time – but marriage was a
step too far. That, to Vincent, was an immoral point of view.

Prostitution, Vincent felt, would have been bad if society
were 'pure and well-regulated'. As it was, materialism and
sanctimonious morality ruled; prostitutes seemed more like
'sisters of mercy' to an outcast such as Vincent. He felt no
scruple about associating with them; he liked their company.
There was something 'human' about them. But he did not
marry Sien.

The partnership between Vincent and Sien was under

attack on several fronts. If Vincent alienated Theo, there was a danger that his allowance would be cut off; on the other hand, the money was not enough for a family of four, with the expense of Vincent's materials. Sien's family suggested she should leave this poor provider and live with someone better off – or perhaps, as Vincent put it, 'fall back into her former errors'.

Under these pressures, Sien's mood deteriorated: 'At times her temper is such that it is almost unbearable for me – violent, mischievous – I am sometimes in despair.' Sien's view was not recorded, but it is likely she had to put up with tirades from Vincent. By the middle of 1883, the household was falling apart. The choice, as Vincent saw it, was between hearth, home and family on the one side and his vocation as an artist on the other. He could not pursue both.

He said goodbye to Sien and the children at the railway station on 11 September 1883 and took the train north. It was a decision that Vincent saw quite explicitly in terms of Christ's agony in the Garden of Gethsemane. 'There is no anguish greater than the soul's struggle between duty and love.' On the other hand, his own future – his vocation as an artist – was 'a cup that will not pass away from me unless I drink it. So *fiat voluntas*' – Thy will be done. Vincent, of course, went on to become a painter.

Thursday 6 December was the day of St Nicholas. In Arles, that always marked the beginning of the Christmas season. A special section of the marketplace was allocated to the merchants of *santons*. These were a charming product of local folk art: small, brightly coloured figures made to people the Christmas crèches which were hugely popular in Provence and in many parts of the Southern Catholic world.

Made from fired clay, papier mâché, cardboard or some

similar material, they represented the gamut of local society – laundresses, shepherds, bakers, grocers – all gathered around the holy family, the baby Jesus and the crib. Most of them were miniature ceramic sculptures, exactly the kind of thing that Gauguin produced in an avant-garde mode. A common *santon* figurine was a woman at a cradle – *la femme au berceau* – a contemporary mother-figure equivalent to the Blessed Virgin. Special songs known as *berceuses* were sung to the crèches, either in French or in Provençal.

These cribs, sometimes containing many figurines, appeared in churches and also in private houses. Did the secular, republican Roulins have one? In Arles, the Christmas season lasted until the beginning of February. Before it was over, Vincent heard Joseph sing a lullaby to baby Marcelle.

At that moment, Roulin reminded him half of an old revolutionary, half of a mother:

When he sang to his child, his voice took on a strange timbre in which one could hear the voice of a woman rocking a cradle or of a sorrowing wet-nurse, and then another trumpet sound like a clarion call to France.

Was it a Christmas song? There was one suitable for a male voice: the '*Berceuse*' or, in Provençal, '*Bressarello*', composed by Theodore Aubanel in 1865 in which St Joseph soothed the infant Christ to sleep.

There were also special Christmas dramas – part farce, part miracle play – like animated versions of the crèches. In January, Vincent went to the local theatre, the Folies Arlésiennes, and saw a play from which he mainly recalled, again, a lullaby. An old woman was led before the mystic crib of the Christ child:

She began to sing in her quavering voice, and then the voice changed, changed from the voice of a witch to that of an angel, and from an angel's voice to a child's, and then the answer came in another voice, strong and warm and vibrant, the voice of a woman behind the scenes.

But by the time he heard that, the great crisis of his life had come. It struck as he was working on a picture he called *La Berceuse*.

Saturday the eighth was the night of the most successful and eagerly awaited ball of the Arles winter season so far. It was given by the society of the local mutual assistance fire brigade at the theatre of Arles. Dancing began at ten in the evening and carried on until one in the morning, when there was a pause; then it continued with even more liveliness and animation, especially in the quadrilles.

According to *L'Homme de bronze*, an American quadrille executed by two groups – one of young men, the other of charming young women in ravishing costumes of pale blue, white and mauve – received acclaim. A pretty quadrille in the military mode, danced by the same two groups of dancers, was dedicated to the man of the moment, Genéral Boulanger. This especially attracted the attention of the officers of the garrison, who were present that evening.

Under the baton of its conductor, the orchestra played to a marvel. The revelry carried on until five in the morning. If such evenings occurred more often, *L'Homme de bronze* reflected, the young people of the town would have less reason to complain of the monotony of the winter in Arles. Jeanne Calment, then a girl of thirteen, remembered such balls over a century later. Her white lace gown was made by one of the best dressmakers in town, Madame Chambourgon.

She recalled dancing to waltzes, polkas, mazurkas and quadrilles while the parents sat around the dance floor. 'It was fun,
great fun,' she recalled. 'I can see the faces now!'

One person who did not carry away entirely pleasant memories of the ball was Vincent. In the next couple of weeks, he
painted a picture of a ball at Arles from memory. It showed
the theatre, with figures looking down from the balcony
above, several of them wearing the distinctive képi of the
French army. The room was brightly illuminated by gas lights,
whose globes hang from the ceiling like artificial suns.

The crowd, however, was as much nightmarish as jolly.
Vincent's viewpoint was from immediately behind a row of
women in Arlésienne costume, each with a long ribbon of
dark blue attached to the little headdress on the crown of her
head. This device of placing heads in the extreme foreground
of a picture was derived from Japanese art. It had been used
by both Gauguin and Bernard.

But in Vincent's picture the viewer felt jammed up against
the bodies of these strangers, nose almost buried in the luxuriant black hair of the nearest Arlésienne. Beyond this row of
women, there is a sea of faces, almost all female and almost
all looking down or away. Madame Roulin, on the right of
the picture, who glances over a little anxiously, is the only
person in this dense mass of individuals who makes eye
contact.

Just behind her is a man in a red Zouave képi. To her left,
a woman in red smiles to herself; otherwise, in all the faces
Vincent painted – some strangely distorted – there is no sign of
enjoyment. The picture gives two contradictory impressions
– of painful exclusion and equally painful, indeed claustrophobic, proximity. Both foreshadowed Vincent's looming
crisis.

★

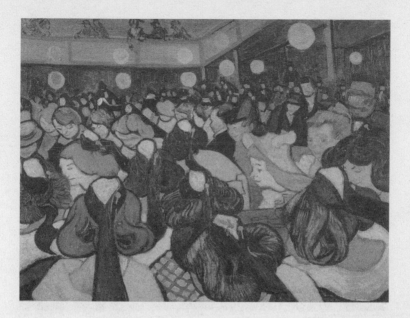

In the first weeks of December, Gauguin composed his own equivalent to Vincent's paintings of the gardens in the Place Lamartine, several of which hung on his bedroom wall. Gauguin's picture was – more or less – of the view from his bedroom window. When he opened the shutters, he looked down on the central garden of the three in the square, the one that had an oval pond in it. At the entrance to the little park there was a gate and, behind that, a path that curved around the water's edge. And that was what he showed in this new painting.

This was very different from Vincent's paintings of late summer and early autumn, which had flowering oleander, women carrying parasols, pairs of lovers, strollers and idlers reading the newspaper in the open air. Gauguin painted a winter garden. The trees were now wrapped in their protective cones of bamboo against the frost – which returned on Sunday

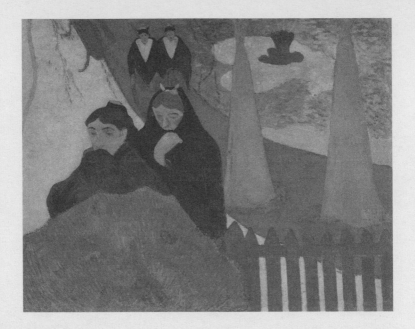

9 December, the day after the ball. Gauguin made a number of drawings in his sketchbook for different features in the painting – the wrapped trees, the park bench, the Arlésiennes who are standing in the park, the little fountain, the pond which reflected blue sky and white cloud. A few dry leaves still fluttered on the trees.

There were four Arlésiennes in the final picture – two standing in the middle distance like Tweedledum and Tweedledee, and two close to the gate, muffling their faces against the biting wind. The one in front, looking towards the Yellow House, is Madame Ginoux. But the most extraordinary aspect of this picture is the bush which she is standing behind.

If the haystack in Gauguin's painting of pigs took on unmistakably female curves and bulges, the bush in this picture was even more improbably masculine. From its green, bristling centre there looked out a male face – two eyes, a nose and a moustache. But was it accidental or intentional? And who was it supposed to be?

Gauguin never discussed or described this picture, nor did Vincent. They were sending far fewer letters. Vincent especially, who had sometimes sent Theo more than one letter a day, was strangely silent. Often, when Vincent did not communicate, it was because there was something he did not want to discuss.

Once again, for the third and last time, Vincent and Gauguin shared a sitting. A middle-aged man with black hair and a white face posed for the two artists. But, this time, it was Vincent who sat directly in front of the sitter and made eye contact, Gauguin who sat to the side.

The sitter peers at the painters, his eyes half-closed, his head tilted back, apparently appraising, perhaps a little suspicious. Behind his head there is an aura of radiance on the wall which suggests that once more the gas light in the studio was on during the sitting. It also recalled one of Vincent's ambitions for his portraits: 'I want to paint men and women with that something of the eternal which the halo used to symbolize, and which we seek to confer by the actual radiance and vibration of our colourings.'

Who was he? He was not, as was later thought, Joseph Ginoux, since Ginoux had grey hair and a moustache. There was one clue: in Gauguin's strange short story, the brothel-keeper, Monsieur Louis, posed for his portrait. Most other incidents in the story were vaguely based on reality – the arrival of the circus in Arles, for example. So, perhaps, 'Louis' really did sit in the Yellow House. The irony of Gauguin's picture suggested it might be him.

In it, the man is seen slightly from above – pale, sickly and

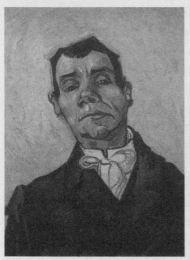 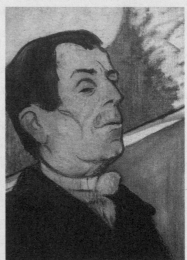

sleazy-looking; he is wearing a frock coat and cravat, which were signs of prosperity. And Gauguin too gave him a saintly attribute: a halo in the form of a big yellow sun-disc from a canvas on the wall behind.

This portrait was one of Gauguin's best done in a natural-istic manner, but he himself did not seem interested by it. He did not bother to finish it, nor sign it, and it was still in the Yellow House, along with his fencing masks, when Vincent came to clear the place out in the spring.

Vincent's portrait was part of another series. After carrying out his long-nurtured plan to paint the baby Marcelle Roulin, Vincent was apparently putting into action another project from the summer. When he first painted Marcelle's father, Joseph Roulin, he had had the idea of doing a series of similar portraits of ordinary working men – the kind of people to be found in Joseph Ginoux's bar, the Café de la Gare (Monsieur Louis, in Gauguin's story, was greeted respectfully in the local café).

Vincent had laid out the project to Theo:

That's what I'm good at, doing a fellow roughly in one sitting. If I wanted to show off, my boy, I'd always do it, drink with the first comer, paint him, and that not in water colours but in oils, on the spot, in the manner of Daumier.

If I did a hundred like that, there would be some good ones among them. And I'd be more of a Frenchman and more myself, and more of a drinker. It does tempt me so – not drinking, but painting tramps. What I gained by it as an artist, should I lose that as a man? If I had the faith to do it, I'd be a notable madman; now I am an insignificant one.

In the weeks leading up to Christmas, it seemed Vincent did just that. It is not obvious why he had waited so long, nor how he overcame the problems that had previously prevented him from painting these people. One answer might have been that, with Gauguin contributing to the finances of the Yellow House and also imposing a little order on them, there was more cash about. These sitters don't seem to have been paid in pictures – there was only one version of each work – so they must have been rewarded for their time with money, or – conceivably – drinks.

Vincent painted a couple of fellows who looked exactly as one would imagine Ginoux's customers might look: down-at-heel and far from wealthy. One of them was wearing a swept-back hat and smoking a pipe; another was a young lad who might have been Armand Roulin after a shave and wearing his everyday clothes. The lines of the nose and the jaw were the same. It was one of Vincent's contentions about painting people that, 'one and the same person may furnish motifs for very different portraits'. That was certainly true of the other two pictures of the eldest Roulin boy; maybe this was a third.

Vincent had long pondered the question of portraits. His stated ambition the previous year was to do 'a really good one'. He meant, it appeared from a letter to Theo written at the beginning of September, 'portraiture with the thought, the soul of the model in it'.

Throughout the history of painting, most portraits had been produced because someone had paid for them – generally the sitter or the sitter's spouse or parents, or subjects if they were a ruler. At any rate, a portrait served a practical purpose – to preserve a record of a certain person's appearance. Vincent was concerned with something different: 'the thought, the soul of the model'. Of course, the greatest artists – Rembrandt, Goya, Titian – had always dealt with those. But Vincent was entirely focused on what one might call the spiritual aspects of portraiture.

Much later, not long before he died, Vincent put the same point in a different way:

I *should like* – mind you, far be it for me to say that I shall be able to do it, although this is what I am aiming at – I *should like* to paint portraits which would appear after a century to people living then as apparitions. By which I mean that I do not endeavour to achieve this by a photographic resemblance, but by means of our impassioned expressions.

This was a thought Vincent perhaps derived from Carlyle: all living people are no more than ghosts, 'shaped into a body, an appearance, and that fade away again into air and invisibility. This is no metaphor, this is simple scientific *fact*.'

Vincent dreamt of an artist who would paint portraits the way a writer such as Guy de Maupassant described his characters or as Monet painted any landscape, however humble, that took his fancy. Similarly, Vincent thought of painting any person who interested him – no matter who they were or who they were related to. His attitude to portraiture recalled his previous ambitions to become a pastor and – later, surprisingly – a doctor. It was diagnostic, but also priestly.

Gauguin heard a great deal of Vincent's views about portraiture, as about everything else. The topic was discussed, Vincent recalled, 'until our nerves were strained to the point of stifling all human warmth'. The odd thing was that Gauguin went along, for a while, with Vincent's obsession.

Normally, portraits were not an important part of his art. The subject was not suited to a painter such as Gauguin, who could exclaim with satisfaction, 'So much for exactitude!' He painted himself frequently, and with brilliance, but even there he was aiming often not at truth but at drama – for example, himself in a role as Jean Valjean.

During this period in early December, however, Gauguin turned out portraits which fitted Vincent's prescription: such as an old chap, with white hair, beard and stick, who could well have been another of Ginoux's customers, perhaps an elderly peasant named Patience Escalier whom Vincent had painted in the summer, except now his beard was longer and he was not wearing a hat. But since Vincent had painted him in August and it was now December, the man might well have become somewhat shaggier.

9. Portrait of the Artist
4–15 December

Around this time, the two painters in the Yellow House each produced a self-portrait to send to Charles Laval in the north. Laval's own portrait of himself – impatiently anticipated by Vincent – had arrived, with Bernard's sea painting, in mid November. Vincent thought it 'extremely good', 'very bold, very distinguished'. He admired the sitter's gaze through his glasses – 'such a frank gaze'.

Vincent now produced a portrait in reciprocation, and dedicated it '*á l'ami Laval*', to his friend Laval. It said something for the seriousness with which Vincent took his views about the brotherhood of artists that he deemed this man, whom he had never met, a friend. The self-portrait was only the second Vincent had done since he came to Arles (not counting a study of himself walking down the road to Tarascon, carrying his painting equipment). In the portrait he had sent to Gauguin in September, he had presented himself in character, as a bonze.

This was a more straightforward representation of Vincent as he looked three months later. His hair and beard had grown considerably in the interval and were a little unruly. Otherwise, Vincent presents an unexpectedly elegant appearance, his collar and jacket taking on an almost stylish turn. A stray lock juts out oddly across his right ear.

Here, Vincent seemed, as he put it later, 'charged with electricity'. This was Vincent as he looked in the weeks before

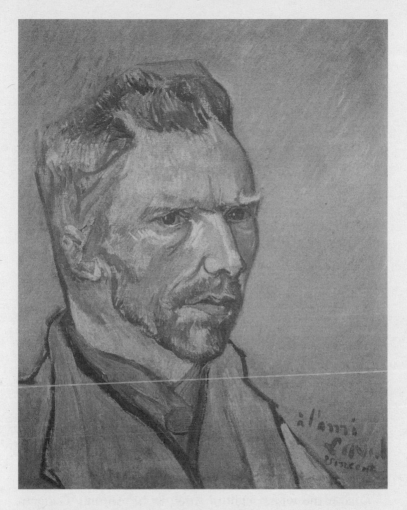

Christmas: nervy, thin, quite youthful, his eyes glittering, their gaze intense. He fairly bristled.

In his new self-portrait, Gauguin also looks quite unlike his earlier presentation of himself as a hunted criminal. He now appears younger, fitter, fatter, sleek, almost placid and pleased with himself. (Vincent attributed this evident improvement in Gauguin's well-being to his sojourn in the Yellow House.)

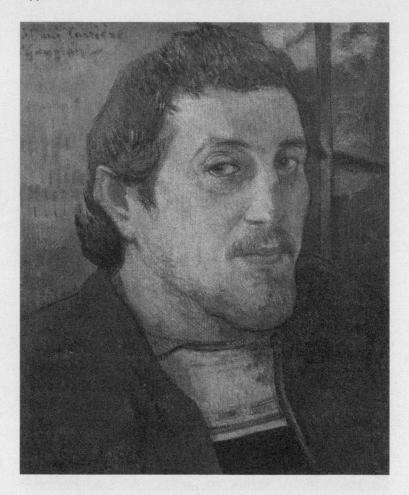

Against the winter chill of Arles, in his portrait, Gauguin is wearing not only a jacket but also one of his Breton pullovers. He sits in front of the window, but the view outside doesn't much resemble the Place Lamartine; there seem to be blue mountains in the distance. Was it a prospect of distant Martinique, where Laval and Gauguin had suffered before, and Gauguin intended to go again?

*

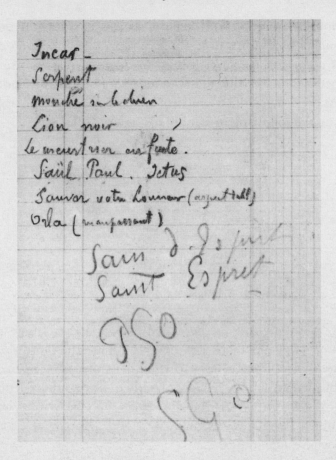

Gauguin made a series of cryptic notes to himself on a double page of his sketchbook. They seem to date either from those wintry December days in Arles or from January, when he had returned to Paris. In either case, these jottings referred to those days with Vincent, and to Gauguin's own most intimate thoughts, in a code so terse as to be almost unbreakable.

A painter, he had come to think, was much more than simply someone who made pictures. An artist might take on a series of interlocking and opposing roles: saint and demon, saviour and criminal, madman and martyr. Several of these thoughts came from observing Vincent, but something else was going on: Gauguin was in the process of transforming Vincent into a mythic figure in his own imaginative world.

At the top of a right-hand page in his sketchbook, Gauguin wrote the following in a column:

> Incas
> Snake ['serpent']
> Fly on the Dog
> Black Lion
> The Murderer in Flight
> Saül Paul. Ictus
> Save your honour (money canvas)
> Orla (Maupassant)

Underneath that list he added in a different, larger and fainter script – perhaps at a different time – the words '*Sain d'esprit, Saint Esprit*'. Below that, in the same, lighter pen, he wrote his signature, 'PGo', and then three others letters, 'SGo'. On the other page, in darker ink, he wrote '*Ictus*' again, enclosed by a ballooning oval shape. Above were some indecipherable squiggles.

What did it all mean? Some of these references were so enigmatic – the Fly on the Dog, for example – that it is doubtful that anyone else would ever be able to make them out. There were too many black lions around to know which one he meant (several on the soot-encrusted façade of Saint-Trophime). Other clues were a little easier to guess. 'Incas' was a reference to Gauguin's own myth of himself as a 'savage from Peru'. The Inca emperor came from the sun and returned to the sun, as Gauguin himself intended to go back to the tropics.

One set of jottings centred on Gauguin's name. He wrote 'Saül Paul'. St Paul was of course his patron saint. Before Paul became a holy man, he had been a persecutor of the Christians, under the name of Saul. In the doodled signatures below, Gauguin seemed to hint at the same ambivalence: a flip from sinful to sacred. Because he formed his 'G' like an 's' and his 'p' with a huge flourish behind the upward stroke, 'SGo' was just like 'PGo' – with the first two letters transposed. 'SGo' suggested 'Saint' or 'Saül' Gauguin', and 'PGo' sounded like slang for penis, so by changing the position of one letter, he transformed himself from prick to apostle.

The word 'snake' fitted the pattern. The following year, Gauguin painted himself as the most notorious of snakes – the tempting serpent in the Garden of Eden. In the self-portrait he is wearing a halo and casually holding a snake or serpent between his fingers like a cigarette: saint and Satan.

In the background, apples dangle; in the foreground, there are leaves like those in a medieval painting. But, despite his halo, simultaneously, Gauguin himself is a satanic serpent, his head growing from a long, jutting, reptilian neck (much like that of the snake in the scene of the Fall carved on Saint-Trophime). Gauguin gave this portrait various titles over the ears: 'Portrait-indictment of the Artist', 'Unkind Character Sketch', 'The Alpha and the Omega'. This was in accord with Gauguin's final view of himself, recorded near the end of his life:

No one is good, no one is evil; everyone is both, in the same way and in different ways.

I wish to love, and I cannot. I wish not to love and I cannot. You drag your double along with you, and yet the two contrive to get on together. I have been good sometimes; I do not congratulate myself because of it. I have been evil often; I do not repent it.

Next to 'Saül Paul' came the strange word '*Ictus*', which was repeated inside the oval bubble on the opposite page. Now, '*ictus*' was derived from *ichthys*, the Greek word for 'fish'. It was used, together with a fish-shaped drawing, by the Early Christians as a symbol for Christ, the fisher of men, several of whose apostles were fishermen.

Gauguin and Vincent seemed to use it as a symbol for themselves: suffering evangelists for a new art (Vincent thought his socialist friend Tanguy had much in common, 'in resignation and long suffering', with the ancient Christian slaves and martyrs). Later, a little drawing of a fish with the word '*Ictus*' appeared at the end of one of Vincent's letters to his friend – like a password exchanged between secret agents – next to a reference to painting *La Berceuse*.

One of Vincent's largely unfulfilled ambitions was to paint 'portraits of saints and holy women from life which would have seemed to belong to another age'. These would be 'drawn from the bourgeoisie of today and yet would have had something in common with the very earliest Christians'. In other words, he wanted to make pictures of ordinary people with the spiritual force of religious art. Shortly, Vincent was to attempt just that.

Gauguin had this same aim – to paint modern people as saints, martyrs, angels and demons – and found it easier to achieve. He had already done something of the sort that September with his *Vision*, in which Breton women watched Jacob wrestle with the angel. In the future, he was to produce many works filled with biblical imagery – Eve, Eden, the Fall, the Nativity, the Agony in the Garden, the Crucifixion. Ultimately, Vincent, with his Protestant devotion to facts he saw before him, found it impossible to paint such subjects. Gauguin, educated in a seminary, found it much easier.

The words – '*Sain d'esprit, Saint Esprit*' – that Gauguin

wrote above his signatures PGo and SGo made up a French pun: 'healthy in spirit, Holy Spirit'. According to Gauguin, Vincent wrote those lines on the wall of the Yellow House. And it is probable that he did, or at least spoke them, because they echoed Wagner's credo, which had greatly struck Vincent in the summer: 'I also believe in the sanctity of the spirit and in artistic truth whole and indivisible.' This was the faith of the Yellow House.

After Vincent's death, Gauguin wrote a story called 'Pink Shrimps'. It was set in Paris in the dead of winter, near Christmas time. The snow was falling hard. Among the pedestrians hurrying along a street in Montmartre was 'a shivering man, bizarrely outfitted'. This lowly figure was wearing a goatskin coat, rabbit-skin hat, his red beard 'bristling', but he showed signs of inward nobility in his 'white and harmonious hand' and 'blue eyes so clear, so childlike'. It was Vincent van Gogh.

Vincent enters a shop dealing – like Tanguy's – in cheap pictures, where he manages to sell a small still life of pink shrimps. The dealer grudgingly gives him a little money so he can pay his rent. As he makes his way home, a starving prostitute, just released from prison, begs for help. 'The beautiful white hand emerged from the overcoat.' And, like Saint Francis, Vincent gave her his only money, then, rapidly, as if ashamed he fled away, 'his stomach empty'.

This never happened. In Paris, Vincent did not have to pay rent, as he lived with Theo. For the same reason, that was one period of his life when Vincent would not have gone hungry. It was a fable.

Another of Gauguin's stories related Vincent's experiences in the Borinage, his family's attempts to put him in an asylum and his preaching. In the story, Vincent – through his devoted nursing – brings back to life a miner who had been left for dead after an explosion, in a conscious echo of Christ's miraculous resurrection of Lazarus.

If he could have read these stories, Vincent would have been horrified. Far from seeing himself as a saint or Christ, Vincent was alarmed even by high praise of his work, when it came. His view of his role was humble, 'altogether secondary'. He was too truthful, too wedded to the facts, too Dutch to imagine himself a saint. 'Pictures and writings,' Gauguin pointed out, 'are portraits of their authors.' And, of course, the author of these poetic, factually vague, mythologizing stories was Gauguin himself.

Around the beginning of December, Gauguin had begun a portrait of Vincent in paint, not words. Vincent reported its start in a curiously indirect fashion. He did not count it, he told Theo, among Gauguin's 'useless undertakings' (raising the question of which of Gauguin's projects he did think useless). This portrait turned out to be a strange piece of work.

Not only was it unlike Vincent's paintings of himself – naturally, one's image of oneself might differ from the view of others – but it was also quite dissimilar to the way that other painters had depicted him. Vincent had been portrayed by his Australian friend John Russell, and by Toulouse-Lautrec, who showed him in a café with a glass of absinthe before him.

There were no photographs of him after the age of eighteen, perhaps because he strongly disliked photography. When, at the beginning of October, he was sent a photograph of his mother, he made a painting from it, as he could not stand its grey and black monotony. Only one snap of the adult Vincent survived, from the back, hunched over a table next to the Seine at Asnières talking to Emile Bernard.

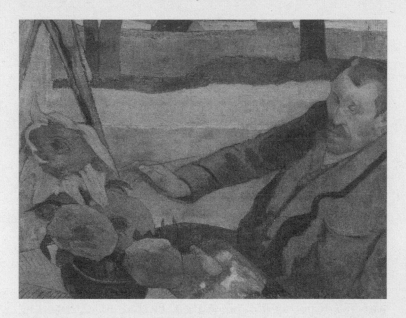

The other portraits show Vincent with a high, slightly sloping forehead and light ginger to blond hair, his beard of a darker reddish tinge. But in Gauguin's painting, Vincent's hair is brownish, his forehead low, his eyes, normally his most dominating feature, half-closed and sunken into his head, and his prominent, hooked nose seems flattened like a boxer's. He is seen from above, as if by someone standing over him at work in the studio.

The most attractive aspect of his image is his hand – 'beautiful' and 'harmonious', as Gauguin described it – holding a brush (sometimes, when he was at work, Vincent felt like a violinist holding a bow, so melodiously did his painting flow).

On the wall behind there is one of Gauguin's own works, greatly enlarged. It was his habit to put his own paintings in the background of these studio interiors, perhaps to suggest that this was a place for the production of images and dreams. In this case it is a landscape, not one that Gauguin actually painted – or that survived if he did – but quite similar to the lower part of *Blue Trees*.

Vincent is painting a bouquet of sunflowers in a majolica vase. That in itself suggests this was not a work of realism. Even in Arles, sunflowers were not in season in December, any more than spring bulbs were sprouting outside. On the other hand, Vincent did do some replicas of his August sunflower pictures in these winter months, perhaps to please his friend, who admired them so. The more Gauguin looked at the *Sunflowers*, Vincent remembered, the more he liked them.

The easel Vincent is using – seen side on and almost invisible – is a portable, folding one for outdoor work. Probably Gauguin painted it because a heavy studio easel would have overbalanced the composition. On one point, however, the picture reflects the reality of Arles in December: Vincent is muffled up against the cold in a thick jacket.

The flowers in their blue vase are placed on a rush chair, similar to the one Vincent has just painted. But the painter seems to have sunk into the floor, since the seat of the chair comes up to his waist. Gauguin did some preparatory drawings for the portrait in his sketchbook: a couple of details of his features, the way his thumb stuck through his palette. These might have been jotted down while Vincent worked on the other side of the studio. He also did a compositional study of the whole picture, in which Vincent was grinning – as if amused at this new project – and chattering in an animated, possibly maddening, fashion.

The final painting, however, was quite different. Vincent looks half asleep, somnolent. Was Gauguin depicting Vincent's deteriorating mental state? Both men later interpreted the portrait in that way. Nine months later, Vincent mentioned it in a letter from the asylum in St Rémy. 'Have you seen that portrait that he did of me painting sunflowers? Afterwards my face got much brighter, but that was really me, very tired and charged with electricity as I was then.'

Gauguin, writing his unreliable memoirs many years later, recalled Vincent exclaiming, 'It's me, but it's me gone mad,' as he examined the painting. On the other hand, Theo, who knew and loved Vincent better than anyone else, didn't see it like that at all. While Vincent was still recovering from the crisis, in January 1889, Theo praised Gauguin's portrait highly: 'It is a great work of art & the best portrait that's been made of him in terms of capturing his inner being.'

When it was finished, Gauguin offered it to Theo — his valued dealer — as a gift:

I've recently completed a portrait of your brother as a subject for a picture the *Painter of Sunflowers* on a size 30 canvas. From a geographical point of view perhaps it isn't a very close likeness, but I think there is something of his inner character in it and if it's not a nuisance keep it, at least if you like it.

Probably, that had been Gauguin's intention all along: to make an elegant gesture of thanks to the most important person in his professional life. Gauguin would scarcely have intentionally depicted Theo's brother as a madman if this were the case. If Vincent really saw madness in the picture, perhaps it was because madness was what he feared.

So what was the truth? To Gauguin, a portrait was a depiction of someone's inner self, not their outer skin. That was why he had painted himself as a haggard and hunted-looking outcast in the character of Jean Valjean, the heroic convict of *Les Misérables*. So his picture shows Vincent as Gauguin felt his companion could be and should be rather than as he looked. The picture wasn't supposed to be accurate 'from a geographical point of view'; it was a symbolic portrait depicting not the outer but the inner reality.

The title was significant. The *Sunflowers* were, as far as Gauguin was concerned, the best things that Vincent had done. In those pictures he had outdone and moved beyond Impressionism; Vincent had made visible the true, hidden significance of the blooms. One day, looking at the sunflower pictures, Gauguin exclaimed, 'It's . . . it's the flower itself.' Vincent stored this tribute away in his memory.

So Gauguin painted Vincent dreaming, as a visionary. There may have been something else. That low forehead, the brownish hair, the small eyes – they belonged not to Van Gogh but to Gauguin himself. Indeed, Gauguin wasn't much of a portraitist except when it came to painting his own features. His pictures of other people tended to slip towards caricature. When shortly he came to paint Schuffenecker and his family, he caused offence by depicting his friend as cringingly obsequious.

In the *Painter of Sunflowers*, consciously or unconsciously, Gauguin had done what painters quite often do – given his subject some of his own features. As a result, the portrait was a perfect metaphor for the intermingling – the exchanging of ideas and methods, the blurring of identities – taking place in the Yellow House.

Meanwhile, on a small piece of jute, Vincent painted Gauguin. The latter was depicted at work on his still life of a pumpkin and apples against a yellow background. The result was not successful; it was indeed so unimpressive that it was over a century before it was generally accepted as Vincent's work at all. Gauguin is wearing his red Breton beret and also, apparently, through an odd use by Vincent of a complementary violet against the yellow picture on his easel, a false nose.

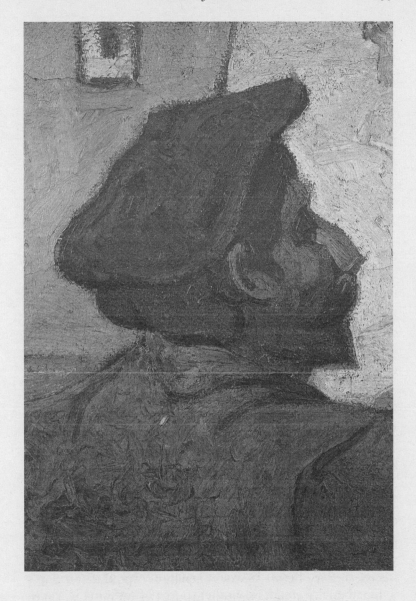

The reason it doesn't work is no doubt that it was – like Gauguin's picture of him – done *de tête*. Vincent needed a model in front of him to produce a good portrait.

Gauguin received another 300 francs from Theo for work that had been sold. Money was raining down on him in a way it hadn't since he had been in the financial markets. From this new remittance, he decided to send two-thirds to his wife, Mette, in Copenhagen; again, this was something that he had not done for quite a while. With the banknotes he sent a brief, stiff, self-justifying letter.

Dear Mette,
    Enclosed is 200 fr.
    I would ask you to acknowledge *receipt* so I can be sure the money has not gone astray. So long as it would not tire you too much, you might take that opportunity to give me some news of the children. It's a long time now since I had any!
    I'm beginning to re-establish myself, but not without setbacks. The state of my affairs is improving, but very slowly. In any case, my reputation is solidly established in both Paris and Brussels.
    I'm sending you a letter from Schuffenecker which will explain better than I can what people are saying about my painting. I'm working fit to bust but I hope to see the benefit from it in the future.
        Your husband
                                Paul Gauguin
                                2 Place Lamartine (Arles)

He did not sign this missive 'PGo' (the cock). Vincent was aware of the tension between Gauguin and Mette and was sympathetic, seeing it as another source of suffering in the *via crucis* of the artist's life.
    Gauguin, Vincent reflected:

is a father, he has a wife and children in Denmark, and at the same time he wants to go to the other end of the earth, to Martinique. It is frightful, all the welter of incompatible desires and needs which this must cause them.

But he also used Gauguin's marital problems as yet another argument to put pressure on him to stay in Arles. Mette, he 'took the liberty' of assuring Gauguin, would certainly support his staying in the Yellow House, 'working here at Arles without wasting money, and earning'; Mette, Vincent was sure, would approve of such 'stability'. Tact was not among Vincent's virtues.

The most sinister of the notes on Gauguin's cryptic list was 'Orla (Maupassant)' – by which he meant Guy de Maupassant's short story of madness, hypnotism and the supernatural, 'Horla'. It had been published the year before. Was Gauguin beginning to fear his housemate was unhinged? After the catastrophe, Gauguin claimed that Vincent had indeed gone mad and that he had lived in fear of some terrible accident. But perhaps it had not been so clear in advance. The horror of 'Horla' lay in the uncertainty as to whether the narrator was deranged or not. Both Gauguin and Vincent read this story; Vincent later used it as a comparison for his delirium.

Writing to Gauguin towards the end of the next month, after he had temporarily recovered, Vincent noted that:

In my mental or nervous fever, or madness – I am not too sure how to put it or what to call it – my thoughts sailed over many seas. My dreams voyaged as far as the phantom ship of the Flying Dutchman, and the Horla.

Gauguin later recalled a disturbing habit Vincent developed during December:

In the latter days of my stay, Vincent would become excessively rough and noisy, and then silent. On several nights I surprised him in the act of getting up and coming over to my bed. To what can I attribute my awakening at just that moment? At all events, it was enough for me to say, quite sternly, 'What's the matter with you, Vincent?' for him to go back to bed and fall into a heavy sleep.

Gauguin's bedroom, remember, was divided from Vincent's by a single door.

This memory – if it was a real event and not one of Gauguin's literary embroideries – was indeed close to the nightmare world of Maupassant's fiction. 'Horla' described the experiences of a man convinced that he is being haunted by an invisible being.

This creature, the Horla, enters his bedroom and drinks his carafe of water at night. Slowly, it takes control over its victim's will: an unseen and more powerful *doppelgänger*. In attempting to destroy it, the man sets fire to his house, murdering his servants. The implication is that this mysterious double came from within, that the man was mad.

Of course, like the narrator and the phantom in the story, Vincent and Gauguin were alter egos, similar in many ways – sharing the same space, dreams and ideas – but also different beings and rival wills. The silent watcher in Gauguin's bedroom – Vincent – resembled the menacing intruder of the story. What would have happened if Gauguin had not awoken and ordered Vincent to return to his bed? The narrator in Maupassant's fiction feared the Horla would climb on his bed, take his neck in his hands and squeeze with all his strength.

Was Vincent going mad? He was certainly acting erratically,

and his mind was full of strange notions. But until this month of December 1888, judgement on Vincent's mental balance was still divided. Soon, however, he was to do something that, in everybody's eyes, including his own, made him seem a genuine and frightening lunatic.

The crisis in the studio came to a head. As Gauguin later told the story, after Vincent had made his remark about the *Painter of Sunflowers* – 'It's me, but it's me gone mad' – they went to the café. Vincent had a 'weak absinthe':

Suddenly he flung the glass and its contents at my head. I avoided the blow and taking him bodily in my arms, went out of the café across Place Victor Hugo. Not many minutes later Vincent found himself in his bed where, in a few seconds, he was asleep, not to awaken until morning. When he awoke, he said to me very calmly, 'My dear Gauguin, I have a vague memory that I offended you last evening.'

Answer: 'I forgive you gladly and with all my heart, but yesterday's scene might occur again and if I were struck I might lose control of myself and give you a choking. So permit me to write to your brother and tell him I am coming back.'

Evidently, Gauguin's story was not to be relied upon entirely. In a triumph of vagueness, he managed to get in a muddle over Place Lamartine, naming it after the wrong romantic poet – and this despite the fact that he had lived in the square for two months and that a poem of Lamartine's was a particular favourite of his mother's. Even so, the other details were quite circumstantial. The 'light absinthe' corroborates other hints that Vincent's tolerance for alcohol was low. He didn't need to swallow much before his behaviour started to become disturbingly agitated.

Vincent was certainly capable, when excited or disturbed, of mild violence. Months later, in the asylum of St Rémy, he kicked one of the guards in the backside, under the impression that the man was a member of the police force of Arles, who were after him and wanted to lock him up.

The quarrel in the café, followed by a deep sleep and confused memories the following day, sounded like one of the three 'fainting fits' that Vincent said he suffered that autumn. At all events, Gauguin did write to Theo, abruptly:

Dear M. van Gogh

I would be obliged if you would send me part of the money from the sale of the paintings sold. All things considered I am compelled to return to Paris. Vincent and I are absolutely unable to live side by side without trouble caused by incompatibility of temperament and he like I needs tranquillity for his work. He is a man of remarkable intelligence whom I esteem greatly and I leave with regret, but I repeat it is necessary. I appreciate the thoughtfulness of your conduct towards me and I beg you to excuse my decision –

> Cordially yours,
>
> Paul Gauguin

Probably in the same envelope, sent between Tuesday and Friday of that week, Vincent also sent a terse, disjointed communication:

My dear Theo,

Thank you very much for your letter, for the 100 Fr. note enclosed and also for the 50 Fr. money order.

I think myself that Gauguin was a little out of sorts with the good town of Arles, the little yellow house where we work, and especially with me. As a matter of fact there are bound to be for him as for me further grave difficulties to overcome here.

But these difficulties are rather within ourselves than outside. Altogether I think that either he will definitely go, or else definitely stay.

Before doing anything I told him to think it over and reckon things up again.

Gauguin is very powerful, strongly creative, but just because of that he must have peace.

Will he find it anywhere if he does not find it here?

I am waiting for him to make a decision with absolute serenity.

The two painters were writing fewer letters, but they still received considerable correspondence. In the post from Paris on Wednesday 12 December, there was an extremely pleasing missive for Gauguin from his friend Schuffenecker. As instructed, the latter had been to Theo's gallery to inspect the new paintings sent from Arles.

Schuffenecker was 'absolutely wild with enthusiasm'; these Arles paintings were even finer than the one from Brittany, 'more abstract and more powerful'. He was 'stupefied' by Gauguin's artistic 'fecundity and abundance'. His self-deprecation was as cloying as his praise was ecstatic: 'Poor unhappy creature that I am, I who grind away at a little canvas for months.'

Gauguin, he predicted – accurately as it happened – was going to become one of the great 'saints' of art; and also one of its martyrs: 'The more I look and I think, the more I become convinced that you are going to pole-axe the lot of them, with the exception of Degas.' Gauguin was a giant, he was 'scaling heaven':

You won't actually reach it, because that's the absolute, which is to say God, but you will shake the hands of those who have most nearly approached it.

Yes, my dear Gauguin, what awaits you is not only success, it's glory beside the Rembrandts and Delacroixs. And you will have suffered like them. I hope that at least now you will be saved from material sufferings.

There was only one discouraging note in the letter; evidently the jute combined with the barium sulphate priming had led the paintings to crack, and the paint was coming off 'in scales'. Otherwise, it was heady stuff. If Vincent read it, it could only have intensified his gloomy feeling that he personally had far to go.

Gauguin, on the other hand, could scarcely have hoped for a better response. It must have made him feel even more restless at being stuck in Arles, where Vincent's behaviour was becoming odder and odder. Instead, he should have been in Paris, receiving this acclaim in person.

The day before, Tuesday 11 December, Second Lieutenant Milliet had penned a letter to Vincent from Algeria. It was a continuation of the conversations of the summer. From Vincent's letters, one might have concluded that Milliet was mainly interested in the women of Rue du Bout d'Arles. But, as his letter clearly showed, the young man of action had been fired by Vincent: more than that, it contained ideas that can only have come from Vincent's head: 'What is truly beautiful here is nature: the sun, the light, the Arab types, the men with floating garments are superb.' Then he said something remarkable: 'Pictures seem to compose themselves in the shadows with the centre dark and the corners in the light. It would seem, if I dare to express myself thus, to be Rembrandt in reverse.'

Now, Rembrandt transposed into the brilliant light of the Mediterranean was one of Vincent's obsessions. The matter of Rembrandt and southern light was one that Vincent felt he and Gauguin had 'broached'. Rembrandt was much on his mind; he felt he was almost the only painter who could evoke 'heartbroken tenderness, that glimpse of a super-human infinitude'. To do just that in the colours of Provence was one of Vincent's most cherished projects.

The Zouave went on to describe a landscape extremely similar to Vincent's views of the Crau at harvest time, which had been done under his eyes in June. It was the view from his barracks window:

My horizon is formed by a line of little mountains running parallel from east to west and lost in the blue. On the other side I have a perfectly flat plain of a debatable colour; the closest levels to the eye are yellowish, the receding parts end up in a violet-grey.

In the far distance there was 'an ash-grey line, but so fine that it would need only a single stroke. These colours defined the extent of the landscape.' This tough young officer, brought up in various military establishments, was seeing with an artist's eye – with Vincent's, to be precise.

The efficient Second Lieutenant had prepared his commanding officer's mind for the expected arrival of Bernard. If the latter did his military service in the 3rd Zouaves, his life would be made as comfortable as possible. Milliet was keen for news of the Yellow House, where things had been going so well when he left on 1 November. 'How are you my dear friend, and Goguin how does he find the life down there? What does he make of it?' He sent Theo his regards, and to 'Goguin' he extended 'a vigorous shake of the hand'.

Over the weekend of the fifteenth and sixteenth it rained heavily.But inside the Yellow House, the storm blew over. The next week began with an unprecedented event. Gauguin and Vincent went on an excursion to visit an art gallery in another town. It was the first time Vincent had been outside Arles since the early summer.

10. Looking at Art
16–19 December

The two painters decided to make a daytrip to Montpellier
to visit the Musée Fabre. This was 68 kilometres to the west
of Arles, in a different region – Languedoc. To get there
involved a lengthy train journey. Neither Gauguin nor Vincent named the day on which they made this expedition, but
it must have been on Sunday, 16 December or Monday the
seventeenth as, except for Thursday mornings, the museum
was only open on those days of the week. The former was
an exceptionally wet day, so it was probably on Monday that
the two painters boarded the train at Arles station; the 8.58
would have been the most convenient departure.

This excursion to Montpellier was Gauguin's idea; he had
been to the Musée Fabre before, in 1884. Then, he had been
in the town, bizarrely, while helping a group of Spanish
republican revolutionaries. Nothing had come of their
attempts to foment a rising across the border but, while
Gauguin was trying to arrange transport for his luckless
friends, he discovered the museum. It was generally regarded
as the finest art gallery in the South of France: rich in French
painting from earlier in the century and with some old masters
as well.

There, Gauguin discovered a picture by Delacroix – a
painter he, like Vincent, revered. It depicted a black woman,
her clothes slipping from her shoulders, one breast revealed.
The extraordinary thing about it, for nineteenth-century

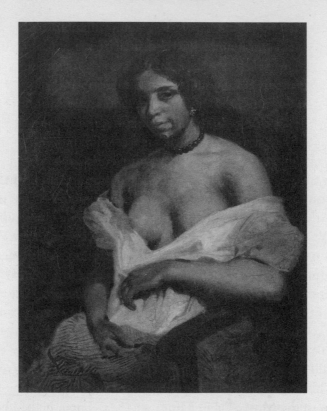

Europe, was that she was both black and beautiful – not in the manner of a classical Venus but nonetheless presented both sensuously and seriously. It must also have struck Gauguin that the woman in the picture had the same name as his mother and daughter: Aline.

The picture affected Gauguin so much that – unusually for him – he copied it. The sight of Aline was perhaps one of the reasons he had begun to think about working in the tropics, and to appreciate a novel, non-Western style of beauty. So, eventually, this Aline may have given rise to his numerous pictures of similarly sensual, bare-breasted Polynesian women.

To Gauguin's mind, there was only one blot in this admirable gallery at Montpellier: a self-portrait by the elderly academic star, Alexandre Cabanel. Gauguin could not stand his slick and glossy work. 'Cabanel!' he snorted. 'Stupidity and fatuity!'

The two painters probably did not arrive at the Musée Fabre until one o'clock.They would have had to return on the 4.09 train, but there was time for a leisurely visit, since the Musée Fabre was not far from the station. Vincent – as ever, sensitive to the cold – found the building 'chilly', but his reaction to what he saw was passionate. So, apparently, was Gauguin's. To Theo, Vincent described the intensity with which the two painters clashed: 'Our arguments are *terribly electric*, we come out of them sometimes with our heads as exhausted as an electric battery after it has run down.'

The generalization, 'sometimes we come out of them . . .', suggests, as was plainly the case, that he and Gauguin had argued much more than once and not only about the pictures in the Musée Fabre. 'Electricity' was Vincent's term for manic energy; evidently his tussles with Gauguin were exhausting them both.

There on the walls in Montpellier were works by several of the painters about whom they had already disagreed. Weeks before, Gauguin had replied, 'Corporal, you're right,' when Vincent expressed controversial views on art – just to get some peace. Now, it seemed, he didn't.

Gauguin had complained about Vincent's reverence for mid-nineteenth-century landscape painters such as 'the great' Théodore Rousseau. Now, there before them was a characteristic Rousseau, the *Pond*, with at its centre a heroic, almost human tree – such as Vincent liked to paint himself. Predictably, Vincent was enthusiastic.

On the other hand, Gauguin expressed his bafflement that Vincent 'hated' Ingres and Raphael. And there at Montpellier was an Ingres of exactly the kind that Gauguin loved and Vincent didn't. Typically, but for once understandably, Gauguin couldn't remember its name – it was called *Stratonice and Antiochus* – but he much admired this picture, with its clear outlines and complex composition, 'a logical and beautiful language' of painting. Vincent, however, though he didn't exactly 'hate' Ingres, only appreciated that painter's portraits, with their 'modern aspect'. The neo-classicism of this kind of picture struck him as 'pedantry'.

But there was much at Montpellier they could agree upon. A little panel was then attributed to the Florentine master Giotto: the *Death of the Virgin*. This 'tiny little' picture whose subject was irrelevant to him – 'the death of some holy woman or other' – made a huge impression on Vincent: 'In it, the expression of pain and ecstasy is so human that, even though we are in the middle of the nineteenth century, one could think and feel one was there, so much does one share the emotion.' Giotto was another artist in whom Vincent saw himself; he imagined the medieval painter, poor in health, 'always suffering and always full of ardour and ideas'.

Gauguin kept a photograph of one of Giotto's frescoes with him in the South Pacific. 'What does it matter whether the conception is natural or unlike nature? In it I see a tenderness and love that are altogether divine.' Giotto was a marvellous example of the stylized, non-naturalistic art that Gauguin admired as 'primitive' – just like the sculpture of Saint-Trophime.

The heart of the museum at Montpellier was the collection of one man: Alfred Bruyas. This was displayed apart from the rest of the museum exhibits in what Gauguin described as 'a very large room, a third of which was raised several steps above the rest'. Bruyas, a wealthy local man, had been an enthusiastic patron of several artists in the 1850s and 1860s –

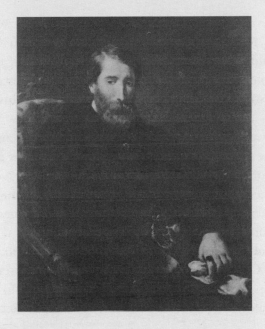

notably Cabanel, Delacroix and Courbet. He had also been markedly eccentric.

A genuine invalid and also a hypochondriac, he had obsessively commissioned portraits of himself. So, from the walls at Montpellier, his image stared down again and again – red-bearded, melancholy and, in one bizarre instance, crowned with thorns in the guise of the martyred Christ. It was possible to take two views of Bruyas – either as an enlightened patron or as a monster of self-pitying vanity.

Vincent and Gauguin praised the Delacroixs, including 'the study of a "Mulatto Woman"', which Gauguin had copied. They were both much struck by Delacroix's portrait of Bruyas. To Gauguin, the sensitivity and anxiety of the man was conveyed by one detail – the way he clutched at a handkerchief with his hand.

As he remarked to Schuffenecker the following week, 'in

painting, a hand touching a handkerchief is able to express the consciousness of a soul'. Therefore, Gauguin went on, why couldn't painters 'create different harmonies' of colour corresponding to the sitter's spiritual state? This was exactly Vincent's ambition – to express feelings and thoughts through colour.

Afterwards, it was Delacroix's paintings that remained in Vincent's mind most of all. The *Women in Algiers* at Montpellier, for example, was very different from the version in Paris. These Delacroixs struck him as 'faded' with age. The memory eventually led him to paint in muted tones himself, rather than 'striking colour effects'.

Vincent also commended the Courbets to Theo. Vincent regarded Courbet as one of those rare, robust painters such as Rubens – and Gauguin – who could make love to women, father children and create pictures without exhausting their life-force.

One picture Vincent particularly singled out – the *Bathers* – was certainly fleshy. The massive buttocks of the nude seen from behind obviously appealed to Vincent. When, at art school, his copy of the Venus de Milo was criticized for having the wide hips of a Flemish matron, Vincent flew into a rage and shouted at the horrified professor: 'You clearly don't know what a young woman is like, God damn it! A woman must have hips, buttocks, a pelvis in which she can carry a baby!' No one could fault Courbet's woman for width of pelvis or lack of buttocks. But there was another Courbet – a famous painting – which Vincent strangely failed to mention: the *Meeting*, otherwise known as *Bonjour, Monsieur Courbet*. Painted in 1854 when Courbet had stayed with Bruyas in Montpellier, this depicts an encounter between the artist and his patron in the countryside. Bruyas, accompanied by a servant, extends his arms in greeting. Courbet, who paints

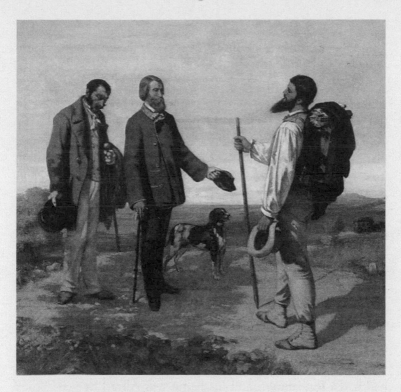

himself as a great, robust fellow – much as he featured in Vincent's mind – has his painting equipment in a knapsack on his back and a staff in his hand.

Looked at through the eyes of compulsive dread, the picture could be read not as a greeting but as a farewell – a sensitive, troubled, red-bearded man bids goodbye to a more vigorous, black-bearded figure. It probably brought to mind what Vincent feared most and what underlay the other disputes: the threat that Gauguin would leave.

This painting also made a deep impression on Gauguin, because a few months later he produced a painting entitled *Bonjour, Monsieur Gauguin*. In this, the figure meeting

Gauguin at a Breton country gate was none other than a woman in black. Like the other black-clad woman in his *Human Misery*, she stood for Solitude.

It was a long, tiring day. The train got into Arles at 7.20 in the evening – just in time for supper. As far as Vincent was concerned, the journey had been extraordinarily exciting; for Gauguin – as may happen to those who revisit a place which they have greatly enjoyed – it was a disappointment. He felt that too many academic pictures had appeared at Montpellier in the intervening four years: 'I returned in Vincent's company,' he remembered, 'and visited this museum again. What a change! Most of the old pictures had vanished, and everywhere their place was filled with – "Acquired by the state, 3rd Medal". Cabanel and his whole school had invaded the museum.'

Vincent's excitement, on the other hand, was almost alarming. The very next day he wrote to Theo to tell him about the amazing discovery he had made: the brothers Van Gogh had had a forerunner, and his name was Alfred Bruyas.

After telling Theo about the museum visit, Vincent went straight to the point: 'Brias was a benefactor of artists, I shall say no more to you than that.' But he did say a great deal more. There were, in Vincent's view, extraordinary parallels between himself, his brother and Bruyas (or Brias, as he spelt the name). To begin with, he had the same colour hair.

Noticing this, Vincent's mind had rapidly made other connections; he deduced that there was a noble brotherhood of red-headed patrons of art, not unlike the Red-Headed League that Arthur Conan Doyle posited in a Sherlock Holmes story a few years later. But Vincent's red-headed league was dedicated to protecting boldly experimental painters and bringing them to the South – just as Bruyas had Courbet and Vincent had Gauguin. In short, in the seventeen portraits of Bruyas's sensitive, suffering features, Vincent saw himself.

Once he had made that connection, in a flash of intuition he leapt to further connections: to a picture by Delacroix, in which he had long seen an image of his own predicament, and a poem by Alfred de Musset. This was all conveyed to Theo with telegraphic speed:

In the portrait by Delacroix he is a gentleman with red beard and hair, confoundedly like you or me, and made me think of that poem by de Musset – 'Wherever I touched the earth, a wretch clad in black came and sat by us, looking at us like a brother.' It would have the same effect on you. I am sure.

It was the same poem, 'December Night', from which Gauguin had adopted the woman in black in his *Human Miseries*.

Vincent was saying that Bruyas was a suffering pilgrim such as he and Theo were. Then Vincent's mind flashed to yet another image:

Please do go to that bookshop where they sell the lithographs by past and present artists, and see if you could get, not too dear, the lithograph after Delacroix's *Tasso in the Madhouse*, since I think the figure there must have some affinity with this fine portrait of Brias.

The relevance of Delacroix's picture of Tasso to Vincent was obvious. The Renaissance poet Torquato Tasso lost his reason as a result of political machinations. He committed an act of violence and was confined to a cell for the rest of his life. Thus, Tasso represented the artist, unhinged and driven out by an uncaring society. In the picture by Delacroix, he looked quite like Bruyas – and also Vincent in his most recent self-portrait, bearded and with unruly hair.

As Delacroix represented it, the inhabitants of Ferrara could mock him through the bars. If the locals were not yet peering through the ground-floor windows of the Yellow House to mock the inmate, they soon would be – especially the children, with their taunt of '*fou rou*' (mad redhead).

Later, looking back on his days in the Yellow House, Vincent regretted not taking a revolver to his persecutors. 'Had one killed gawking idiots like that,' he believed, most implausibly, 'as an artist one would certainly have been acquitted.' He wished he had defended his studio more vigorously: 'It would have been better had I done that, but I was cowardly and drunk – ill too, but I wasn't brave.'

The letter to Theo about the Musée Fabre whirled from subject to subject even more than was normal in Vincent's correspondence. As it went on, it became quite worryingly odd. First Vincent quoted a beautiful saying from the novelist and art critic Eugène Fromentin, but one that was strange in this context, because it suggested that Vincent and Gauguin were bewitched: 'We were in the midst of magic, for as Fromentin well says: Rembrandt is above all else a magician.'

Then, after these words, Vincent later inserted another startling line in smaller handwriting: 'and Delacroix a man of God spreading fire and brimstone in the name of God who didn't give a bloody damn'. This bizarre exclamation was without parallel in Vincent's letters. It was as if for a moment he had lost the control he normally maintained, at least while writing, and revealed the wild and angry thoughts swirling within his mind. Delacroix was, of course – like Bruyas, Monticelli and others – another predecessor in whom Vincent saw himself.

After this, the letter continued calmly, though somewhat weirdly: 'I tell you this in connection with our Dutch friends de Haan and Isaacson, who have so sought after and loved

Rembrandt, so as to encourage you all to pursue your researches. You must not be discouraged in them.'

This was peculiar, because there were no works by Rembrandt in the Musée Fabre. But there was a hidden link in Vincent's mind between Courbet's *Meeting*, Gauguin, Rembrandt and Delacroix: a 'strange and magnificent "Portrait of a Man"', by Rembrandt' in the Lacaze collection at the Louvre (in fact, scholars later decided, not by Rembrandt at all).

This painting depicted a man with a distant look in his eye and, like Courbet in his picture, a pilgrim's staff. The sight of the *Meeting* was presumably what brought it to Vincent's mind. He had pointed out to Gauguin that he saw in this Rembrandt a family resemblance to Delacroix and to Gauguin himself.

'I do not know why,' he added, 'but I always call this portrait "The Traveller", or "The Man Come from Far".' The connections that whirled about within Vincent's head were becoming looser and looser; with bewildering speed, pictures he had seen, people he knew and texts he had read were blurring together. Vincent, Gauguin and Delacroix merged together into one solitary outsider.

This image of the 'man come from far' had been in Vincent's imagination for twelve years – since he had preached his first sermon in Richmond. That had been a meditation on the theme of pilgrimage, ending with these words: 'We are pilgrims on the earth and strangers – we come from afar and we are going far.' So, to summarize Vincent's sequence of thought: Bruyas = Vincent (and Theo); Courbet = Gauguin = Delacroix = Rembrandt's portrait = pilgrim = Vincent. It was the logic of delirium.

Vincent wanted Theo to pass on an important message to the most eminent artist in Paris:

Say to Degas that Gauguin and I have been to see the portrait of
Brias by Delacroix at Montpellier, for we must make bold to
believe that *what is, is*, and the portrait of Brias by Delacroix is as
like you and me as a new brother.

It was most improbable Theo did so but, if he had, Degas
might have had second thoughts about coming to Arles.

Vincent would have written to Isaacson and de Haan as
well, to tell them about everything he had seen and thought
in Montpellier, if he had felt 'the necessary electric force'. That
word kept coming up. Later, looking back on these days, he
thought of himself as 'extremely tired and charged with electricity'. This surging force was fighting exhaustion within
him. Sometimes he bristled with sparks, sometimes not.

Strangely, after that contentious trip to the Musée Fabre,
Gauguin was feeling better. The next morning Vincent asked
him how he felt, and Gauguin replied 'that he felt his old self
coming back'. This pleased Vincent greatly. Instantly he saw
Gauguin's rise in morale in terms of his own experience:
'When I came here myself last winter, tired out and almost
stunned in mind, before ever being able to begin to recover
I had a strain of inward suffering too.'

Vincent hoped that everything might still turn out well,
but he was far from confident. 'As for founding a way of life
for artists chumming it together,' he remarked darkly to Theo,
'you see such queer things, and I will wind up with what you
are always saying – time will show.'

Before Vincent sent his disquieting missive, Gauguin had
composed a much more prosaic letter to Theo. He withdrew
his previous announcement that he was leaving Arles immediately and would therefore like all the money owing to him.
'Please consider,' he began, 'my journey to Paris as a figment

of the imagination and thus the letter I wrote to you as a bad dream.'

Gauguin went on to discuss a number of mundane business matters: he thought Theo had forgotten to deduct the price of the picture frame from a statement of account he had been sent. If the *Human Miseries* picture was developing cracks, it was doubtless because of the priming: 'If necessary send the picture back to me and I will put it in good order.'

At this point, Gauguin revealed that his departure from Arles was postponed, not cancelled. 'I am increasingly nostalgic for the Antilles and naturally as soon as I've sold a few things I'll go over there.'

Finally, he made the offer of the portrait of Vincent, the *Painter of Sunflowers*, as a gift, which kept the whole tone 'cordial', as he signed himself after noting that, 'We have been to Montpellier and Vincent will write you his impressions.'

Theo would have received both of these letters on Wednesday 19 December, but for once his attention was entirely distracted from events in Arles by the drama of his own life. Theo was going to be married.

For years, since before Vincent arrived in Paris, he had been secretly in love with Johanna Bonger, sister of his Dutch friend in Paris, André Bonger. In July of the previous year he had declared his feelings to her, but to Johanna, or Jo, they had come as a complete surprise. She felt she could scarcely say 'yes' to his proposal that she share his life full of intellectual stimulation, working for the good cause of the new art. Furthermore, at that time, she was in love with somebody else.

At the beginning of November, unknown to Theo, Jo moved to Paris. That week, when madness was threatening in the Yellow House, the two of them met once more. Johanna, it turned out, had engineered the meeting. One

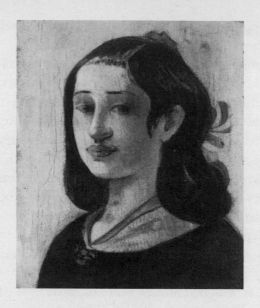

thing rapidly led to another, as Theo wrote euphorically to his mother on Friday the twenty-first.

Johanna had said she loved him and would take him as he was. 'I am actually very worried,' Theo added with characteristic self-deprecation, 'that she is making a mistake & that she will be disappointed in me, but I am so very happy, & I will try my best to understand her and make her happy.' That day Jo and Theo wrote to her parents asking permission to marry.

Meanwhile, in Arles, relations were once more fraying. Gauguin wrote to Schuffenecker, asking whether he could put him up at his house in Paris if it became necessary to leave Arles in a hurry. But, work continued.

Perhaps it was at this time that Gauguin painted a portrait of his mother, Aline. He did this – very unusually for him – from a photograph; just as Vincent, also extremely uncharacteristically, had earlier painted his own mother.

Gauguin's painting was based on a photograph of his mother as a young woman, around 1840, before he had even been born. At that date Aline Gauguin *née* Chazal had been only fifteen. She had a difficult life. Her father, André Chazal, was a figure of fear, having kidnapped and attempted to rape her. He almost murdered her mother, who never entirely recovered from having been shot in the chest and died when Aline was nineteen years old. Her husband, Clovis Gauguin, a republican journalist, died on the voyage to Peru in 1849, when Paul was one year old.

In the painting Aline looks very young and distinctly exotic. There is a hint of Goya about the image, in accordance with Gauguin's memory of his mother as 'a very noble Spanish lady'. The period in Peru was the time at which they were closest. On the family's return to France in 1855, the father-less, Spanish-speaking Paul began to prove difficult. He was sent away to the seminary in Orléans when he was eleven and went to sea at seventeen.

While he was on a voyage, his mother died, in 1867. During the Franco-Prussian war, her house at St Cloud, together with most of the family heirlooms, had been burnt in a fire. Perhaps, therefore, this photograph was the only image of his mother that Gauguin had.

That didn't explain, however, why he exaggerated her exotic look, giving her the nose and lips of Delacroix's black Aline. He also altered his mother's costume so that it had a somewhat Arlésienne appearance, her headdress and gaze growing close to Vincent's summer picture of a teenage girl, *La Mousmé*. During the process of painting, he changed the background from red to yellow.

Odder still was the next picture in which he included his mother. Eighteen months later, anticipating his departure to the South Pacific, Gauguin painted an *Exotic Eve*. Her naked

body was derived from a Buddhist sculpture, but her face –
down to details of the hair, including the little curl in front
of the ear – came from his painting of Aline Gauguin.

11. The Crisis

22–25 December

Vincent had had an idea for a new picture featuring Madame Roulin. It had come to him while he was talking to Gauguin about Pierre Loti's book, *Icelandic Fisherman*. They discussed the Breton fishermen and 'their mournful isolation, exposed to all dangers, alone on the sad sea'. Vincent frequently compared life – especially his own life – to a frail vessel at sea, tossed by every storm. During that week in Arles, he must have felt that the waves were mounting ominously.

'Following those intimate talks of ours,' he recalled to Gauguin:

the idea came to me to paint a picture in such a way that sailors, who are at once children and martyrs, seeing it in the cabin of their Icelandic fishing boat, would feel the old sense of being rocked come over them and remember their own lullabies.

A passage at the start of Loti's book did indeed describe the snugness of the sailor's cabin – a warm refuge not unlike the studio in the Yellow House. Even when the night was cold and wet, inside the cabin, there was a comfortable fug of tobacco smoke. The men's merry conversation, over their wine and cider, was of love, sex and marriage. Above them there was a holy figure: a china statuette of the Virgin Mary – painted 'with very simple art' in red and blue – was fastened to a bracket, in the place of honour. 'She must have listened to many an ardent prayer in deadly hours.'

But the picture Vincent actually painted depicted not a cabin in a fishing boat but Augustine Roulin sitting in the best chair in the Yellow House – Gauguin's chair – and holding in her hands the string which rocked her baby's cradle. The cradle itself was outside the picture – indeed, anyone not familiar with the mechanics of cradle-rocking would not guess it was there.

In Vincent's mind, the occupants of this little cot were Breton fishermen. 'I'm sure,' he later explained to Gauguin, 'that if one were to put this canvas just as it is in a fishing boat, even one from Iceland, there would be some among the fishermen who would feel they were there, inside the cradle.' No doubt Vincent imagined himself being thus soothed and comforted.

Behind Madame Roulin, however, was not the wall of the cabin, nor the icy waves of the North Atlantic, but stridently patterned French wallpaper. This came from reality – and the people of Arles were fond of loud wallpaper – but also linked with yet another book.

It was a Dutch novel, *De Kleine Johannes* by Frederik van Eeden, the first volume of which had come out in 1885, the year before Vincent moved to Paris. It dealt with the pilgrim-age through life of the eponymous central character, who grew up – like Vincent – in idyllic countryside. During his happy, rural childhood, Johannes slept in a bedroom decor-ated with huge flowers in 'gaudy' colours. That was what Vincent painted now, which implied it was Johannes in the cradle, as well as the fishermen, which meant, again, that it was really Vincent.

Augustine Roulin sat again for this picture. No real wall-paper, however garish, was quite as extreme as the one in the

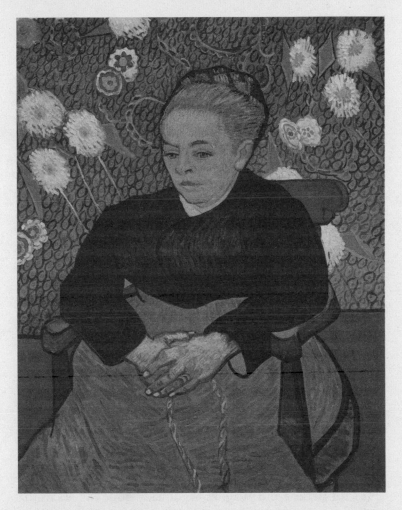

painting. Behind Madame Roulin a luxuriant garden rears up. Huge white blossoms – dahlias, according to Vincent – sway on long thin stalks, tendrils and leaves twine against a background of thousands of small blue-green forms, each with a red dot in the middle, like a bud, or a pod, or a breast.

Nor does this exhaust the references that Vincent poured into this picture. There was an echo of the *santon* figures in the crèches lit with candles all over Arles. He compared the picture with a cheap religious print, a chromo-lithograph and barrel-organ music.

It also suggested the *ex voto* figures of female saints giving blessing from a boat that he had seen in the church of Stes Maries de la Mer on the coast of the Camargue. Then there was a memory of a stained-glass window – Mary, Star of the Sea – he had admired in Antwerp three years before, and a suggestion of Flemish Madonnas he had also seen there by painters such as Van Eyck. Perhaps there was an echo, in this densely woven picture, of the embroideries described in Zola's *The Dream*.

He imagined hanging several versions of *La Berceuse*, with his *Sunflowers* in between, so the whole would amount to an altarpiece of seven or nine canvases. By and by, he demonstrated this arrangement to Roulin. The *Sunflowers*, those radiant southern blooms, would act as 'candelabras' between the multiple mothers – just as the Christmas crèches were displayed with candles on either side.

Vincent wanted the picture to be equivalent to a holy image of the early Christian era, yet modern. He thought perhaps it should be displayed on the wall of a sailors' tavern in a fishing village such as Stes-Maries. He hoped it would comfort the suffering. 'Ah!' he exclaimed to Gauguin a fortnight later, 'my dear friend, to achieve in painting what the music of Berlioz and Wagner has already done . . . an art that offers consolation for the broken-hearted! There are still just a few who feel it as you and I do!!!'

The strange aspect of it was that all these tumbling associations which evoked such powerful feelings in the artist were virtually invisible. All that could be seen on the canvas was a boldly styled, audaciously coloured portrait of a woman sitting in a chair.

The picture did indeed have an impact on younger artists
– unknown to Vincent – such as Henri Matisse, Pierre Bon-
nard and Edouard Vuillard, but it was a formal not a spiritual
one. It lay in that amazing expanse of crazily exuberant wallpaper. *La Berceuse* was a daring step into an unexplored art in
which space and mood were created by colour and pattern,
which made a whole world of its own.

There had been a hard frost on Wednesday, followed by three
days of heavy rain. *L'Intransigeant* reported on Saturday the
twenty-second that the murderer Prado, so defiant and
insouciant at his trial, had been reduced to a state of terror
haunted by nightmares while awaiting execution in his prison
cell. The day of his death was drawing near.

On that evening, Gauguin sat down to write a long, long
letter to Schuffenecker – the longest communication he had
sent to anybody since he arrived in Arles. Its copiousness
suggested that he no longer had anyone to talk to closer to
hand. Communications had broken down completely in the
Yellow House.

Schuffenecker had offered Gauguin hospitality in Paris,
but Gauguin still wasn't quite ready to leave Arles. Gauguin
thanked him for his offer; he wasn't coming straight away,
but he might on an instant:

My situation here is painful; I owe much to Van Gogh and Vincent
and despite some discord I can't bear a grudge against a good heart
who is ill and suffers and wants to see me. Do you remember
the life of Edgar Poe in which as a result of sorrows, a nervous
temperament became alcoholic? One day I'll explain it all to you
thoroughly.

I'm staying here for now, but I'm poised to leave at any moment.

His comparison was drawn from the biographical essay on Poe by the poet Charles Baudelaire that served as a preface to his translation of Poe's *Tales of Mystery and Imagination* – which themselves contained plenty of Horla-like insanity and haunting. But Gauguin was not saying Vincent was actually insane.

Baudelaire presented Poe as a heroic, almost saintly victim. It was 'sorrows' that had driven the American writer to the bottle. Gauguin's implication was that Vincent was not only a boozer but also a creative spirit of rare quality.

To Baudelaire, Poe was a:

man who had climbed the most arduous heights of aesthetics, and had plunged into the least explored abysses of the human mind, he who, in the course of a life which seemed like a storm without respite, had found new means, unknown techniques, to make an impact on man's imagination, to enchant all minds athirst for beauty.

That described Vincent's achievement exactly.

If Gauguin stated that Vincent was a drunkard, there was no reason to doubt him. He had been spending virtually every moment of every day with Vincent for two months. Gauguin might have been vague about facts, but not that vague. If he thought that Vincent was a problem drinker, then he evidently was. That was exactly what Vincent's neighbours in Arles complained of: that he behaved oddly when he had been drinking.

At the close of December, Vincent might have been drinking more heavily than usual, as he had been working flat out for several weeks. In the previous month, he had painted twenty-five paintings, several of them among the finest he ever produced.

Furthermore, the picture on which he was currently

engaged, *La Berceuse*, was a complex chromatic combination – 'the reds moving through to pure orange, building up again in the flesh tones to the chromes, passing through the pinks and blending with the olive and malachite greens'. Subsequently, he was extremely pleased with it: 'As an impressionist arrangement of colours I have never devised anything better'. But working out such combinations was precisely what led Vincent to 'stun' himself with alcohol. Added to this was the worry that Gauguin was about to leave.

Two considerations still restrained Gauguin from going. One was that he felt guilty about deserting Vincent. The other was that he was concerned about how Theo might react if he did. 'I need Van Gogh,' he confided to Schuffenecker. Gauguin wanted to leave Arles, when he did, in such a way that Theo would be 'bound' to him even more rather than feel able to withdraw from their agreement. Gauguin swore Schuffenecker to secrecy about the whole matter and also asked him to make enquiries about the possibility of Gauguin doing some casual work in the pottery workshop where he had worked before – in case the worst should come to the worst.

The letter went on and on, quite unlike the brief notes Gauguin had sent Schuffenecker earlier in his stay. He was concerned that his sales through Theo had dried up. This was because the financial outlook was grim. The *Human Miseries*, which had not been sold, meant a lot to him; he would like Schuffenecker, who had a private income, to buy it (as he eventually did). He described the frame it should have: black with a yellow line on the inside edge.

'If I am able to leave,' he announced, 'in May with life assured in Martinique for 18 months I will almost be a happy mortal.' He hoped to be followed there by his disciples, 'all those who have loved and understood me'. Gauguin elaborated his ideas of a better world in which men would live happily together under the tropical sun. But simultaneously he foresaw that his path in life would be lonely. In doing so he revealed how completely he had now absorbed Vincent's mental landscape. 'Vincent,' he noted, 'sometimes calls me "the man who has come from far away and will go far".'

'You remember Manfred' – as usual, Gauguin got the name wrong: he meant de Musset – 'Wherever I go to settle down in some corner of the earth I see a man dressed in black who looks at me like a brother.'

Gauguin wrote on, for nine pages. Eventually, he closed his letter, even though, that 'rainy evening', he could have gone on until morning. Under his signature, he did a little drawing of a memorial plaque he had invented for himself, presumably as a joke about his new status as a great artist. It was a cartouche, bearing the date and the initials PGo, once again spelling out 'pego', or 'the prick'.

Gauguin wrote Schuffenecker's address with a flourish, and then walked out into the rain to post the letter. He had missed the last collection of Saturday the twenty-second, which went at 10 o'clock, but his letter was in time for one of the first express trains on the following day, Sunday the twenty-third. That was the day on which the catastrophe, so long impending, finally occurred.

Vincent continued to paint *La Berceuse*. In an attempt to lure Gauguin into staying at the Yellow House, he reminded him that the great Degas had said he was 'saving himself up for the Arlésiennes'. If the women of Arles were good enough for Degas, surely the place had enough interest for Gauguin?

At some point he asked Gauguin point-blank if he was about to go. Gauguin described the encounter to Bernard a few days later:

I had to leave Arles, he was so bizarre I couldn't take it. He even said to me, 'Are you going to leave?' And when I said 'Yes' he tore this sentence from a newspaper and put it in my hand: 'the murderer took flight'.

These words were printed at the end of a small news item in the day's edition of *L'Intransigeant*. An unfortunate young man, one Albert Kalis, had been stabbed from behind while walking home at night. He had been taken to Bicetre hospital in a desperate condition. 'The murderer took flight.'

The painters – according to Gauguin's much later recollection – proceeded to have their supper, cooked by Gauguin, as usual. Gauguin 'bolted' his and went out to walk in Place Lamartine. He gave two quite different accounts of what happened next, and he was the only witness, because Vincent's memory of that night was very vague. He told the following story to Bernard, who narrated it to the critic Albert Aurier:

Vincent ran after me – he was going out; it was night – I turned round because for some time he had been acting strangely. But I mistrusted him. Then he told me, 'You are silent, but I will also be silent.'

Fifteen years later, Gauguin gave a more sensational version of the encounter:

I felt I must go out alone and take the air along some paths that were bordered by flowering laurels. I had almost crossed the Place Victor Hugo when I heard behind me a well-known step, short, quick, irregular. I turned about on the instant as Vincent rushed towards me, an open razor in hand. My look at that moment must have had great power in it, for he stopped and, lowering his head, set off running towards the house.

This was vivid, but there were several indications that it is also partly imaginary. Not only did Gauguin again muddle Place Lamartine with Place Victor Hugo, he also confused its vegetation. He wrote of *lauriers* – laurels – in flower. There are certain varieties of laurel which bloom in winter, but what he probably meant was *Laurier-rose*, or oleander, the flower 'that speaks of love', which Vincent had painted in September. When he wrote this passage, in his mind Gauguin was walking through Vincent's paintings of these gardens which had hung in his bedroom.

Was there any more reality to that sinister blade, glittering in Vincent's hand? The indications were that it was also a product of his imagination. The knife had been employed as a weapon by both Jack the Ripper and Prado in recent times, and their crimes had been widely reported. And that powerful gaze with which the crazed Vincent was subdued recalled the authority that the brothers Pianet exercised over their wild beasts.

It was true that Vincent was capable of acts of mild violence when deranged – kicking his nurse up the backside, for example. It was also the case – and the only evidence that led any credence to Gauguin's story – that Vincent later regretted not using greater violence in defending the Yellow House against the citizens of Arles.

But – assuming the razor existed only in Gauguin's mind – why did he make up this grave accusation against his by then dead friend? The next paragraph of Gauguin's narrative supplied the motive:

Was I negligent on this occasion? Should I have disarmed him and tried to calm him? I have often questioned my conscience about this, but I have never found anything to reproach myself with. Let him who will cast the first stone at me.

Obviously, Gauguin felt guilty; and he had examined his conscience.

By the time he wrote those words Vincent had already been established as a great painter and a saint of art. If Gauguin had not turned on his heel, if he had returned to the Yellow House and soothed his friend, perhaps the disaster would have been averted – although, in the long term, the fate that was overtaking Vincent was probably inexorable. So, Gauguin supplied a very good reason for leaving. Nobody, after all, could blame him for refusing to spend the night under the same roof with an armed madman who had threatened to attack him. As it was, Gauguin had had enough. He spent the night in a hotel.

Vincent returned to the Yellow House, perhaps after he had completed the mission on which he was going out, according to Gauguin's first account. Possibly he posted his letter to Theo, or he went and had a drink, or both. Later in the evening, around ten-thirty to eleven, he took the razor with which he sometimes shaved his beard and cut off his own left ear – or perhaps just the lower part of it (accounts differ). In this process, his auricular artery was severed, which caused blood to spurt and spray.

As Gauguin remembered the scene the following day:

He must have taken some time to stop the flow of blood, for the day after there were a lot of wet towels lying about on the tiles in the lower two rooms. The blood had stained the two rooms and the little staircase that led up to our bedroom.

This indicated either that Vincent was in the studio, in the presence of his new painting, *La Berceuse*, when he mutilated himself – or that he had done so in the bedroom and then walked downstairs.

After he had staunched the gore pumping from his head with the linen which he had bought so proudly for the Yellow House, he put the little amputated fragment of himself – having first washed it carefully, according to Gauguin – in an envelope of newspaper (perhaps that morning's *L'Intran-sigeant*').

Then he put on a hat, pulled right down on the injured side of his head – Gauguin recalled that it was a beret, perhaps Gauguin's own, left lying around after his abrupt departure. Vincent went out across Place Lamartine once more, through the gateway in the town wall, turned left and then took the second turning on the left, and walked to the brothel at No. 1, Rue du Bout d'Arles. There he asked the man on the door if he could see a girl named Rachel, and delivered his grisly package.

There are two slightly different accounts of how he did this. The following week the *Forum républicain* carried this item in its local news section:

Last Sunday at 11.30 p.m. one Vincent Vaugogh painter, of Dutch origin, presented himself at the *maison de tolérance* no. 1, asked for one Rachel, and gave her . . . his ear, saying, 'Guard this object very carefully.' Then he disappeared.

Gauguin told Bernard that Vincent gave a more biblical-sounding instruction when he handed over his nasty package: 'You will remember me, verily I tell you this.'

Not surprisingly, Rachel fainted when she discovered what she had been given. Somehow, Vincent got home. He climbed the blood–spattered stairs, put a light in his window and fell – as he had before during these attacks – into a deep, deep sleep.

★

What had been going on in Vincent's mind that led him to do something at once so horrible and so oddly specific? It was as though he was following a ritual of his own devising. People suffering from mental disturbances do many strange things, but very, very few cut off their own ears (though, following Vincent's example, more were to do so in the future).

Vincent himself claimed afterwards to have only the vaguest recollection of what had occurred. But perhaps he just preferred not to go into it. When questioned by his doctor, he replied that the reasons were 'quite personal'.

However, there were some clues. It seemed that Vincent, who could not normally sing, had sung in his madness. He had sung 'an old nurse's song', because he was 'dreaming of the song that the woman rocking the cradle sang to rock the sailors to sleep'. That was, he explained to Gauguin, the same subject 'for which I was searching in an arrangement of colours before I fell ill'.

After subsequent attacks, Vincent confessed he was plagued by religious fears, and also by what he dubbed 'religious exultation':

I am astonished that with the modern ideas that I have, and being so ardent an admirer of Zola and de Goncourt and caring for things of art as I do, that I have attacks such as a superstitious man might have and that I get perverted and frightful ideas about religion such as never came into my head in the North.

So his wild thoughts that evening seemed intimately bound up with the subject of the picture he was painting: a mother rocking a cradle, who was also, at least in his mind, a Madonna comforting sailors who were afloat on perilous seas. Looking back on this project of painting a holy woman from life, he reflected that the emotions it aroused were 'too strong'.

There were other hints at the thoughts that whirled in his head that night: two narratives that obsessed him, both connected with the previous occasion on which he had had a household and a studio — 'a studio with a cradle' — and lost it. Both of these stories involved the cutting off of ears.

The first story was the drama of Christ's agony in the Garden of Gethsemane. Foreseeing his arrest, torture and crucifixion, Christ prayed, saying, 'If thou be willing, remove this cup from me: nevertheless not my will, but thine, be done.' Vincent had seen his decision that he should leave the reformed prostitute Sien Hoornik and her two children in terms of the Agony in the Garden.

In the New Testament, after Christ accepted his fate, Judas burst into the garden accompanied by armed men, come to arrest him. When the disciples saw what was going to happen, they thought of defending Christ by force, 'And one of them smote the servant of the high priest, and cut off his right ear.'

The other narrative was Zola's novel, *The Sin of Father Mouret*. Vincent read it shortly after the birth of baby Willem, in July 1882. A fantasy rather than a realistic novel, this dealt with a crisis in the life of Serge Mouret, a priest in a small village in Provence. It was luxuriantly overwritten, in terms that mixed allegory and dream; many readers might have concluded it was just bad. But its literary deficiencies were unlikely to have bothered Vincent, who must have found a remarkable number of parallels to his own life in this book.

The central character, Father Serge Mouret, was ecstatically pious — just as Vincent had been in the Borinage. Then he suffered a crisis — as the young Vincent had. He collapsed, 'his teeth chattering', before a statue of the Virgin.

When Mouret awakes, he is in paradise — or rather in *Le Paradou*, a huge, overgrown garden to which Doctor Pascal Rougon has taken him to recover. He is nursed by Albine, a wild teenage girl who lives there with her grandfather. Under her care, he recovers, and together they explore the paradise garden. This is described by Zola in paragraph after paragraph of overheated – indeed, hothouse – prose. Great stress is laid on the sexuality of the plants and trees. The effect is of a horticultural *Kama Sutra*.

Finally, the inevitable fall occurs: Albine and Serge make love and Serge is driven from the garden by the stern and violent local friar, Brother Archangias (or 'Archangel'). He returns to his life as a priest and resists Albine's entreaties to return to her, the garden and love. Eventually, she kills herself, poisoned – rather improbably – by flowers. The final scene of the book is that of her funeral.

The characters of the novel gather in the cemetery beside Albine's grave. Then a new figure appears: Jeanbernat, Albine's grandfather:

He stood behind Brother Archangias and seemed for an instant to be gazing intently at the back of his neck. Then, as Father Mouret was finishing the prayers, he calmly pulled a knife from his pocket, opened it, and chopped off the friar's ear.

Vincent had this book – and the drama in the Garden of Gethsemane – in his mind when he was making the decision to leave Sien. Then, he wrote that 'a Paradou is beautiful, but a Gethsemane is even more beautiful' – the implication being that spiritual struggle was a more compelling subject than an erotic idyll. And he was certainly reminded of Zola's novel when he saw the rampant vegetation of Provence at Montmajour. Very probably, he also knew that one of the farms there, whose fields he painted, was called *Le Paradou*.

Vincent's action on the evening of 23 December suggested that he again recalled this strange fiction. But if so, why did he inflict the punishment of Brother Archangias on himself? In the novel, the friar, rough and unpleasant, stands for the unbending laws of the Old Testament. He makes it his business to persecute the local children for their natural, sinful behaviour, his favourite punishment being to pull their ears. A prominent victim of the friar is the altar boy, Vincent, who has unruly red hair – a detail that would have impressed the other Vincent, who could claim Bruyas as a brother partly on grounds of hair pigmentation.

Near the start of the novel, Archangias catches Vincent in the churchyard, looking at a bird's nest. This place is the child's 'paradise of nests, lizards and flowers'. Archangias destroys the nest and suspends the boy by his ear in mid air. Vincent van Gogh, too, had been obsessed by nests – he painted and drew them at Nuenen, where his studio had been full of them.

There might have been one more connection in his mind: the ear of Catherine Eddowes, sliced off by Jack the Ripper on 30 September. It was characteristic of Vincent's mind that it skipped from one association to another. In the Musée Fabre at the beginning of the week he had shot along a helter-skelter of associations.

Now, in the anguish of Gauguin's departure, Vincent must have experienced another such typhoon of thoughts and feelings. In his agony of mind and whirling confusion, Vincent did what the voices in his head did, as he later revealed: he blamed himself. He was responsible for the terrible, solitary life he led (isolated again now that Gauguin had left); he was guilty of causing the collapse of his dream of a shared studio. Vincent punished himself as Archangias had been punished in the novel, as St Peter punished the soldier in Gethsemane, as the red-haired altar-boy, Vincent, had been chastised for his misdemeanours, and as Catherine Eddowes had suffered at the hands of the Ripper.

He took his razor, and slashed. Then he wrapped what he had removed, and gave it to one of those 'little good women' of Rue du Bout d'Arles.

Contact with Rachel and her colleagues was the nearest thing to a sensuous or emotional life he had, a little taste of paradise at 2 francs a time. To Vincent, they were sisters of mercy. The murderers of the autumn made prostitutes suffer; he punished himself and gave the result to a prostitute. Not surprisingly, she didn't understand, and nor did anyone else. And when he came to his senses, even Vincent claimed to have forgotten why he had done such a strange and horrible thing.

There was understandable consternation at the brothel. The following morning a passing gendarme named Alphonse Robert was summoned. There, Virginie Chabaud, who ran the establishment, showed him the ghastly offering that Vincent had presented to the girl Rachel.

He questioned them, opened the package and certified that it did indeed contain an ear. 'It was my duty to inform my superior immediately.' Forthwith, Commissioner Joseph d'Ornano and other officers went to look for Vincent in the Yellow House.

While this drama was being played out a few hundred yards away in the Yellow House, Gauguin was tossing and turning in his hotel bed. He did not get to sleep until three and woke up later than usual, around seven-thirty. When he was dressed, he walked over to Place Lamartine, perhaps intending to make amends for the row the night before, or at least to say goodbye in a more amicable fashion and collect his belongings. Possibly, he was a little concerned as to what had happened to Vincent on his own.

The sight that met his eyes as he approached the Yellow

House was not reassuring. There was a great crowd of on-
lookers gathered in the square. 'Near our house there were
some gendarmes and a little gentleman in a bowler hat who
was the Commissioner of Police.' This was d'Ornano, the
man who had been caricatured so cheerfully in Gauguin's
sketchbook.

Gauguin had no idea what had happened. But he must
have been extremely alarmed; he no sooner appeared than
he was arrested because the house 'was full of blood'. Presumably Gauguin came along before the police had entered the
Yellow House, otherwise they would rapidly have established
that Vincent was still alive. They had probably seen the
evidence of carnage through the glass at the top of the
studio door.

This must have been a terrible moment for Gauguin. As he
knew well, it was quite possible that Vincent had committed
suicide; it was also possible that his death might look like
murder. D'Ornano apparently assumed the worst.

Gauguin recalled:

The gentleman in the bowler hat said to me straightaway, in a tone
that was more than severe, 'What have you done to your comrade,
Monsieur?'

'I don't know . . .'

'Oh, yes . . . you know very well . . . he is dead.'

I would never wish anyone such a moment, and it took me a
long time to get my wits together and control the beating of my
heart.

Anger, indignation, grief, as well as shame at all the suspicious
looks that were tearing my entire being to pieces, suffocated me,
and I answered, stammeringly: 'All right, Monsieur, let us go
upstairs. We could talk about it up there.'

Perhaps Gauguin then produced his own key; at any rate, they climbed the stairs. Gauguin's starring role in the next part of the story made his account a little suspect:

In the bed lay Vincent, rolled up in the sheets, curled up in a ball; he seemed lifeless. Gently, very gently, I touched the body, the heat of which showed that it was still alive. For me it was as if I had suddenly got back all my energy, all my spirit.

But perhaps he really had been the first to touch the body.

Then in a low voice I said to the Police Commissioner, 'Be kind enough, Monsieur, to awaken this man with great care, and if he asks for me tell him I have left for Paris; the sight of me might prove fatal to him.'
I must own that from this moment the Police Commissioner was as amenable as possible and intelligently sent for a doctor and a cab.

Vincent regained consciousness, though it does seem that Gauguin took care to remain out of his sight:

Once awake, Vincent asked for his comrade, his pipe and his tobacco; he even thought of asking for the box that was downstairs and contained our money – a suspicion, I dare say! But I had already been through too much suffering to be troubled by that. Vincent was taken to a hospital where, as soon as he had arrived, his mind began to wander again.

Gauguin was more specific, if not necessarily more accurate, when he gave his report to Bernard in Paris. He did not mention Vincent's worry that he had absconded with the houschold's petty cash, but he did describe what happened when Vincent was taken to the hospital, the Hôtel Dieu, on the other side of Arles: 'His state is worse, he wants to sleep with the patients, chases the nurses, and washes himself in the coal bucket. That is to say, he continues the Biblical mortifications.'

This remark suggested that Gauguin connected the ear amputation with the Bible, that is, with Gethsemane. Once he was released by the gendarmes, Gauguin sent a telegram to Theo telling him what had happened. The ear itself – or fragment of ear – was placed in a bottle and carefully handed over by the police to the doctors at the hospital, but far too late to sew it back again. So eventually it was thrown away.

On Monday 24 December, Christmas Eve, Theo was sitting in his office in an exceptionally euphoric mood. He had already written to his middle sister, Elisabeth, or Lies, telling her of his engagement, when Gauguin's telegram arrived.

Theo then wrote to Jo, who was staying with her brother in Paris. 'Vincent is gravely ill,' he scribbled on some Boussod et Valadon paper. 'I don't know what's wrong, but I shall have to go there as my presence is required. I'm so sorry that you will be upset because of me, when instead I would like to make you happy.' He gave the letter to her brother.

Then he wrote to her again, enclosing some letters from his mother and Wil and expressing the wish that Vincent, though very sick, might still recover. He caught a PLM express to the South, probably the 7.15 p.m. train; Jo, who had a heavy cold, came to see him off at the Gare de Lyons.

Next morning, Theo found Vincent in the hospital at Arles. The 'people around him' – which meant Gauguin – told Theo of Vincent's 'agitation', that he had for a few days been showing symptoms of madness, culminating in this 'high fever' and self-mutilation.

'Will he remain insane?' Theo raised the question.

The doctors think it is possible, but daren't yet say for certain. It should be apparent in a few days' time when he is rested; then we will see whether he is lucid again. He seemed alright for a few minutes when I was with him, but lapsed shortly afterwards into his brooding about philosophy and theology.

Vincent told Theo that in his delirium he had wandered over the fields of their childhood home, Zundert, and reminded his brother of how they had shared a little bedroom there, both boys' heads on one pillow:

It was terribly sad being there, because from time to time all his grief would well up inside him, and he would try to weep, but couldn't. Poor fighter & poor, poor sufferer. Nothing can be done to relieve his anguish now, but it is deep and hard for him to bear. Had he once found someone to whom he could pour his heart out, it might never have come to this. In the next few days they will decide whether he is to be transferred to a special institution.

When Theo talked to Vincent about his engagement and asked if he approved of the plan, Vincent replied that, yes, he did, but marriage 'ought not to be regarded as the main objective in life'. Vincent, for all his loneliness, had doubts about conventional wedlock.

Vincent asked for Gauguin 'continually', 'over and over'. But Gauguin didn't go to visit him in the hospital that Christmas Day. He claimed that seeing him would upset Vincent; perhaps he shrank from the pleading to which he would certainly have been subjected.

Theo left Arles on the night train to Paris on Christmas Day. Probably, Gauguin went with him, leaving so rapidly that he left several paintings and possessions in the Yellow House. He and Vincent never saw each other again.

12. Aftermath

26 December–2005

Roulin took over the task of looking after the invalid. He had promised Theo that he would report on Vincent's condition, which he did – bleakly – on Wednesday the twenty-sixth:

I am sorry to say I think he is lost. Not only is his mind affected, but he is very weak and down-hearted. He recognized me but did not show any pleasure at seeing me and did not inquire about any member of my family or anyone he knows. When I left him I told him I would come back to see him; he replied we would meet again in heaven, and from his manner I realized he was praying.

On the twenty-eighth, Roulin wrote again with even worse news. Vincent had had a visit on Thursday from Madame Roulin, *La Berceuse* herself:

He hid his face when he saw her coming. When she spoke to him, he replied well enough, and talked to her about our little girl [the baby Marcelle] and asked if she was still as pretty as ever.

Today, Friday, I went there but could not see him. The house doctor and the attendant told me that after my wife left he had a terrible attack; he passed a very bad night and they had to put him in an isolated room, he has taken no food and completely refuses to talk. That is the exact state of your brother at present.

Evidently, the sight of Augustine Roulin brought back with full intensity all the feelings that he had had in front of her picture on Sunday night. Perhaps it was then that Vincent sang himself those lullabies – in a surprisingly good voice – consoling himself for his loneliness, his pain, his desperation, his lost studio, his lost companion, and all the many sufferings of his life.

The next day, Vincent's mother, Anna van Gogh, wrote to Theo, noting her conviction that Vincent had been mad all along: 'I believe he was always ill and his suffering and ours was a result of it. Poor brother of Vincent, sweetest dearest Theo, you too have been very worried and troubled because of him.' She was divided between joy at Theo's engagement and grief at Vincent's breakdown. She wanted to know where Aix was. The best thing, she felt, would be for Vincent to die: 'I would ask, "Take him, Lord."'

Vincent's youngest sister Wilhelmina was filled with pity – and curiosity. She would go and visit him if he were dying – she had the money for the journey – but was he? Could he ever find peace? Or was the disease he suffered from irreversible, and physical? What a difficult life her poor brother had had. Did Gauguin see the catastrophe coming? That last question was one to which no one – perhaps not even Gauguin himself – really knew the answer.

Meanwhile, events were closing in on Prado, the murderer whose case Vincent and Gauguin had been following and whose fate seemed curiously intertwined with theirs. On the same Thursday, the twenty-seventh, that Vincent had been visited by Augustine Roulin, Prado's appeal for clemency was turned down.

Gauguin asked a friend in the Municipal Guard to let him know when the inevitable sequel was to occur. Late that

evening he was in the *Nouvelle Athènes*, a well-known haunt
of the Impressionists, when he got a telegram reporting that
Prado's execution was about to take place. There was of course
another death of which Gauguin was expecting to hear at any
moment: a sad announcement from the hospital in Arles.

Gauguin had had only one good night's sleep in several
days, yet, exhausted as he was, he went to see Prado die. In
France at that time the death penalty was still inflicted in
public. Often a large crowd gathered to watch, amounting
sometimes to thousands. At half-past two in the morning
Gauguin was on the Place de la Roquette, outside the prison,
stamping his feet, for it was extremely cold that night. His
interest in Prado's death must have been intense.

Already the area with the best view – the space around the
site of the guillotine – was crowded with dark, motionless,
waiting figures. Eventually, the moment came. The gates of
the prison opened and the guard marched out, the gendarmes
drew their sabres, many of the spectators doffed their hats.
Gauguin ran forward to get a better view, dodging between
the gendarmes.

Prado seemed small to Gauguin, but sturdy, holding his
handsome head proudly. He looked good 'in spite of the evil
appearance of his closely shaven head and his coarse white
linen shirt'. Later, and implausibly, Gauguin claimed to have
overheard Prado question his executioner: 'What is that?'
Answer: 'The basket for the head.' 'And, what is that?'
Answer: 'That is the box for your body.' Gauguin was utterly
fascinated by the panoply of judicial death.

When Prado's head was on the block, a triangular blade
weighted by a 66-pound wooden block was released by the
executioner. It fell 14 feet 9 inches on to the neck of the
prisoner. In this case, most unusually, it missed:

Instead of the neck it was the nose that was hit. The man struggled with pain, and two blue-blouses, brutally pushing on his shoulders, brought the neck into its proper place. There was a long minute, and then the knife did its work. I struggled to see the head lifted out of its basket; three times I was pushed back. They went off a few yards to get water in a pail to pour over the head.

Why did the execution of this criminal so obsess the painter, so much so that he later wrote two accounts of the event? In Gauguin's mind, Prado was innocent, a victim of an unjust society. He was, in other words, a martyr like the early Christians, whose code word, '*ictus*', Gauguin and Vincent used. To Gauguin, the contemporary artist – himself – was just such another outcast. Was there something else? Did Gauguin wonder if he was indeed a murderer, as Vincent's square of newspaper seemed to accuse him of being? Was he guilty of the death of his deserted friend?

In Gauguin's imagination, the horrible image of Prado's decapitation merged with the memory of Vincent's mangled ear. About a month later he produced a response by crafting – of all things – a vase.

It was, again, a self-portrait: a depiction of his own head severed, the ears shorn off, his eyes closed as in death. Once more, his own image and that of Vincent merged in Gauguin's mind – this time with that of St John the Baptist and the convicted murderer Prado. It was a portrait to match that of himself as Jean Valjean of *Les Misérables*: the artist as outlaw, criminal and suffering saint.

Against everybody's expectations, Vincent recovered rapidly. The house doctor, Félix Rey, predicted (correctly) that he would always retain the 'extreme excitability' that was 'the

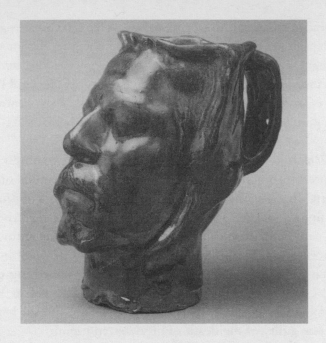

basis of his character', but within a few days Vincent had
returned to a normal state of lucidity. He was now concerned
that Theo had been anxious over him and that Gauguin had
had a shock.

Vincent still hadn't been told his housemate had departed
from Arles. 'Have I terrified him? In short, why hasn't he
given me any sign of life?' Vincent deduced that he must
have left with Theo but missed his companion badly. 'Tell
Gauguin to write to me, and that I think about him all the
time.'

By Friday 4 January Vincent was well enough to leave the
hospital and walk over with Roulin to the Yellow House,
where they stayed for four hours while Vincent delightedly
reacquainted himself with his paintings. During his days in

hospital, Roulin and the charlady had scrubbed the blood off the studio floor and the stairs and tidied up.

While he was there, Vincent took the opportunity to write a letter to Theo and another to Gauguin. He informed his brother that he hoped soon to start work again on the orchards of spring. To Gauguin he sent a message of mingled affection and reproach:

My dear friend Gauguin, I take the opportunity of my first outing from the hospital to write you a couple of words of my profound and sincere friendship. I have often thought of you in the hospital and even in full fever and relative weakness.

Then, abruptly, he shot out what seemed to him the crucial question: 'Tell me – was my brother Theo's trip necessary – my friend?'

Evidently, Vincent thought the answer was no. He sent his regards to the 'good Schoeffenecker' (Vincent, too, was capable of mangling names) and begged Gauguin to desist 'from speaking ill of our poor little yellow house'. On the margin, pathetically, were the words, 'Please reply soon.'

On Saturday the fifth Dr Rey came with a couple of medical friends and inspected Vincent's paintings. They were, Vincent reported, 'uncommonly quick at understanding at least what complementaries are'. Vincent was beginning to take a strong interest in Félix Rey. He was planning to paint his portrait.

Forty years later a journalist caught up with the now senior doctor, who had a slightly different recollection of his former patient:

He often complained that he was the only painter in town and therefore could not talk to anyone about his art. For lack of such a colleague, he would talk to me about complementary colours. But I really could not understand why red should not be red, and green not green!

A couple of days later, on Monday the seventh, Vincent was released from hospital and back in the Yellow House. He celebrated by having dinner with Roulin at the Restaurant Venissat. Altogether, it seemed that Vincent had been positively refreshed by his stay in hospital; he embarked on painting again, beginning with some still lifes and two self-portraits, in which he was bandaged, shaken and muffled against the January chill.

He also painted Roulin again, and young Dr Rey. The latter portrait had a strange feature: the young doctor's ear was almost entirely blood-red.

However, Vincent's return to the Yellow House was not to last. By the third week in January his mood had begun to slump. The old financial anxieties were back. He itemized his expenditure since he had come out of hospital at length – so much for paying for the blood to be washed out of the linen, so much to pay the attendants who changed his dressings, and so on. As a result, he had run out of money and gone without food for days. There was more bad news: Roulin had been promoted, and would leave to take up a new post in Marseilles.

Vincent brooded on Gauguin's departure, his sending of the telegram summoning Theo. In a letter, he hinted at grave flaws in his ex-housemate's character:

On various occasions I have seen him do things which you and I would not let ourselves do, because we have consciences that feel differently about things. I have heard one or two things said of him, but having seen him at very, very close quarters, I think that

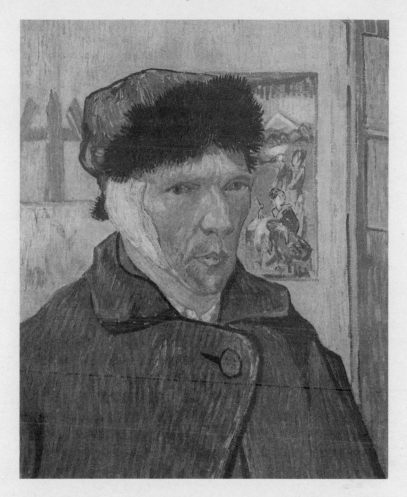

he is carried away by his imagination, perhaps by pride, but . . .
practically irresponsible.

Then Vincent's anger faded. He reflected that all artists
were a little unbalanced. 'Old Gauguin and I understand each
other basically, and if we are a bit mad, what of it?' They
would be vindicated – he thought, entirely correctly – by

their pictures. Vincent wrote to Gauguin advising that he should consult a doctor, as he too was doubtless a little cracked.

Towards the end of the month Vincent finally completed *La Berceuse*, the hands of which had been left unfinished at the time of the attack. Then he started to produce replicas of the composition. It was at this point that Vincent went to see the Provençal Christmas play and described hearing Roulin singing to his baby. He thought of himself as being like a *Santon* figure from a crèche, made out of cardboard with a papier-mâché ear, too flimsy to go travelling about the world any longer. He had lullabies on his mind again.

Again *La Berceuse* seemed perilous to his sanity; it called forth emotions that were 'too strong'. He had completed two more *Berceuses* and was working on a third on Sunday 3 February when he wrote a sad letter to Theo. His hopes of recovery had drained away. Evidently, Vincent felt the same old agitation rising in him again. Waves of mania passed over him, but he tried to disguise them:

I have moments when I am twisted with enthusiasm or madness or prophecy, like a Greek oracle on his tripod. I display great presence of mind then in my words, and speak like the Arlésiennes, but in spite of all that, my spirits are very low.

Four days later, he was back in the hospital. This was effectively the end of his free life in Arles.

Another doctor, Deloy, wrote a short report on 7 February. His patient, he wrote, was suffering from a state of complete over-excitement, a veritable frenzy in which he spoke incoherent words and failed to recognize the people around him. Vincent was prey to auditory hallucinations in which he heard reproachful voices; he was in the grip of a fixed idea that the people around him were trying to poison him.

Ten days later he was once again pronounced recovered and released, but this time his neighbours were horrified. A petition or protest was organized and delivered to the Mayor, Monsieur Tardieu. 'We the undersigned, inhabitants of the city of Arles,' it began:

have the honour of informing you that a certain Vood [Vincent], a Dutch citizen, landscape painter, and inhabitant of the said place, has for some time and on several occasions given sundry proofs that he is not in possession of his mental faculties.

Essentially, they protested that Vincent was just too alarming as a neighbour:

He indulges in excessive drinking after which he finds himself in such a state of over-excitement that he knows neither what he is doing nor what he is saying. His instability frightens all the inhabitants of that quarter, and above all the women and the children.

The petition suggested that he should either return to his family, who would look after him, or he should be sent to an asylum. It was signed by thirty people. The first name was François Crevoulin, the grocer who lived next door, and in the middle column was the signature of Joseph Ginoux. When this was received, Vincent was again locked up, after a week of independent life, and there was an investigation by the police into the accusations that had been made.

On 3 March, central police Commissioner Joseph d'Ornano presented his conclusions. Five witnesses had been questioned. Bernard Soulé, who lived at no. 53, the hotel on Avenue de Montmajour and was the manager of the Yellow

House on behalf of the landlord, testified that Vincent's reasoning was impaired and his speech incoherent. He also said he touched the local women and wandered into their houses. Marguèrite Crevoulin, who ran the grocer's shop in the other half of the same building as the Yellow House and from whom Vincent had bought the ingredients for Gauguin to cook, had similar complaints. Jeanne Conial, a forty-two-year-old dress-maker living at 24 Place Lamartine added that Vincent had grabbed her on the pavement outside the Yellow House and lifted her into the air. The final witness simply supported what all the others had said. He was Joseph Ginoux. Vincent never found out about this betrayal; he remained on good terms with the Ginouxs until the day he died. They looked after his furniture, whose fate continued to concern him.

As a result of the petition and the police investigation, Vincent was locked up in a private cell in the hospital without tobacco, books or paints. Once again, after a couple of weeks, he regained some semblance of lucidity. This time, however, there was to be no rapid return to normal life.

On Saturday 23 March he had a visitor from another world. His old friend Paul Signac, the pointillist painter, was passing through Arles on his way to work on the Mediterranean coast at Cassis. This was a sign that Vincent, all along, had been right to think the South of France was the new land of art. From now on, with increasing frequency, the painters of Paris would take flight like migratory birds for Provence and Languedoc. The Fauves, the Cubists, Matisse, Picasso: all of them would follow Vincent to the South.

He and Signac went to the Yellow House, which had been sealed by the police. After a negotiation with the authorities, Signac made a forcible entry and was able to inspect the treasures of painting that were lying within. Signac did not quite know what to make of what he saw. Many, he reported to Theo, were 'very good', and all 'very curious'. Much later, he remembered only the 'splendour' of the whitewashed walls, on which Vincent's paintings 'flowered in their full freshness'. The next day, the two men went for a walk. Signac suggested that Vincent might join him in Cassis.

There it was: a chance once again to set up a studio in the South with a new companion, another gifted painter fascinated by colour. But Vincent did not take it. His confidence had gone. He no longer felt up to living with another person, nor to living alone. He began to see himself as a person with chronic mental problems: 'Now and then,' he recorded, 'there are horrible fits of anxiety, apparently without cause, or otherwise a feeling of emptiness and fatigue in the head.'

Vincent now lived in fear of another attack. He decided that he would prefer to spend the next few months in a nursing home. On his behalf, the Protestant clergyman in Arles, Revd Salles – who was looking after his interests – made contact with an institution a few miles away, outside St Rémy.

Before he departed, Vincent paid a visit to Place Lamartine, where the 'real neighbours' – presumably the Ginoux rather than the Crevoulins at the grocer's shop – assured him that they had not signed the petition nor cooperated with the police investigation. But Vincent was beginning to feel that the petitioners had had a point. Part of his anxiety about living outside an institution was that he might act oddly and make scenes.

Since Christmas, he told his sister Wil, 'I have had in all four great crises, during which I didn't in the least know what I said, what I wanted and what I did.' Sometimes he had 'moods of indescribable mental anguish, sometimes moments when the veil of time and the fatality of circumstances seemed to be torn apart for an instant'.

But the problems, he now saw, had been going on for longer than just the previous few months. 'I have been "in a hole" all my life,' he told Theo. 'And my mental condition is not only vague *now*, but *has always been so*, so that whatever is done for me, I *cannot* think things out so as to balance my life.'

On Wednesday 1 May, the anniversary of that exciting day when he had signed the contract for the Yellow House, he was back there, packing up his pictures. While he had been in hospital the Rhône had flooded – as it almost had in November – to within a stone's throw of the house, which was uninhabited and unheated. When Vincent returned, 'water and saltpetre were oozing from the walls'.

Some of the paintings had been damaged by the damp and, over those, Vincent stuck newspaper before putting them in a packing case together with Gauguin's fencing masks and gloves and the pictures his friend had left behind.

Vincent felt terrible sadness, since:

not only the studio had come to grief, but even the studies that would have been reminders of it. It is all so final, and my urge to found something very simple but lasting was so strong. I was fighting a losing battle, or rather it was weakness of character on my part, for I am left with feelings of deep remorse about it, difficult to describe. I think that was the reason I cried out so much during the attacks – I wanted to defend myself and couldn't do it.

Two days later, he left for St Rémy, in the company of Revd Salles.

In all, Vincent had four more attacks while he was at St Rémy. The first did not come until 16 July, after a long remission during which Vincent once more hoped he was cured. But when it came, it stayed for a long time; it did not lift for a month and a half. The attacks, Vincent reported, 'tend to take an absurdly religious turn'.

Then, almost on the anniversary of his ear amputation, he became deranged again on 24 December 1889. This lasted only for a week, as did a second crisis commencing on 21 January. There was a short interval before another wave of madness hit him on 23 February, which for a while looked as if it would never recede. It was over two months before he recovered, a long period, during which, according to Dr Peyron, he would seem about to rally, then fall back into silence and suspicion.

At St Rémy, the first attempt was made to diagnose what the matter was with Vincent. Dr Peyron believed he had a form of epilepsy. It was not a bad diagnosis. Evidently, Vincent did not have full epileptic fits, but a variety of attack known as a partial seizure might indeed explain many of his symptoms. It would account for the sudden onset of the attacks – one came on while he was painting a picture of the mouth of a quarry at St Rémy, which he managed to complete before succumbing. These partial seizures could be associated with depression, hallucinations and delusions.

Dr Peyron, however, had not had an opportunity to chart Vincent's moods and behaviour from day to day over a period of years. Nobody, except Theo, ever did. Strangely, that was an examination that could be carried out – to some extent at least – posthumously and at a distance, through the medium of Vincent's letters, which were slowly silting up in Theo's desk. Few people have left a fuller self-portrait in words than Vincent did.

Despite the interruptions of his attacks, at the hospital Vincent had long intervals of steady and productive work. He painted again with great power and intensity, but by and large he avoided the complementary colours and brilliant palette of the previous year in Arles. He associated this 'high yellow note' with the life he had then led – keyed up by alcohol and coffee, and without regular meals.

At St Rémy his regime was much more sober. He and the other inmates consumed large quantities of dull food, mainly pulses (Vincent made a joke of the farting this caused). He took long, cold, therapeutic baths and worked either in the hospital itself or its garden. For periods he was intensely nervous of encountering strangers. And, when alone in the fields, he was overwhelmed by a feeling of loneliness, 'to such a horrible extent that I shy away from going out'.

Rather than working from memory or imagination, Vincent developed a method of making copies from other artists' works – or as he preferred to describe them, with reason, 'translations'. Among the sources he used were prints after paintings by Delacroix, Rembrandt and Millet, and prints by Daumier and Gustav Doré. Vincent also made a series of paintings from Gauguin's drawing of Madame Ginoux, which had been left in the Yellow House and which he had brought with him to the hospital. Borrowing ready-made compositions was a way of solving his eternal problem: how to invent a composition, without a subject in front of him that he could see.

Vincent achieved some notable paintings *de tête* while he was at St Rémy. Of these, the most extraordinary depicted a starry sky, the sight he had once written would soothe him when he felt himself becoming agitated. But this was a most unsoothing starry sky, in which the heavenly bodies swirl through the night rather than hanging motionless and far away. In the foreground, a huge cypress tree rears up and, in the centre, almost overwhelmed by the humming power of natural forces, is the sharp steeple of a church – not a Provençal church but a northern one such as one might have found in Holland.

But Vincent remained unable to paint a Gethsemane. When both Bernard and Gauguin painted exactly that subject in the autumn of 1889, Vincent reacted with rage. Gauguin's Christ had his own features but Vincent's red hair. The mingling of roles that had gone on in the Yellow House continued still.

Vincent denounced Gauguin's painting, in which he felt nothing was 'really observed'. About Bernard's effort, he was savage – 'roaring my loudest, and calling you all sorts of names with the full power of my lungs', he implored Bernard to become himself again.

Vincent had finally tired, he claimed, of working *de tête*:

When Gauguin was in Arles, I once or twice allowed myself to be led astray into abstraction, as you know, for instance in the Berceuse, in the Woman Reading a Novel, black against a yellow bookcase. At the time, I considered abstraction an attractive method. But that was delusion, dear friend, and one soon comes up against a brick wall.

I don't say one might not try one's hand at it after a whole life long of experimentation, of hand-to-hand struggle with nature, but personally, I don't want to trouble my head with such things.

He even regretted his *Starry Night*: 'once again I allowed myself to be led astray into reaching for stars that are too big – another failure – and I have had my fill of that.'

After a month in Paris Gauguin returned to Pont-Aven; at the same time he exhibited, as planned, with *Les XX* in Brussels. In May he was back in Paris making preparations for an exhibition of work by himself and his friends for the Universal Exhibition (the Eiffel Tower was now finished and dominating the skyline of the city). Then he returned to Brittany and settled in Le Pouldu – a more primitive spot than Pont-Aven – with Theo's Dutch protégé de Haan.

Gauguin had not given up his plan to move to the tropics, and applied to the Colonial Office for an appointment in Tonkin, where Second Lieutenant Milliet had served. When this was turned down, he decided to go to Madagascar instead, with – perhaps – de Haan, Vincent, Bernard and Schuffenecker.

At the beginning of 1890, there were signs that Vincent was about to become a success. On 18 January, the exhibition of *Les XX* opened in Brussels; this year it included six paintings by him. And the January issue of *Le Mercure de France* contained a long and laudatory piece on Vincent by the critic Albert Aurier. Even better, a painting of his was sold for a decent price: 400 francs.

The article by Aurier was essentially Vincent as seen by Gauguin and Bernard, a friend of Aurier's. He presented Vincent, eloquently, as a realist, but also as a visionary and a symbolist.

'The fixed idea that haunts [Vincent's] brain,' thought Aurier, was of the 'coming of a man, a messiah, a sower of truth, who will regenerate our decadent and perhaps imbecilic industrial society'. He had an obsessive passion for the 'solar disc' and, at the same time, 'for this vegetal star, the sumptuous sunflower'. The critic hailed his 'brilliant and dazzling symphonies of colour and lines' and evoked the painter's delight in imagining an 'art of the tropical regions'. The legend was born of Vincent van Gogh, the mad, inspired artist.

Vincent himself was flattered, but also appalled. He wrote to Aurier, offering a picture in gratitude, thanking him for his praise but pointing out that there were others, especially Monticelli and Gauguin, who were more worthy to receive it, particularly in the matter of colour and the art of the tropics: '*For the role attaching to me, or that will be attached to me, will remain, I assure you, of very secondary importance.*' Vincent was a little hurt that Aurier was rude about Meissonier.

He wrote to Theo, confessing that:

Aurier's article would encourage me if I dared to let myself go, and venture even further, dropping reality and making a kind of music of tones with colour, like some Monticellis. But it is so dear to me, this truth, *trying to make it true*, after all I think, I think, that I would still rather be a shoemaker than a musician in colours.

In any case he felt that remaining faithful to what he saw before him was 'perhaps a remedy in fighting the disease which still continues to disquiet me.'

Of the first four months of 1890, Vincent spent all but a few weeks in a state of insanity or withdrawal. Vincent regarded the most prolonged of these attacks as a punishment for his success. It did not lift until the very end of April. Before he departed from the South, he did one more picture *de tête*: the one of two walkers – he and Gauguin – strolling down a Provençal road at evening.

On 16 May he finally left St Rémy to live under the supervision of Doctor Paul Gachet – a medical man with an interest in advanced art – in the quiet village of Auvers-sur-Oise north of Paris.

When Vincent arrived en route at Theo's apartment on 17 May 1890, he impressed his sister-in-law, Jo – who had never met him – with his robust healthiness. Rested after a year in St Rémy, he looked sturdy in comparison with Theo, whose constitution was weakening rapidly. Vincent also met a young nephew – named 'Vincent Willem' after him – who had been born in February. He renewed some old acquaintances and saw again his own paintings, gathered in

Theo's flat. But he found Paris too agitating. After three days, he moved on to Auvers.

There he enjoyed again, for the last time, an astonishing burst of productivity. In a little over two months he painted seventy-six pictures; sometimes he must have turned out two canvases a day. Dr Gachet pronounced him cured. On 8 June there was a happy reunion with Theo and his family, who took the train from Paris and lunched with Vincent and Gachet. Vincent gave his baby nephew a bird's nest as a toy.

The Ginouxs dispatched Vincent's furniture from Arles to Auvers, where Vincent thought of renting a cottage and establishing another studio. He wrote to thank them, adding that he regretted not having said goodbye to Arles:

I often think of you all, one cannot do what one wants in life. The more you feel attached to a spot, the more ruthlessly you are compelled to leave it, but the memories remain, and one remembers – as in a looking glass, darkly – one's absent friends.

He corresponded with Gauguin.

At the beginning of July, the shadows started to close in again. Jo was ill, the baby was ill, and Theo appeared to be in a terminal dispute with Boussod et Valadon, raising the spectre once more that Vincent might lose his allowance. All of this caused Vincent great anxiety. On the evening of Sunday 27 July he walked out into the fields and – either in depression, or fearing another attack, or in the throes of a crisis – he shot himself through the chest.

Typically, he made a mess of his suicide. The bullet missed his heart. After a while, he got up and staggered back to his lodgings, where his landlord found him lying wounded in bed. Vincent asked for his pipe, always a source of comfort, and lay in bed silently smoking.

Theo, who initially had hopes his brother might recover, was summoned, as he had been to Arles. Dr Gachet told Vincent he, too, was positive about his chances, but Vincent replied that then he would have the work of killing himself once more. Theo wrote to Jo that Vincent asked after her and the baby and said, 'You could not imagine there was so much sorrow in life.' The suffering, he said to Theo, goes on for ever. And towards the end, 'I wish I could pass away like this.' He died at 1.30 a.m. on Tuesday 29 July 1890.

Emile Bernard described the funeral which took place the following day to Aurier. On the walls around the coffin, Vincent's paintings were nailed up:

On the coffin, a simple white linen, masses of flowers, the sun-flowers which he loved so much, yellow dahlias, yellow flowers everywhere. It was his favourite colour, as you will remember, a symbol of the light he dreamt of in hearts as well as in paintings.

Gauguin's reaction was calm:

Sad though this death may be, I am not very grieved, for I knew it was coming and I knew how this poor fellow suffered in his struggles with madness. To die at this time is a great happiness for him, for it puts an end to his sufferings and if he returns in another life he will harvest the fruit of his fine conduct in this world (according to the law of the Buddha).

He must have remembered Vincent's *Self-Portrait* as a bonze.

Theo did not long outlive him. In September he suffered hallucinations and nightmares. After a violent dispute with his employers, he abruptly left the gallery. Then he sent Gauguin a telegram reading, 'Departure for tropics assured, money follows.' The offer was an empty one: Theo had gone mad.

He was taken to a Parisian hospital, then to a clinic run by a Dr Blanche in Passy. There was a diagnosis: general paralysis of the insane, one of the most horrible symptoms of tertiary syphilis. At the end of November Theo was transferred to a clinic near Utrecht, where he died on 25 January 1891, speechless and paralysed, at the age of thirty-three.

Naturally, Gauguin never received the money for his tropical exploration from Theo. But he remained determined to go. Since Bernard had reread Pierre Loti's book about Tahiti, that had become the destination. In February 1891 he held a successful sale of paintings in Paris to raise money for the trip. With the help of Charles Morice, author of 'The Blue Sow' and now a firm supporter of Gauguin's art, he was sent on an official government mission to paint in the South Pacific.

After a last visit to Mette and the children in Copenhagen, he set sail in April. He was alone. De Haan had returned to Holland; Bernard and Laval did not go with him. As he had always predicted, the dark figure of solitude was his only companion.

Gauguin returned to France in 1893 but was disenchanted with his native land. Again he set sail for Tahiti in July 1895, alone despite plans that others would accompany him. By this time he and Bernard had quarrelled bitterly, the latter accusing Gauguin of stealing his ideas in Pont-Aven at the time that the *Vision* was painted.

In 1901 he moved on from Tahiti to Atuona, on the island of Hivaoa in the remote group of islands called the Marquesas. By that stage he was chronically ill, with unhealed sores on his legs. Later, phials of morphine and broken bottles of absinthe were excavated from the well behind his house. The problem, almost certainly, was syphilis.

In those last years, Vincent was often in Gauguin's mind. In 1901 he painted his pictures of sunflowers in which some of the blooms have eyes – just as he had imagined the painted decorations in his bedroom at Arles had. Towards the end of his life he wrote a manuscript entitled *Diverses choses*, or 'Various Topics'. It included meditations on colour, religion and, at the end, the short story into which the circus, the brothel and other memories of Arles had been fused.

On the title page he wrote a description of his manuscript: 'Scattered notes, without sequel, like dreams, and like life itself made up entirely of fragments.' Under that, he wrote that several people had collaborated in 'the love of beautiful things glimpsed in the house of the future'. He must have been thinking of the Yellow House and his erstwhile companion in Arles because, as an afterthought, he pasted a drawing by Vincent where he had originally written the title. It was of the teenage girl Vincent called *La Mousmé*, after the Japanese courtesans in *Madame Chrysanthème*. Beside this, Gauguin wrote '*du regretté Vincent van Gogh*' – 'by the much-missed Vincent van Gogh'.

He was perhaps also thinking of Vincent and himself when he wrote in the manuscript of his memoirs, *Avant et après*, that 'it is so small a thing, the life of a man, and yet there is time to do great things, fragments of a common task.' Gauguin died on 8 May 1903, a month short of his fifty-fifth birthday. By that time he had become, like Vincent, almost a figure of myth among the artists of Paris: the painter who rejected civilization and went to live on the other side of the world in a primitive Eden.

As the years went by, Emile Bernard became increasingly religious and reclusive. He died in Paris in 1941, but by far the best work of his career had been done in the brief years when he was very young and in contact with Vincent and

Gauguin. The last surviving person who had had any role in the events of autumn 1888 in Arles was Second Lieutenant Milliet, who had risen to become a lieutenant-colonel and a Commander of the *Légion d'honneur* (though not, as Vincent had predicted, a general). Milliet, too, died during the Second World War.

Over the century that followed Vincent's death, the paintings which had once hung on the white walls of the Yellow House became familiar around the world. The story of Vincent's life was transformed into the fable of a mad artist painting under the raging southern sun, obsessed by massive, drooping sun-flowers. This was the portrait of Vincent as crazy saint and martyr that had first appeared in Gauguin's mind that autumn in Arles.

But what had really been the matter with Vincent? That was a question that embarrassed the world of art. Here was one of the greatest painters who had ever lived – as everyone now agreed – but he had gone mad and sliced off his ear. On the other hand, the unscholarly revelled in this gory episode. There were those who knew nothing much of art at all except that an artist once had done this crazy thing.

Vincent has been posthumously diagnosed with innumer-able conditions. An overdose of digitalis, lead-poisoning (from paint), absinthe-induced hallucinations, a condition of the inner ear named Ménière's disease, severe sun-stroke and glaucoma have all been put forward. So, too, have schizo-phrenia, syphilis, acute intermittent porphyria – a metabolic imbalance once believed to have caused the madness of George III – and borderline personality disorder (a contro-versial term for all those who were irritable, impulsive, drunken and had difficulty in getting on with their fellow men).

The most puzzling feature of Vincent's case was its inter-

mittent nature. He would be utterly out of his mind for a
spell, then quite shortly afterwards paint great pictures and
write letters of heart-breaking eloquence. All the explanations
listed above might illuminate some parts of his problem but
not the depth of his derangement and the suddenness with
which it could disappear.

Syphilis, for example, might have caused mania, but it is a
progressive condition caused by the destruction of the brain
and nervous system by the bacterium *Treponema pallidum*.
Vincent may well have been harbouring these creatures, as
would anyone who visited cheap prostitutes in 1888. But
tertiary syphilis would not descend and rise like fog. If Vincent
had it, the condition was still latent – hence, not the problem.
Similarly, it couldn't have been absinthe that gave him his
hallucinations, partly because he gave up drinking in St Rémy
and his problems didn't go away; partly because, it later turned
out, absinthe was not a hallucinogen anyway. And so on
down the list.

But evidently something had been ailing Vincent. Were
there any clues? Well, whatever it was, other members of his
family seemed to be afflicted by it. Vincent's younger brother,
Cornelius, migrated to South Africa and killed himself in a
'fever' in 1900. That same year, Wil – Vincent's beloved
younger sister, who was still living with her aged mother –
started behaving oddly and expressing 'bizarre ideas'.

She was admitted to a hospital in The Hague, then, in
1902, into another at Veldwijk in the area of Ermelo. There
she stayed for the rest of her long life, at first angry and
suicidal, later almost catatonic. She died on 17 May 1941, the
last of Vincent's siblings to survive. Theo also suffered – apart
from the syphilis that killed him – from 'melancholy', or, as
it was to be described in later years, depression.

Depression is one of the commonest ailments of Western

man and tends to run in families. Closely allied is another condition not properly analysed until long after Vincent died: manic depression, or bipolar disorder. This is, essentially, a disturbance of moods. What is known as sanity, it seems, is in part a biochemical affair: an ability to keep happiness and sadness within limits. Most of us go up and down in spirits. But in some individuals, for reasons that are still not known, the swing from one to the other is extremely violent. They are plunged into black and icy despair and rocket up into a frenzy of energy and exhilaration.

In the second stage they need little sleep; they can work at an inspired speed; their thoughts are supercharged with speed and audacity; they make connections that seem extraordinary to common sense (as Vincent did in his letter about the trip to Montpellier). The bipolar person may talk and talk, uncontrolled and uncontrollably, driving others away – as Vincent had Gauguin.

At the extreme top end of the mood curve, a manic depressive may shift into a shadowy world of unreality – as did Vincent when he saw things and heard voices that weren't there. They may develop paranoid delusions (such as that their neighbours are poisoning them).

One word much used of that manic mood did not often fit Vincent: 'euphoria'. At times he did have a feeling he described as 'exaltation' when he was working – in September in the sunny gardens of the Place Lamartine, for example. Some bipolar sufferers, however, enter a 'mixed' state in which they are neither exactly manic nor depressed: combining the rushing mind of mania with the fears and frantic anxiety of depression. That sounds very like Vincent, especially in November and December 1888.

At all times he had a see-sawing flux of morale dropping and rising constantly. That was how Second Lieutenant

Milliet – grown old and transformed into a retired colonel –
remembered Vincent when questioned decades later:

He didn't have an easygoing personality, and when he was angry
he seemed crazy.
Was he, then, irascible?
Yes and no. Rather agreeable, on the whole, but quite change-
able from day to day. Very nervous. Furious when I offered a
criticism of his painting. But that didn't last. We always ended up
reconciling.

Irascibility is characteristic of manic moods, especially
mixed ones. Another indication is recourse to drugs or alcohol
to deaden the agony of the down swings and quieten the
ferment of the highs. That is precisely what Vincent said he
did: 'if the storm within gets too loud, I take a glass too much
to stun myself.' It was also the reason why Edgar Allen Poe,
almost certainly bipolar, drank so much; so Gauguin was
closer than he realized when he compared the two.

Vincent's case, in fact, was almost a textbook one. Many
details of his behaviour tally: the gloomy religious thoughts
that came on him, much to his surprise, during his attacks
and the loss of sexual inhibition that led him, if only mildly,
to molest the women of Place Lamartine: lifting a middle-aged
dressmaker clean off the pavement. Both are typical.

The puzzling feature was the speed at which his attacks
came on and then receded, but this is explained by another
phenomenon connected with manic depression: rapid cycling. A patient is undergoing rapid cycling if they have more
than four major episodes per year – Vincent's exact rate in
1889. It is relatively common among those who are afflicted
by mixed states.

So, had Vincent been examined by Doctors Rey or Peyron

a century or so later they would probably have found a ready diagnosis. They would also have had a cure to prescribe. In the mid twentieth century it was discovered that violent mood swings could be controlled by drugs such as lithium. But would Vincent have accepted the prescription?

The question is not empty. Taking the pills would have reduced his mental pain, but a number of bipolar writers and artists, given the drug, gave it up. They miss the excitement of the highs when – as the composer Hugo Wolf, another sufferer, put it – 'blood becomes changed into steams of fire'. Sane life feels flat to them.

The last surprise about Vincent – apparently such a unique individual – is that he was not alone. Bipolar affective disorder occurs in about 1 per cent of modern Western populations, but its incidence among creative people – poets and writers in particular – appears to be much higher. Thus Vincent had many distant companions – the composer Schumann, Byron, Poe, the architect Borromini – who shared some or all of his distress and exaltation. He was right in a way when he suggested he just suffered from 'an artist's fit'.

Bipolar disorder is a terrible and often, as in Vincent's case, fatal disease. Around two-thirds of suicides are either depressive or manic depressive (so the manner of Vincent's death was also characteristic). But living so near the edge may allow a person to see further. The rushing thoughts, the connections seen where no one in a normal mental state might see them, the keenness of feeling and suffering – all these might fuel a creative voyage. The madness of artists is not entirely mythic.

That leads us to a final question about Vincent. Was he a painter who happened to suffer from a mental illness, or was he, as Gauguin came to present him, a crazy martyr and seer? The answer is complex. Art historians have been inclined to ignore Vincent's problems as unrelated to their investigations. And it is true that bipolar patients are demented, if at all, for limited periods and otherwise may be capable, like Vincent, of brilliant, disciplined and deeply pondered work.

But Vincent's condition was not irrelevant: it permeated his mind and personality. Given a mood-stabilizing medicine in 1889, he would have retained remarkable skills of hand and eye, but he would have been a different – and probably a duller – artist.

In part, his painting was therapeutic: it kept him steady. He said this over and over again. But this was the case only when he was depicting something that was in front of him – a chair, a person, a flower. Even when he did that, his mind was apt to swarm with associations. For him to work from memory or imagination was perilous: he might be overwhelmed by teeming thoughts, some of them dark. That was part of his inner story that autumn in Arles. Vincent feared to work *de tête*, yet risked it in Gauguin's company. But the danger still remained.

In a way, Gauguin got him wrong. Vincent wasn't an inspired, mad artist; he was a great painter desperately trying to remain sane. He saw the world with a rare intensity which gave great power to his work. And it was while looking and painting that he knew the greatest pleasure of which his tormented nature was capable.

After Vincent's departure, the Yellow House itself was used in many ways, finally serving as one half of a bar named *La Civette Arlésienne*.

On 25 June 1944 the little building was hit in a bombing raid. The explosion reduced Vincent's bedroom to rubble, but part of the old studio and Gauguin's bedroom survived for a while longer.

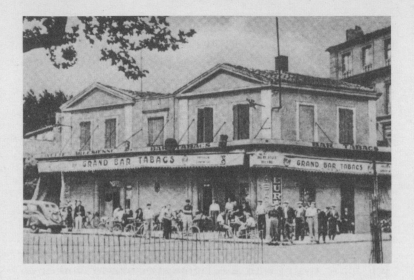

After the war, the site of the Gendarmerie became a super-market; the gardens of Place Lamartine were replaced by a car park and a roundabout. The brothel at No. 1, Rue du Bout d'Arles was demolished. Little remained of the scruffy, marginal quarter of the town that Vincent and Gauguin had inhabited. The Café de la Gare was no more, but still in somewhat similar bars, not quite shaven men drank at tables around a billiard table. At night, no doubt, a prostitute or two came out. Only the atmosphere lingers – that, and the pictures.

Notes on Sources

I felt it would be cumbersome to footnote every point in a book of this kind. This is a subject which has been studied by generations of scholars, to many of whom I am indebted. In particular, I owe a great deal to Douglas Druick and Peter Zegers and their brilliant catalogue for the *Studio of the South* exhibition in 2002 – especially to the technical examination which enabled them to sort out decisively which paintings had been done in the period from October to December 1888.

I accept, as they do, and it is believed the forthcoming new edition of Van Gogh's letters will do, that letter LT 565 was sent around 12 December, not 23 December, as previously believed. All my quotations from Van Gogh letters are from the excellent searchable edition to be found on *www.webexhibits.com*. The quotations from Gauguin's *Avant et après* are from Van Wyck Brooks's translation (entitled in English *The Intimate Journals of Paul Gauguin*), revised by me. The translations of his letters are in some cases by me; others are taken from *Writings of a Savage* (ed. Guérin), *Gauguin: A Retrospective* (ed. Prather & Stuckey) and *Gauguin By Himself* (ed. Thomson). The translations of 'The Blue Sow' and Gauguin's story in *Diverses choses* are mine, as is that of the letter from Milliet.

My discussion of Gauguin's and Vincent's religious background in Chapter 4 and of the Arles Christmas festivities in

Chapter 8 is largely based on the work of Debora Silverman in her book *Van Gogh and Gauguin: The Search for Sacred Art* (though the notion that the Roulins might have had a crèche is my own).

There are several other works which I would like in particular to acknowledge. I found Victor Merlhès's *Paul Gauguin and Vincent van Gogh, 1887–1888, Lettres retrouvées, sources ignorées* of great use, especially for its inclusion of several Gauguin letters not available elsewhere. I have depended on Jan Hulsker's *Vincent and Theo van Gogh: A Dual Biography* for many points concerning Vincent's earlier life. Ronald Pickvance's catalogue for the exhibition *Van Gogh in Arles* at the Metropolitan Museum of Art, New York, in 1984 was frequently highly useful.

I found Kay Redfield Jamison's *Touched With Fire* completely convincing regarding Vincent's medical condition, and Martin Bailey's excellent re-examination of the facts surrounding the drama of the severed ear appeared in *Apollo* in September 2005, just as I was finalizing this text, so I was able to incorporate several of his points.

The details of Wilhelmina van Gogh's illness are culled from an article by Dr Erik van Faasen, of Veldwijk psychiatric hospital in Ermelo, where she was a patient (this was translated for me by Dr Murray Pearson). Much of my information about the Roulins comes from J-N Priou's article in the *Revue des PTT de France*, 1955; but my information about Camille Pelletan comes from Stone's *Sons of the Revolution*. The suggestion that Roulin was probably an admirer of the fiery Camille rather than his father Eugène – dead for some years in 1888 – is my own, as is the idea that he might have named his second son after the Republican politician.

I believe I am the first writer who has noted the names of the neighbours who signed the petition against Vincent and gave evidence to the police about him. Ginoux's name is clearly legible on the petition; so, too, are several others on the police investigation report. Both are published in facsimile in Arles (2003). I discussed this discovery at more length in a piece for the *Daily Telegraph* arts section, 25 June 2005.

A good deal of what I have written consists of straightforward deductions from the letters, pictures and the plan of the house (for example, that there must have been a smell of tobacco smoke in a smallish room in which two keen pipe-smokers worked all day), but there are some new conjectures and pieces of evidence in *The Yellow House* on which more detail might be useful.

1. *Gauguin, Vincent and the brothels*

The brothels of Arles play a prominent part in the story, but little information has been available on them. This is for several reasons. The Arles police files for the relevant period are missing and the files concerning the administration of the brothels closed for 150 years. Furthermore, Vincent, though he made repeated references to the subject of brothels and prostitution, did not go into much detail (the more one reads the letters, the more one suspects that there were aspects of his life he was shielding).

Recently, a few new points have been established, however. The closed brothel dossier has been examined by the archivist for Martin Bailey, so we now know that the brothel at No. I *Rue du Bout d'Arles* was run by a certain Virginie Chabaud.

There are passages that concern the brothel in Arles in a short story by Gauguin to be found at the end of his manuscript *Diverses choses* (pp. 269–73 in the manuscript). This is an extremely odd narrative, which begins with a reverie, after which the narrator adopts various personae. First, he is a soldier – resembling Generals MacMahon and Boulanger and Second Lieutenant Milliet – then he is the owner of a circus-cum-menagerie and, finally, Monsieur Louis, who is married to the madame of a brothel in Arles. In this guise he sits for a painter – Manet, since the story is set in the 1870s.

The story has not been transcribed in full – probably because the ink is badly faded in places. The point that has not been appreciated is that 'Monsieur Louis' also appears in a passage in Gauguin's *Avant et après*, in which he describes being shown the smart salon in an Arles brothel by a man he describes as *père* Louis – or Old Louis – and ironically praises as a '*très splendide maquereau*' – or magnificent pimp (p. 192, Merlhès, 1989). Louis showed off his prints of a Madonna and a Venus by the academic painter Bouguereau. The Arles census of 1886 shows that there were two brothels in Rue du Bout d'Arles, Virginie Chabaud's No 1, and apparently next door the smarter establishment of one Louis Farce, which had six prostitutes, two male servants and a cook. Gauguin and Vincent were presumably on social terms with Louis Farce. I go into more detail about this in 'Gauguin and a Brothel in Arles', *Apollo*, March 2006, pp. 64–71.

Hence my very tentative suggestion that he may be the individual painted by the two in December, previously identified as Joseph Ginoux. It is intriguing that Van Gogh seems here identified with Manet, since Degas's etched portrait of Manet (*c.* 1861) looks like a partial template for Gauguin's portrait of Vincent, the *Painter of Sunflowers*. It may well have been one of the Degas prints he asked Schuffenecker to send to Arles.

2. *Gauguin and 'The Blue Sow'*

The title of this story from *Le Courrier français* was mis-transcribed in many editions of Van Gogh's letters – as '*Le trace bleue*' not '*La Truie bleue*' (though Pickvance has it correctly (New York, 1984). Apart from the rather startling implications as to Vincent's feelings for Agostina Segatori – this story about a pig dressed up as a woman reminds him of her, according to letter 538a – it seems to me that it throws a lot of light on Gauguin's hitherto mysterious painting, *In the Heat*.

My hypothesis – not an extravagant one – is that the magazine was still lying around in the Yellow House six weeks after Vincent had read it and that he recommended the story to Gauguin as he had to Theo. If Gauguin read it and it had made an impression, it would help to explain not only the subject of this strange picture but also why Gauguin took pains to cultivate its author when they met, probably the following spring.

The second literary connection I suggest, with *The Sin of Father Mouret*, by one of Vincent's favoured authors, Émile Zola, is more conjectural. But the reiteration of the word '*chaleur*' in the farmyard scene is highly suggestive in view of Gauguin's title, *En Pleine Chaleur* (*In Full Heat*). There is more below about this novel (the fact that a farm near Montmajour was named *Le Paradou* is in Allard, Michel *et al*, *Jeanne Calment: From Van Gogh's Time to Ours: 122 Extraordinary Years*).

I have not mentioned in the text that the pose of the woman in the picture seems partly based on an etching of a brothel scene by Degas that Gauguin certainly owned (and associated with Arles, since it appears in the background of one of his late sunflower paintings (*see* Druick & Zegers, 2001–2, p. 353)). I go into more detail about this and also the effect I believe that the sculptures of Saint-Trophime had on Gauguin – mentioned briefly in Chapter 4 – in an article scheduled to appear in *Apollo* in spring 2007.

3. The Drama of the Ear and Vincent's Madness

Here I am offering not so much new fact as a new hypothesis. Vincent's mad action – not just cutting off the ear, or part of it, but also taking it to a brothel – was too carefully structured to be haphazard. It was highly irrational, to be sure, but there was some hidden pattern.

I rejected the notion that he cut off the ear because he was bothered by auditory hallucinations because it does not explain the sequel – the delivery of the ear. The theory that he was mimicking the removal of the bull's ears at the climax of a *corrida* seems very dubious for the same reasons – all the more so because it is unclear whether Vincent saw a bullfight in Arles. The event described in the letters is a *Course Camarguaise*, in which the animal does not die.

We are therefore left with three possibilities. The close connections between Van Gogh's life and work and Zola's *The Sin of Father Mouret* were first pointed out in Tsukasa Kodera's book *Vincent van Gogh: Christianity versus Nature* (pp. 79–92). Kodera, however, regarded the fact that this book also contained an ear amputation (and multiple ear-pullings of a character named Vincent) as coincidence. That seems highly unlikely to me. Professor W. N. Arnold (1992) also noted the Zola novel as a possible cause of Vincent's self-mutilation. But why repeat the injury suffered by Brother Archangias?

The association with Christ's Agony in the Garden – the picture which Vincent repeatedly tried to paint but could not – has long been noted. But the ear amputation is suffered by a minor character – the armed man attacked by St Peter. So why did Vincent inflict it on himself? The answer seems to be self-punishment. He associated the agony in the garden with his decision to leave Sien Hoornik. The basic conflict in the Zola novel is the same: a choice between a sexual partnership and a vocation.

After the failure of his surrogate family with Gauguin, Vincent's anger must have turned on himself. But to explain his subsequent actions, it is necessary to recall the details of the Ripper case. Again, the link between the ear amputation perpetrated on his victims by the Ripper and Vincent's has been seen before. But not how it fitted in. The connection between ear-cutting and punishment was already in his mind. The Ripper case, like that of Prado, was big news that autumn.

These sensational murder cases, and murder in general, were clearly on Vincent's mind – hence the newspaper clipping with the words 'The murderer took flight' pressed into Gauguin's hand. Vincent's characteristically oblique response was to reverse the Ripper's horrible threats. The Ripper said he hated prostitutes and cut off their ears as a sign of his hostility. Vincent thought of them as 'sisters of mercy' and gave one his own ear as a proof of his self-punishment. The fact that the Ripper's 'Dear Boss' letter, with its threat of ear-cutting, was printed in full in a newspaper Van Gogh often read has not been previously noted (*Le Figaro*, 3 October 1888, p. 3).

I suggest there need not be any *one* reason why Vincent mutilated himself. All three above, I believe, were interacting in his mind. Indeed, I suggest it was characteristic of Vincent's thought when agitated that he constantly connected very disparate things – often via his reading, as in the riff about Petrarch, Gauguin and the public gardens in Place Lamartine. This vertiginous thought-association is symptomatic of sufferers of bipolar affective disorder at certain points in their cycle.

Selected Bibliography

The literature on Van Gogh and Gauguin is vast. Below are simply listed the works which I found most useful in writing this book.

Allard, Michel *et al, Jeanne Calment: From Van Gogh's Time to Ours: 122 Extraordinary Years*, translated by Beth Coupland, New York & Basingstoke, 1998.

Arlésienne: Le Mythe?, exhibition catalogue, Musée Arlatan, Arles, 2000

Arnold, W. N., *Vincent van Gogh: Chemicals, Crises and Creativity*, Berlin, 1992

Bailey, Martin, 'Drama at Arles: New Light on Van Gogh's Self-Mutilation', *Apollo*, September 2005, pp. 30–41

Callen, Anthea, *The Art of Impressionism: Painting Technique and the Making of Modernity*, New Haven/London, 2000

Carlyle, Thomas, *Sartor Resartus*, London, 1841

Cate, Phillip Dennis & Welsh-Ovcharov, Bogmila, *Émile Bernard: Bordellos and Prostitutes in Turn-of-the-Century French Art*, exhibition catalogue, Zimmerli Art Museum, New Jersey, 1988

Crimpen, Han van (ed.), *Brief Happiness: The Correspondence of Theo van Gogh and Jo Bonger*, Amsterdam, 1999

Dorn, Roland, *Décoration: Vincent van Goghs Werksreihe für das Gelbe Haus in Arles*, Hildersheim/Zürich/New York, 1999

Druick, Douglas W. & Zegers, Peter Cort, *Van Gogh and*

Gauguin: The Studio of the South, exhibition catalogue, Chicago and Amsterdam, 2001–2

Gauguin, Paul, *Gauguin Écrivain (Noa noa, Diverses choses, Ancien culte mahorie)*, on DVD, *Réunion des musées nationaux*, Paris, 2003

Gauguin, Paul, *Paul Gauguin 45 Lettres à Vincent, Théo et Jo Van Gogh*, Douglas Cooper (ed.), The Hague, 1983

Gauguin, Paul, *The Writings of a Savage*, Daniel Guérin (ed.), New York, 1978

Gauguin, Paul, *Paul Gauguin's Intimate Journals*, translated by Van Wyck Brooks, New York, 1921 (English translation of *Avant et après*)

Gauguin, Paul, *Avant et après*, Paris, 1989

Gayford, Martin, 'Gauguin and a Brothel in Arles', *Apollo*, March 2006, pp. 64–71.

Hartrick, Archibald, *A Painter's Pilgrimage through Fifty Years*, Cambridge, 1939

Hulsker, Jan, *Vincent and Theo Van Gogh: A Dual Biography*, Ann Arbour, Michigan, 1993

Hulsker, Jan, 'Vincent's stay in the hospitals at Arles and St Rèmy', *Vincent* no. 2 (1971), pp. 21–39

Huyghe, René, *Le Carnet de Paul Gauguin*, Paris, 1952 (facsimile of sketchbook from Brittany and Arles, 1888–91, Israel Museum, Jerusalem)

James, Henry, *A Little Tour of France*, Boston, 1884

Jamison, Kay Redfield, *Touched With Fire: Manic Depressive Illness and the Artistic Temperament*, New York, 1993

Janson, Leo, Luijten, Hans & Fokke, Erik, 'The Illness of Vincent van Gogh: A Previously Unknown Diagnosis', *Van Gogh Museum Journal*, pp. 113–19, Amsterdam, 2003

Kodera, Tsukasa, *Vincent van Gogh: Christianity versus Nature*, Amsterdam/Philadelphia, 1990

Lees, Sara (ed.), *Bonjour, Monsieur Courbet!: The Bruyas*

Collection from the Musée Fabre, Montpellier, exhibition catalogue, Richmond, Williamstown, Dallas, San Francisco, 2004–5.

Merlhès, Victor, *Paul Gauguin and Vincent van Gogh, 1887–1888, Lettres retrouvées, sources ignorées,* Taravao, Tahiti, 1989

Morice, Charles, '*La Truie bleue*', *Le Courrier français,* 16 September 1888, pp. 5–8

Pickvance, Ronald, *Van Gogh in Saint-Rémy and Auvers,* exhibition catalogue, Metropolitan Museum of Art, New York, 1986

Pickvance, Ronald, *Van Gogh in Arles,* exhibition catalogue, Metropolitan Museum of Art, New York, 1984

Prather, Marla & Stuckey, Charles, *Gauguin: A Retrospective,* New York, 1987

Priou, J-N, '*Van Gogh et al famille Roulin*', *Revue des PTT de France,* May–June 1955, pp. 26–32

Rewald, John, *Post-Impressionism from Van Gogh to Gauguin,* New York, 1956

Silverman, Debora, *Van Gogh and Gauguin: The Search for Sacred Art,* New York, 2000

Stein, Susan Alyson (ed.), *Van Gogh: A Retrospective,* New York, 1986

Stone, Judith F., *Sons of the Revolution: Radical Democrats in France 1862–1914,* Baton Rouge & London, 1996

Sund, Judy, *True to Temperament: Van Gogh and French Naturalist Literature,* Cambridge/New York/Victoria, 1992

Thomson, Belinda (ed.), *Gauguin's Vision,* exhibition catalogue, National Galleries of Scotland, Edinburgh, 2005

Thomson, Belinda (ed.), *Gauguin By Himself,* London, 1993

Traulbaut, Marc Edo, *Vincent van Gogh,* New York, 1969

Van Gogh à Arles: Dessins 1888–1889, Documents Originaux, Photographies, exhibition catalogue, Fondation Vincent van Gogh–Arles, Arles, 2003

Van Gogh, Vincent, *The Complete Letters of Vincent van Gogh*, translated by J. van Gogh-Bonger & C. de Dood, London, 1978 (3 vols.)

Van Gogh: Face to Face: The Portraits, exhibition catalogue, Detroit, Boston, Philadelphia, 2000–2001

Van Gogh-Banger, J. (ed.), *Verzamelde Brieven van Vincent van Gogh*, Amsterdam, 1952–4 (4 vols.)

Van Meekeren, Erwin, *Starry, Starry Night: Life and Psychiatric History of Vincent van Gogh*, Amsterdam, 2003

Welsh-Ovcharov, Bogmila, *Van Gogh à Paris*, exhibition catalogue, Musée d'Orsay, Paris, 1988

Wilkie, Ken, *The Van Gogh File: The Myth and the Man*, London, 1978, 1990, 2004

Zola, Émile, *The Sin of Father Mouret*, translation of *La Peche de l'abbé Mouret* by Sandy Petrey, Lincoln and London, 1983

Picture Credits

Every effort has been made to trace copyright holders. The publishers will be glad to rectify in future editions any errors or omissions brought to their attention.

245: The Israel Museum, Jerusalem; p. 207: Saint Louis Art Museum. Funds given by Mrs Mark C. Steinberg; p. 208: Collection Oskar Reinhart 'Am Römerholz', Winterthur, Switzerland; p. 211: Museum Associates/LACMA, George Gard de Sylva Collection. Photo © Museum Associates/ LACMA; p. 215: Philadelphia Museum of Art: Bequest of Lisa Norris Elkins, 1950; p. 235: © Photo RMN – © Hervé Lewandowski; p. 236: Mr and Mrs Lewis Larned Coburn Memorial Collection, 1934–391. The Art Institute of Chicago. Photography © The Art Institute of Chicago; p. 244: Collection of Mr and Mrs Mellon, Image © 2005 Board of Trustees, National Gallery of Art, Washington; p. 266: © Photo RMN – © Bulloz; pp. 269 & 271: © Photo RMN; p. 278: Staatsgalerie Stuttgart; p. 283: Museum of Fine Arts, Boston. Bequest of John T. Spaulding 48.548. Photograph © 2006 Museum of Fine Arts, Boston; p. 306: Museum of Decorative Arts, Copenhagen. Photograph © Pernille Klemp; p. 309: The Samuel Courtauld Trust, Courtauld Institute of Art Gallery, London

Endpapers: Van Gogh, *Sunflowers*, The Bridgeman Art Library © The National Gallery, London

Acknowledgements

The genesis of this book lies in a delightful journey I made in 1999 in the company of George Shackelford and Dawn Griffin of the Museum of Fine Arts, Boston. We travelled in the footsteps of Vincent van Gogh, from the Netherlands to Paris, Arles, St Rémy and Auvers. En route we met Professor Jacques Chabot, great-nephew of Marcelle Roulin, the baby who sat for her portrait in the Yellow House. By the end of the journey, I was hooked on Vincent and his story.

The next impetus came from the great exhibition *Van Gogh and Gauguin: The Studio of the South*, which I saw in Amsterdam in 2002. This – and the admirable catalogue which accompanied it – demonstrated just how much interest, information and excitement could be extracted from these few short weeks of Van Gogh's life.

The book which I have written is the result not only of fascination with Vincent and Gauguin but also of dissatisfaction with conventional biography.

However long a life in words may be, it seems to me, it generally fails to give the reader a sense of what it would have been like to meet the subject face to face. I wanted to write a biographical work which does just that – to put you in the same room as the person you are reading about, even inside their head. *The Yellow House* is my attempt to do just that.

In writing it, I have been helped by numerous people. First of all, my agent, David Godwin, whose enthusiastic certainty that there was a need for a new book about Van Gogh got the project in the air. My publisher, Juliet Annan, has been equally positive and supportive throughout. I am also extremely grateful to Martin Bailey for initial encouragement, helpful conversations about Van Gogh and, most of all, for undertaking the task of reading and commenting on the manuscript.

During many occasions while I was sitting for two portraits, Lucian Freud and I discussed Van Gogh and Gauguin; the opportunity to share the life of an artist's studio while I was writing about the Yellow House was enormously valuable. He also kindly read and commented on my translation of Charles Morice's 'The Blue Sow' (though the Freudian *Portrait of a Pig* which I hoped it would inspire has not yet appeared). George Shackelford – in addition to being my guide around several Van Gogh sites on that memorable MFA Boston trip – gave me an expert assessment of some of my notions about Gauguin's artistic influences in Arles.

I am most grateful to Nigel Lowe and Elizabeth Mack for their assistance in research in France (and to Nigel for his advice on my translations from French). Murray Pearson performed similar services in the Netherlands. Sylvie Rebuttini kindly examined the Arles census of 1886 for me. Claire Lawton has assisted me hugely in my understanding of Vincent's mental problems – firstly by steering me gently away from various tempting but improbable diagnoses and then by proposing the one that I finally adopted. In addition, she kindly read through the manuscript.

The book has benefited from the work of my text editor, Sarah Day, and my picture researcher, Sally Nichols. Most of all, I am grateful to my wife, Josephine, who has – heroically – read through successive drafts of *The Yellow House* and made innumerable perceptive suggestions for improvement.

Index

Note: Page numbers in *italic* refer to illustrations.